SNOOP

'Sam Gosling is an engaging writer, a brilliant psychologist and a charming individual, and he must never, ever be allowed inside my office!' Mary Roach, author of *Stiff* and *Bonk*

'A tour de force! A riveting read, packed with fascinating information. I devoured the book and then rushed over to clean up my desk and change my iPod playlist.' Richard Florida, author of *The Rise of the Creative Class* and *Who's Your City?*

'A must-read for anyone who wants to learn about the cutting edge of psychological research' Eric Abrahamson, co-author of *A Perfect Mess*

'Snoopology is a science with a right way and wrong way of doing it … I was blithely going about it entirely the wrong way. A fascinating book.' Lucy Kellaway, *Financial Times*

'It works, not least because it has the huge advantage of being exclusively concerned with the one topic that most people find endlessly fascinating: themselves.' *New Scientist*

'It's fascinating … On he goes, writing better than American social psychologists usually do – because he's a Brit.' *Management Today*

'I look forward to more of this from Gosling.' *Spectator*

'A wry primer into how to decode other people's private lives through their worldly goods. Warning: side effects may include paranoia.' *Tatler*

SAM GOSLING is an associate professor of psychology at the University of Texas at Austin. He has spent the last decade conducting research on how personality is expressed and perceived in everyday contexts. The world's expert on snooping, he has been profiled by many publications, including the *New York Times* and *Psychology Today*, and is featured in Malcolm Gladwell's *Blink*. This is his first book. Born in London, and educated in Leeds and California, he now lives in Austin, Texas.

SNOOP

What Your Stuff
Says About You

SAM GOSLING, PH.D.

P
PROFILE BOOKS

This paperback edition published in 2009
First published in Great Britain in 2008 by
PROFILE BOOKS LTD
3A Exmouth House
Pine Street
London EC1R 0JH
www.profilebooks.com

First published in the United States of America by
Basic Books, a member of the Perseus Books Group

5 7 9 10 8 6 4

Printed and bound in Great Britain by
CPI Bookmarque, Croydon, Surrey

The moral right of the author has been asserted.

A CIP catalogue record for this book is available from the British Library.

ISBN 978 1 84668 028 1

Mixed Sources
Product group from well-managed
forests and other controlled sources
www.fsc.org   Cert no. TT-COC-002227
© 1996 Forest Stewardship Council
FSC

In appreciation of their wisdom,
creativity, and loving support
I dedicate this book to Mum and Dad,
and to my mentors, Oliver and Ken.

CONTENTS

The Arrival of
the Mystery Box

A FedEx package awaited me in the mailroom. Nothing much distinguished the box from other boxes. It was your standard box, brown and about the size of a shoebox, but squarer. What made this delivery different was the unusual set of instructions that came with it. I was not to open it until given permission to do so. Just in case I was in doubt, the words *DO NOT OPEN* were boldly inscribed in black ink across the top flap. According to instructions left on my voicemail, at a prearranged time I was to videotape myself opening the package. So at 3:00 P.M. the next day I took the box to a small room equipped with a video camera. Once inside, I pointed the camera to the spot where I would be standing and switched it on. I moved into view of the camera lens and pulled a small scrap of paper from my pocket. There was a number scribbled on the paper. I punched it into my cell phone.

"This is Dr. Gosling. I'd like to speak to Gary."

"I'll put you through."

A click. Then a pause.

"Gary speaking."

"It's Sam here. I'm ready."

"Go ahead and open it up."

Free at last to exercise my Pandoran urges, I slit the box open. "Inside you will see some things belonging to one person," said Gary. "They're all taken from that person's bathroom." (I noticed he was

1

careful not to say *his* or *her*). "Take the objects out one by one," he continued, "and tell me what they say about the owner."

As I removed the objects, I turned each one over in my hands. A small tube of skin cream, a CD, slightly scratched, of dance music, a brown plastic hair brush, and a Polaroid photo of the owner's sink area. As I inspected each item for clues I narrated my reasoning to the camera. "Well, the brush is quite large, probably belonging to a man." My theory was supported by the Polaroid photo, which showed a sink area with the surrounding surfaces generally devoid of sweet-smelling stuff and with levels of grime and (dis)organization more likely to be associated with males than females. I noted that the hairs trapped on the brush were short, straight, and dark. Perhaps the person was Asian or Hispanic. The photo showed that the door on the bathroom vanity wasn't closed properly and the hairdryer cord was hanging out; the tube of skin cream had been squeezed in the middle, not from the end, and some crusty residue was stuck to the cap. The CD was a compilation of house music, a genre stereotypically associated with gay clubs. Combine that with the evidence that the person is concerned with his (I'm now pretty sure the owner is a male) appearance and a coherent picture begins to emerge.

After a few minutes, Gary asked: "So, what can you tell me about the owner of these items?" On the basis of what I'd inspected, I said I believed the owner was an Asian male in his mid to late twenties and that he was quite possibly gay. I had underestimated his age by a few years—he was in his early thirties—but I was right about the rest. Gary seemed pleased.

What was going on here? What was I doing talking to this faceless voice under such strange circumstances?

The mysterious caller was a television producer planning a new reality series that would deal with the familiar, almost irresistible, human urge to snoop. If you're anything like me, you do more than passively observe the surroundings when you enter someone's living space for the first time. I find it hard not to look around and collect, filter, and process information about the occupant. Would I be so kind as to excuse the host while she goes to the bathroom? Absolutely! She's gone. Right. Hightail it over to the bookcase. Scan the books. A guidebook to budget travel in Madagascar. A tiny gift edition of Virginia Woolf's *A Room of One's Own*. Interesting. Now the photos. Hmm, all but one show my host with a big group of friends, and each picture projects an image of drunken hilarity. No time to dwell, I just heard the toilet flush and there are still the CDs, the trash basket, and that pile of junk on the windowsill. And all this is before I've had a chance to look through her medicine cabinet . . . I mean, kindly be excused to powder my nose. (Medicine cabinets are such quintessential snooping sites that I've often thought it would be fun to surprise guests with a "visitors' book" inside.)

The television producers were taking this common impulse to its logical endpoint: What can a physical space tell you about someone you have never met or even seen? The vision for the program—unlike MTV's popular show *Room Raiders*—included a role for an expert who would provide insight into the snooping process.

Why were the producers talking to me? I am a professor of psychology at the University of Texas, and I specialize in the study of personality differences and how people form impressions of others in daily life. My research focuses on the same question driving the television program: how people's possessions can tell us even more about their personalities than face-to-face meetings or, sometimes, what their best friends say about them. Indeed, my first study on this topic, which I conducted when I was still a graduate student at UC Berkeley, was the scientific equivalent of what the producers had in mind for their show. The study examined what observers could learn about men and women they had never met purely on the basis of snooping around their bedrooms.

The "bedroom study," as it came to be called, yielded fascinating findings in its own right (more about these later), and, to my surprise, the research and the ideas underlying it sparked significant interest beyond the halls of academe. Although other psychologists have looked at personality impressions based on small snippets of information, like video clips or short interactions, no one had examined rooms before. And no one had come up with such a rich bounty of information. The media reported our results with obvious glee. They gave their stories headlines such as "Object Lessons," "Behind Enemy Lines," and "Room with a Cue."

I continued my research in graduate school and have developed it further since taking up my post at the University of Texas in 1999. My graduate students and I have conducted many studies on personality in everyday life: We've peeked under beds and peered into closets; we've riffled through music collections; we've scrutinized Facebook profiles. We've visited eighty-three dorm rooms and nearly a hundred offices in banks, real estate firms, business schools, advertising agencies, and architecture studios. And we've examined how people reveal their personalities in such ordinary contexts as their Web pages, their books, the words they use in casual conversation, and where they live.

In the years we've been doing this research my teammates and I have learned how people form impressions of others based on their stuff, and we have trained our eyes to exploit clues that will tell us what a person is really like. Did the Virginia Woolf volume mean that my friend was an ardent feminist? Or perhaps the book was merely one of many she was assigned for a course on British literature? Did the photos of drunken hilarity mean she was using alcohol as an escape? Or was she just a party girl? Some ten years into the research, we'd assembled an enormous amount of information showing how people portray and betray their personalities.

So perhaps the television people were on the mark. Maybe I could say something useful about this topic.

* * *

Two weeks after the arrival of the box, I found myself in Los Angeles. We were to shoot a pilot episode the next day. As I stood on Hollywood Boulevard in front of Mann's Chinese Theater and stared down at the famous footprints on the sidewalk, I thought about how I could contribute to the program. I hoped I would be able to explain the different ways people leave behavioral footprints in the places they occupy. I hoped I would be able to guide the contestants away from common errors of judgment such as jumping to conclusions on the basis of only one clue or being misled by the things that tend to grab your attention. And I hoped to do this without oversimplifying the science underlying my research.

As I mulled these questions over in my mind I began to realize that there was no single source that brought together all the different strands of snooping research. So, soon after my Los Angeles adventure, as I returned to Texas to continue my work, I began formulating my plans for this book.

The task facing me in my research—and thus here in *Snoop*—is not much different from the task we all face as we attempt to make sense of the social worlds in which we live; that is, we draw meaning from artifacts. Of course, we usually don't realize that we're doing this because we do it unconsciously and with great ease. When you first meet someone, you don't notice that you're forming an impression by integrating information—from his shaved head or the maps on his living room wall, from the first words that pop out of his mouth or the firmness of his handshake. But underlying the apparent ease with which we paint these portraits is a set of complex mental processes that have only recently been systematically investigated.

And sometimes these processes go awry. For example, our dorm-room snoopers were pretty good at judging students' political values just by glancing around their living spaces. But they were far from perfect judges. They correctly used obvious cues such as explicit political décor—bumper stickers, posters of political icons such as Malcolm X, Che Guevara, or Ronald Reagan. But there were clues that they shouldn't have used but did, and clues that they should have used but didn't. In our studies, judges used the presence of art and books on art to infer that occupants leaned to the Left. But despite what you might think, these things bore no relation to political affiliation. What *did* give clues to (conservative) political leanings, though, was sports-related décor, a clue that our judges completely overlooked. This tells us that although common sense often gets it right, it can also lead us in the wrong direction. And without learning about the studies we can never know whether we're using the kind of common sense that's useful or misleading.

What's more, our common sense can fool us into thinking that the results of studies merely confirm what we already know. I was struck by this 20/20 hindsight bias during a recent presentation. Before I begin a talk I usually ask my audience to guess what the bedroom studies showed. This turns out to be difficult to do. Few people are able to predict that attractiveness is easy to pick up in bedrooms but that nervousness is tougher to crack. On this particular occasion I made the mistake of unveiling the findings without asking the audience to guess in advance. And this time, something different happened: the attendees did not seem at all surprised by the results. Thus, I learned once again that just because something makes sense after the fact doesn't mean it was obvious all along. In the chapters that follow, I'll show you how snooping can shed new light on all these "obvious" conclusions.

*　　*　　*

The goal of my décor-decoding research and the work of scientists who study the nature of personality itself is to create portraits of people based on the clues they leave—just as detectives and FBI profilers create a complete picture of someone by strategically assembling seemingly disparate information. Besides discerning the basics, such as sex and age and ethnicity—as I did with the mystery box—I will show how we can capture something about a person's character and personality, values and habits, hopes and dreams, just from looking closely at their rooms or offices.

One of my goals in writing this book is to share what I've learned about the special brand of voyeurism I'm calling *snoopology* and to describe how you, too, can become an expert snooper. So the next time you call on someone in his office or interview a prospective job applicant or cast your eyes around a date's digs, you'll know to ask yourself questions like: What does that collection of cheesy trinkets on the computer monitor say about its owner? And why are they all pointing toward the visitor's chair? What's the story behind those inspirational messages stuck on the mirror over the dresser? You'll learn how to use items like these to figure out whether someone is extraverted or introverted, friendly or suspicious, conscientious or weak-willed.

You'll also learn to be on the lookout for fake messages and how to peer behind the propaganda set up to fool you. People go to great lengths to mask their identities in person, but in a room, with its gradual build-up of clues, it's much more difficult to fake it. And most people don't even think about what they're broadcasting about themselves with that pile of shoes under the desk, the wilting plant in the corner, or the small rubber chicken dangling from the lamp. Can people manage the impressions others have of them? And if they can, how often do they do it, and what clues can you use to decide whether someone is trying to pull the wool over your eyes?

You may also be interested to discover, as I was, that there's no exact correlation between clues and their meaning. As we'll see, a messy desk doesn't always signal a messy mind (you'll need more clues to draw that conclusion), and a crucifix over the mantelpiece doesn't always mean your companion is a saint.

You can distill clues from all kinds of stuff—e-mail usernames and exercise equipment, CD collections and cars—but not all domains are created equally. If you want to learn about your date's dependability, his music collection won't help much; that would be a better place to find out about his interests and values. But if it's his political stance you're after, you'll figure that out within two minutes of entering his apartment—should you make it that far.

Knowing where and how to look for personality cues in other people is essential to mastering the art of snooping. But what about how others pick up on the cues *you* leave? Does your workspace tell your boss you deserve a promotion or does it permanently confine you to cubicle hell? Do your car radio's pre-sets give away more than your taste in music? And why is it that dates take one look at your apartment and then promptly make their excuses and depart for good? Learning about others requires that you first understand the connections between your own personality and the space around you.

Of course, the science of snooping entails much more than simply noticing what's on the walls or under the bed. It also demands that we combine the discoveries that psychologists have unearthed over the past decades with cutting-edge contemporary research on human behavior. In this book I will take you on a tour of that research. Together we will explore the new and notable ideas emerging from the science behind snooping.

Along the way, I'll show how your tastes and habits provide particularly useful portals into your personality. I'll explore what it means to know someone well—and what it takes for an acquaintance to become a friend. We'll visit the curious habit of hoarding, the bewildering world of personal Web sites, and why stereotyping gets such bad press. Finally, I'll share what I've learned about an exciting business enterprise that builds homes designed to match people's personalities. But first we've got to get back to basics—we have to learn how to snoop.

ONE

—⫘—

Less Than Zero
Acquaintance

O NE BRIGHT SEPTEMBER morning in 1960, John Steinbeck and his French poodle, Charley, embarked on a grand tour of the United States. The writer and his beloved pooch spent the next three months traveling around the country in a truck specially modified for their expedition. Together they went in search of the real America. *Travels with Charley* chronicles their journey.

Partway into his travels, Steinbeck arranged to take a break from the road and spend some time with his wife, who was to meet him in Chicago. He arrived early to find that his room was not ready, but the hotel was happy to accommodate his request for a place to rest and take a bath. Another guest had left early, so the hotel allowed the eminent writer to wash up and nap in the recently vacated but as yet uncleaned room. As Steinbeck undressed, he became distracted by the traces the room's previous occupant had left behind, a man he dubbed Lonesome Harry:

> An animal resting or passing by leaves crushed grass, footprints, and perhaps droppings, but a human occupying a room for one night prints his character, his biography, his recent history, and sometimes his future plans and hopes. I further believe that personality seeps into walls and is slowly released. . . . As I sat in this unmade room, Lonesome Harry began to take shape and dimension. I could feel that recently departed guest in the bits and pieces of himself he had left behind.

Steinbeck's observation draws on an intuition that the environments people craft around themselves are rich with information about their personalities, values, and lifestyles. From some laundry receipts, an unfinished letter in the wastebasket, an empty bourbon bottle, and other assorted clues, Steinbeck pieced together a portrait of Lonesome Harry.

SPACE INVADERS

Each of us faces similar challenges every day. You piece together bits of evidence, wherever you can find them, to form coherent portraits of the characters who populate your social spheres. You draw on information from your long history with dear old friends, you make snap judgments from thin slices of behavior in brief social interactions—the so-called zero-acquaintance contexts—and, if you're a snooper, you use clues left by people you've never met. You integrate new information, toss out current beliefs, and fill the gaps with new working hypotheses. But what are the mechanisms by which personality reaches out and connects to the physical world? How exactly does the self send its signals?

These were the questions driving my research when, in 1997, I assembled my first team of environmental assessors to help me develop a science of snooping. One of our goals was to explore the ways in which people have an impact on their personal spaces. What evidence of their characters do they leave behind? What elements of personality are most likely to leave traces? I also wanted to examine the judgments my assessors made on the basis of these spaces. I was not trying to improve the judging process, but to examine ordinary, everyday evaluations—the kind you and I might make, not the sort that would interest the FBI.

After much discussion with my graduate advisor, I formulated a plan. I would recruit a bunch of volunteers who, at a specified time, would vacate their rooms. While they were gone, I would send in a team of judges to form an impression of the recently departed purely from evidence in their rooms. Next, I would send in another team of coders to assess the physical features of the space. We would also give the rooms' occupants personality tests and collect information about them from their friends.

As an impoverished graduate student, all I could offer the volunteers as an incentive was feedback on how others viewed them on the basis of their rooms. To my surprise, almost a hundred people signed up; then, as word of the study got out, others came around, virtually begging to be included.

As soon as I set foot in the first room, I knew we were on to something. The rooms varied much more than I had expected, not only in the quantity of objects but also in the nature of the objects themselves. Some rooms contained little more than a modest bed in the corner. Others were so full of objects and so adorned with decorations that our assessors had to be careful not to crush the evidence they were there to examine. And even in the overflowing rooms there was much variation in the objects that fought for territory on the shelves, chairs, beds, floors, and windowsills.

One such room exhibited a magnificent collection of *Star Wars* figurines and toys, a theme echoed in the posters adorning the walls and ceiling. Winnie the Pooh and friends were featured in a surprising number of rooms. Some spaces were meticulously arranged; others suggested that the occupant was aiming for a level of organization best described as "somewhere in the room." Some spaces were dark and stale, others light and breezy. Some were cozy, others cold.

As we examined the rooms, we began to notice their occupants' psychological footprints and to glimpse the different ways personality is expressed. Three broad mechanisms—identity claims, feeling regulators, and behavioral residue—seemed to connect people to the spaces that surrounded them. These mechanisms stood out especially clearly in the rooms of occupants I'll call Cindy, Duncan, and Gideon.

IDENTITY CLAIMS: CINDY'S SIGNALS

We spend many hours in our personal environments, but there is no obvious functional reason why we should decorate them. The strawberry motif on the quilt hardly guarantees sweet dreams, and the stuffed piranha on top of the computer monitor won't help an ad writer produce snappy copy. Nonetheless, we continue to decorate our spaces, and the decorating is far from random; these changes to a space, which on a superficial level seem "non-functional," may have a big impact on what is done there. Indeed, the results of one survey on worker comfort and engagement in the *Gallup Management Journal* reported that "employees working in a comfortable environment are much more likely to be engaged and to make a positive contribution to the organization's financial success." The survey was careful to point out that "comfort" extends well beyond physical conditions. The psychological environment that people craft is also crucial. This is certainly consistent with observations we have gathered—the extensive and persistent efforts by many of our subjects to decorate and modify their spaces strongly suggest a need to affect their psychological surroundings.

One way we make spaces our own is to adorn them with "identity claims"—posters, awards, photos, trinkets, and other mementos—that make deliberate symbolic statements. Cindy's room was laden with such symbols. My research teammates and I noticed them even before we stepped into the room. A sorority sticker stuck to the door announced an allegiance to one group. A bumper sticker, "Be Your Own Goddess," broadcast public self-affirmation with a feminist twist. Once across the threshold, we found more. On the dry-erase board was a quote from Nietzsche, "Where the will to power is lacking, there is decline," and written in caps along the bottom of the board was "Think Positive!" Hanging from the wall were cheerleading pompoms.

Identity claims are either directed toward others or directed at the self, and both kinds have their own psychological functions. People use other-directed identity claims—like Cindy's pompoms and the goddess bumper sticker—to signal how they want to be regarded. Since it is crucial that a person's audience understand the intended message, other-directed identity claims rely on objects that have shared meanings. The bumper sticker conveys pride in Cindy's gender and the pompoms affirm her loyalty to the university.

In workplaces, office doors (or, these days, the outside of cubicle walls) are great repositories of other-directed identity claims. Next time you're visiting someone at work, I encourage you to cruise the corridors and trawl for the messages people are sending about themselves. Should your hallway wanderings lead you to my door, you will find a large poster produced by despair.com, a company that parodies inspirational posters promoting teamwork, trust, and other wholesome values. My poster shows a stunning photo of the Leaning Tower of Pisa set against a spectacular sunset. The message below reads: "Mediocrity. It takes a lot less time and most people won't notice the difference until it's too late." I didn't think deeply about the symbolic value of the poster when I first hung it up, but I now realize I was trying to convey an image of someone who not only has an ironic sense of humor but also has a broader distrust of facile feel-good moments.

Posters on the outside of office doors (as opposed, of course, to those hung on the inside where they face the occupant) are particularly interesting because the owners rarely see them. They are thus paragons of other-directed identity claims. As we shall see later, these statements are typically intended to convey honest messages about their owners. But they can also be strategic, even deceptive. The student who adorned his dorm room with images of such hip icons as Bruce Lee and Tupac and cult movies such as *Reservoir Dogs* clearly wanted his visitors to see him as "cool." But we'd need to look further to see how cool he really is.

Your other-directed identity claims may vary, depending on whom you're trying to influence—the things you do to impress your boss might overlap only partially with the things you would do to wow a potential mate. However, it is increasingly difficult to keep our audiences separate, as the freelance television producer Colleen Kluttz discovered. According to a story in the *New York Daily News,* a friend posted a picture of Kluttz on her MySpace profile showing Kluttz with half-closed eyes; the caption indicated that she had smoked an illegal substance. Although the photo and caption were a joke between two friends, there was nothing to stop prospective employers from Googling her. After losing a couple of jobs at the eleventh hour, Kluttz suspected that her professional and personal worlds had collided so she had the photo removed.

As we begin to live out more and more relationships online, it's harder and harder to keep our various identities distinct. And it's harder to project the approved identities only to the audience we want to target. I'm not wild about the nerdy, decidedly uncool high-school picture of me easily discoverable online by all those people who I am hoping will view me as a sophisticated, devastatingly cool international man of mystery.

In addition to making statements to others about how we would like to be regarded, we can make symbolic statements for our own benefit. These self-directed identity claims reinforce how we see ourselves. In Cindy's room, objects on her desk included an inscribed gavel and a button expressing support for a local mayoral candidate. Their placement, right where Cindy would get to see them, suggests they were primarily there for her own benefit—reminders, perhaps, of her accomplishments on the debate team and her involvement as a volunteer during the previous local elections. Both symbols raised hypotheses about some core features of Cindy's identity to be supported or rejected by further evidence.

Mass-produced posters are a good source of cultural symbols. A former colleague of mine displayed a small poster of Martin Luther

King, Jr., on her office wall. Like Cindy's gavel and political buttons, MLK's placement above my colleague's desk was deliberate and significant. It would be easy to miss the poster because, from the visitor's perspective, it was partially obscured by the computer monitor; but if you sat at her desk you would notice that the image was hung in a spot that didn't even require my colleague to move her head to see her idol—a quick rightward flick of the eyes, away from the document she was reading on the computer screen, is all that was needed. The arrangement suggested to me that she used this icon of progressive thought and values to inspire and reinforce the way she viewed herself. The poster appeared to be there more for her benefit than for that of visitors.

As with many cultural icons, the meaning of MLK is reasonably clear, but identity claims directed at the self can also make use of artifacts whose meaning may be obscure to outsiders. As long as the items have personal meaning, they work. A pebble collected from a beach during a vacation in Morocco could provide someone with a connection to her Moroccan heritage. A fountain pen awarded to the occupant at her high school science fair could bolster her current identity as a chemist. Private artifacts can convey a broad message to the snooper even if the exact significance is unclear. In combination with other objects, the pebble or fountain pen could suggest that the collector is sentimental about a certain era in her life.

One simple experimental method for measuring identity—a person's view of who he or she is—is the Twenty Statements Test, which consists of twenty lines, each beginning, "I am . . ." followed by a blank space. Participants fill in as many of the blanks as they can in twelve minutes. (Think for a moment of the kinds of things you might come up with.) Typically, people generate about seventeen responses in the allotted time. The "Twenty Answers" can vary widely and include such responses as a girl, an athlete, a blonde, married, and from Chicago. Some respondents refer to themselves simply as *religious* or *a student;* others describe themselves more specifically as

Christian, Baptist, or *a poor Christian,* or *pre-med, studying engineer-ing,* or *a pretty good student.* Even this small set of responses gives us a sense of the potential range of identities that can be expressed by this method.

Photographs on display are the pictorial analogs of the "I am . . ." test because they capture a moment the person wanted to record ("Here I am being me"): "I am a freewheeling world traveler" (a picture of a grungy young man on the roof of a train as it climbs through the mountains of Rajasthan). "I am a loving daughter" (a teenager hugging her parents as she arrives home from a trip). "I am a successful student" (a young man collecting an award during a graduation ceremony).

In fact, the Twenty Statements Test has been adapted for pictorial use. Instead of filling in the blanks, people are given a camera and a twelve-exposure roll of film (this test was developed long before the advent of digital cameras) and given the following instructions: "We want you to describe to yourself how you see yourself. To do this we would like you to take (or have someone else take) twelve photographs that tell who you are. These photographs can be of anything just as long as they tell something about who you are." This exercise mirrors closely what people do informally when they select and display photographs in their homes, offices, cars, and wallets.

Tattoos are usually regarded as classic other-directed identity claims. Not only do they proclaim a particular value or attitude or allegiance, the permanence of tattoos signals that the wearer anticipates a continued commitment to that value—you don't tattoo yourself with a message you believe is going to be transitory; "Perot for President" is better expressed on a T-shirt or bumper sticker than inked across your forehead. But not all tattoos are for the benefit of others. Before heading to California to attend graduate school, my friend Amanda had her arm tattooed with an outline of the state of Texas. Not surprising—she had a strong allegiance to her home state. But the placement of the tattoo is what made this a striking self-directed identity claim: It was on her inner forearm and, from my perspective, it was upside down. This might seem odd until we realize that it was there to remind Amanda herself of her home state, not to signal to others where she was from. The placement meant that she could look down and think of Texas; it couldn't have served this purpose had she put it on her biceps or shoulder blade. This example underscores the importance of paying attention to location when considering identity claims. Placement determines the psychological function that the clue serves.

Identity claims can be made on T-shirts, buttons, necklaces, nose rings, tattoos, e-mail signatures, posters, flags, bumper stickers, and just about any other space big enough to accommodate a symbol of some sort. In his book about iPods, *The Perfect Thing,* Steven Levy describes "wars" in which iPod wearers thrust their digital music players into one another's faces to demonstrate how hip they are. In the 1980s, when "ghetto blasters" or "boom boxes" were de rigueur, it was easy (unavoidable, actually) to broadcast your musical tastes to others. But as headphones took these acoustic emblems off the streets and directly into our skulls, we were denied this form of expression. Although less intrusive than filling a subway car with the latest number from the Fat Boys, the screen of the iPod has rescued, at least partially, the opportunity to let others know what's currently rocking your world.

And now we have music players that let you broadcast your musical tastes to anyone within wireless range. Although "squirting," as it has been called, was designed to allow you to share your songs with those who have compatible players, it can also be used to check out other people's music libraries and playlists. As we shall see in chapter 7, a glimpse of a person's music collection can put you on the fast track to learning about his or her personality, political views, artistic tendencies, and even preferences in alcohol.

In practice, it can be hard to tell whether an identity claim is self-directed or other-directed. Displaying a poster of Martin Luther King, Jr., may simultaneously reinforce your view of yourself and communicate your values to others, but it is useful to treat the two kinds of claims as separate because they reflect separate and distinct motivations. For example, this distinction may help us understand the difference between public and private spaces. In a home, what distinguishes the hallway, dining room, living room, and guest bathroom, which are sure to be seen by others, from spaces that require a higher security clearance, such as the bedroom, study, or private bathroom? Perhaps there is religious iconography, such as a cross or menorah, in the public places but reminders of family in the private places. Or, if the occupant is less concerned with privacy for the family and instead experiences his spiritual identity at a more private level, it could be the other way around, with the iconographic symbols hidden away and the family photos displayed for all to see.

For the snooper, it is invaluable to detect such distinctions because they hint at a potential fractionating of the self. Several years ago, my scientist friend Genevieve was in town for a conference on stem-cell research; I met up with her in a bar, where she was chatting with a fellow neurobiologist from the conference. This wasn't my area of research and I didn't really know anyone at the conference, so I was a little more cavalier in my choice of conversational topics than I might have been had I been politely chatting in my own professional circles. On a whim, I brought the conversation around to morality and religion, but I soon noticed that Genevieve's colleague went strangely quiet. It then emerged that, in contrast to the vast majority of biological scientists, he was a deeply religious person but had kept his beliefs under wraps—until they were unexpectedly flushed out by the rapid turn of conversation. Given my predilection for places, I couldn't help but imagine how this uncomfortable schism must be reflected in the physical places he occupies—I was certain there would be no sign of the forbidden beliefs in his research office or laboratory but, given how shaken he seemed by the revelation, I suspected that there would be few spiritual symbols in the public places in his home; perhaps we would find them only in places where he felt really safe, such as his bedroom or a study.

So as a snooper you need to be on the lookout for discrepancies in the signals that people send to themselves and others. But also be ready to notice the absence of a discrepancy—the projected persona may match the occupant's self-view—because this could reflect less of a struggle between inner and outer selves. Sometimes, a space that at first appears to be public can include private areas within it. Many offices are like this, the theater being set up with the orchestra seats on the front side of the desk, psychologically separated from the backstage area behind the desk. You can use this public/private distinction to guide your snooping for identity claims within a single space. In an office where the occupant is separated from visitors by a desk, check to see which way the items on the desk face. Do the photos of the person's spouse and kids face him or her ("I'm so proud to be part of this fabulous family")? Or do they face outwards, primarily for others to see? ("Look at my beautiful spouse and marvel at the fruits of my loins.")

Another place to look for discrepancies is in the differences between front and back yards. The back yard tends to be a place to spend time and relax. The front yard is where most people make their statements to the outside world. If you want to fly a flag, it makes sense to fly it in front of the house, not at the back. Front-yard spaces, which can be seen by anyone who passes by, also provide clues to homeowners' personality.

In a fascinating study, Carol Werner from the University of Utah and her colleagues examined how we can learn something about people's sociability by looking at how they decorate the fronts of their houses. First, she collected photographs of houses in Salt Lake City at Christmas time (all the houses were occupied by people who celebrate Christmas). Then researchers interviewed the female heads of the households and determined their level of sociability. Photos of sixteen houses were then given to fifty-two judges; on the basis of what they saw in the pictures, the judges rated the owners' sociability. Of the eight houses that were decorated, four belonged to sociable residents and four to unsociable ones; of the eight that were undecorated, the split between sociable and unsociable residents was again even.

As one might expect, the judges perceived the inhabitants of the homes decked out for Christmas as more sociable than inhabitants of nondecorated homes. But the researchers also showed that homeowners can put forth an other-directed identity that's different from a self-directed one. Among the decorated houses, the nonsociable occupants sent the strongest sociability message; this finding suggested to Werner that they were hoping the appearance of their homes, including their Christmas decorations, would project an affable image that would help them make friends in the neighborhood.

But even where there were no decorations, judges were able to identify the sociable families from their houses. The judges described the homes of social occupants as more "open" and "lived-in" compared to the homes of less sociable people, which were seen as relatively closed and abandoned (in upkeep, neatness, and attractiveness, the judges saw no differences in the homes of high and low sociable occupants). Thus, perceivers draw not only on deliberate identity statements, such as Christmas decorations, but also on inadvertent betrayals of personality, such as a "lived-in" appearance.

FEELING REGULATORS: DUNCAN'S SANCTUARY

Psychologists have long known that optimal performance is associated with an optimal level of arousal—to do something well, you must be alert and engaged but not so excited that you can't focus on the task at hand. Moreover, there are vast differences among people in conditions that promote their optimal arousal levels. Some people work most effectively in a place that's free of visual and auditory

stimulation—in a library or in a room that is quiet and plainly decorated. Others prefer to have things going on around them. I like to
work in bustling cafés where music is playing, people are coming and
going, and chitchat is all around, but I have colleagues who couldn't
even read a newspaper in such places.

Much of the stuff we gather about us and the environments we create are there not to send messages about our identities but specifically
to manage our emotions and thoughts. "Feeling regulators"—family
photos, keepsakes, the CDs in the stereo, even the color of the walls—
can help a person reminisce about bygone happy times, focus on an
important task, or get pumped up for a night on the town.

One of the spaces our team assessed, Duncan's room, seemed
crafted specifically to let him immerse himself in a vast collection of
music, books, and videos and thus create a soothing ambiance for
himself. It was a luxurious (at least by student standards) hideaway
designed to allow him to enjoy his treasured possessions. A king-sized
bed took up most of the space; it was enveloped in a generously
stuffed comforter and crested at one end by a ridge of plump pillows.
Facing the bed was a state-of-the-art multimedia entertainment
system that consisted of a huge high-quality television and a stereo system. Speakers surrounded the room. All the wall space was occupied
by bookcases laden with hundreds of videotapes, CDs, and books.

Unlike most high-tech environments, which tend to be cold
and off-putting, this space was warm and inviting. The wooden
bookshelves and the voluptuous bedding suggested a place you might
like to stay a while and revel in the sensory experiences the room offered. All your needs would be met. Should you be watching a movie,
you would have no need to torment yourself trying to recall an actor's
name or the film he appeared in with Audrey Hepburn because a collection of movie and music reference books was in easy reach (we
assessed Duncan's room long before Google and IMDB had rendered
such sources nearly obsolete). Need a little more treble for that Haydn
symphony? No problem. The remote was at hand. I could see that

instead of heading to the next room the judges on my team were being sucked into Duncan's sanctuary. He had masterfully created a personal space that left clues about the type of person he is. Unlike many students who find a perverse joy in the frugal life and nurture an almost puritanical suspicion toward anything giving a whiff of self-indulgence, Duncan took pleasure in pampering himself; he could switch off from the worries of work and life—indeed, he was prepared to devote considerable effort to doing so. Some people can't switch off or don't want to—Duncan evidently could.

En suite bathrooms are another place to look for feeling regulators. The privacy they afford (in contrast to guest bathrooms) and the fact that they don't have to accommodate the needs of anyone but the owner can make them into a psychological refuge. As part of a research project, my collaborators and I visited one such sanctuary. A huge, deep bathtub surrounded by candles and jars of bath salts, a deep-pile bathmat to indulge the toes, and magazines within easy reach invoked someone who wanted to leave the world behind. By providing the environmental means to pamper herself, she left clues to the psychological space she was aiming for and the means by which she hoped to arrive there. We knew that tranquility is a desirable state for her to be in, and we knew she retreated to that quiet state by stealing away to her private sanctum where the distractions of the outer world seemed far, far away (others might find their peaceful moments sitting on top of a mountain or sitting with a spouse in a street-side café in a sleepy town in Tuscany).

People also use music to manipulate and maintain their feelings and thoughts, and their choices can be a useful clue to personality. When I see a CD collection that has a preponderance of smooth jazz, it suggests to me that the owner is someone who maintains a calm demeanor; those who boast extensive collections of Stan Getz, Duke Ellington, and Billie Holiday are, on average, slightly less anxious than people who don't like jazz. Music is a widespread and highly flexible means of manipulating how we feel. In fact, the effects of music are so strong that they are sometimes used in psychological experiments to affect the moods of the research subjects.

There were one or two exceptions (such as jazz music) but, to our surprise, living spaces housed exceptionally few clues to how anxious people were. However, one interesting clue stood out: inspirational posters. Apparently, anxious people high on neuroticism are using the self-affirmations and inspirational messages of posters to regulate their tendency to worry about things and become blue. The posters are a visual form of self-medication.

Recently, I was reminded of the versatility of such symbols as regulators of emotions. I was invited to a university to present some of my findings, and before the talk, I had one-on-one meetings with several faculty members. One man, I'll call him Larry, seemed a little bitter; just by chatting with him I got the message that it's a hard life out there—you've got to fend for yourself because nobody else is going to watch out for you or do you any favors. So being tough on students is actually doing them a favor because they'll learn all the sooner what a brutal place the world is. He said at one point, "You can work all you like but no one's going to give you any prizes."

As he continued to rant, a series of elements in his otherwise standard faculty office began to stand out as psychologically important. Of the few items hanging on Larry's walls were several framed degrees and awards. More interesting were the novelty awards placed on bookshelves around the room—plastic trophies or small plush animals with ribbons attached declaring "World's Best Dad" and "You Deserve a Medal." Of course, these could all be brushed off as a bit of fun. But why was he, of all the faculty members I visited, having this particular kind of fun? The novelty awards in combination with the real awards told me that at a fundamental level Larry felt unappreciated. When one of his colleagues gets recognition, such as a pay raise or an award, I bet it bugs the heck out of him.

Most of us like to know we are appreciated, but Larry deeply needed praise from a world he saw as hard and hostile. I predicted that his departmental head and colleagues would find that the occasional unsolicited note of appreciation for what he does and what he has accomplished would go an extraordinarily long way. His family and whoever gave him all those novelty awards have already learned that lesson.

Larry's awards sat permanently in his office, but some forms of self-regulation are used on an as-needed basis. My colleague Bill Swann has a photo in his office of Ned Jones, a famous social psychologist, now deceased, who was Bill's greatly admired good friend. The photo is in an unusual location—it is taped to the inside of the door of a small cupboard above Bill's desk. The picture of Ned brings back happy memories of their friendship and inspires Bill in the work he does. But having the photo out in the open, pinned to his bulletin board, on the windowsill, or even taped to the outside of the cupboard, would be too intense. Bill wants to be able to dip into the warm feelings and memories that Ned elicits but not be swamped or constantly distracted by them. So he has devised a system that regulates the doses of Ned. Whenever Bill feels like a hit of Ned, he just opens up the cupboard and takes a look. His system tells us not only about Bill and his esteem for his friend but also about his style of regulating his emotions.

BEHAVIORAL RESIDUE: IN GIDEON'S WAKE

On opening the bedroom door of Gideon's apartment, a visitor is faced with what can best be described as a cascade of stuff—stuff upon stuff on the desk, table, shelves, chairs, bed, and floor. A cascade of files and clothes and paper flowed into a pool of socks and towels and books and CDs. Stacks on every flat surface had collapsed.

Against one wall, a set of metal shelves was crowned with several smaller shelves. At one point long ago, the empty metal shelves must have seemed like an inviting resting place for whatever happened to be in Gideon's hands at the time. Looking at them now, it was hard to discern any physical or thematic order. Take the stack on the second level: The bottom layer was composed of a handful of loose change, assorted receipts, a spool of green thread, a piece of paper with some notes scribbled on it, and one of those red-and-white striped mints that come with the check at a restaurant. The next layer consisted of a small upturned white cardboard box, a bottle of Wite-Out, a small Ziploc bag containing an assortment of vitamins or other pills, and a semicrumpled brown-paper bag. Layer three held a white shoelace, an opened box of pens, and a small pile of envelopes from banks or utility companies. Layer four was mainly comprised of loose-leaf notes. The top layer looked unstable. Skidding off one edge of the stack was a folded pink receipt. Hanging over another was a lonely athletic sock. And perched precariously at the front of the pile was an empty tissue box, on its side.

I use the term *behavioral residue* to refer to the physical traces left in the environment by our everyday actions. Sometimes it is the *lack* of an act that leaves a residue. The soiled empty coffee mug on your desk is residue of your not bothering to wash it. Not all behavior leaves physical remains. Smiling doesn't, and neither does walking or talking. But the residue of actions that do leave their mark can tell us a lot about a person's traits, values, and goals.

The residue left in Gideon's wake—that is, the objects and their arrangement (or disarrangement)—suggested actions undertaken haphazardly, moment-to-moment. To be fair, the composition of the stacks did not appear to be entirely arbitrary. With the exception of the sock, things seemed to be more or less corralled into a specified sector of the room. The book sector, for example, was about 90 percent books; the rest consisted of notes, software disks, index cards, and a Kinko's envelope. The recycling crate contained mostly paper, though a plastic bag lay on top and an unopened box of Cocoa Pops rested just a few sheets down.

As with all the subjects, we gave Gideon personality tests and examined reports from people who knew him well; both the tests and the friends confirmed what the behavioral residue suggested—that he did not devote much time to planning and was not widely renowned for his organizational skills.

The analysis of behavioral residue falls squarely within the tradition of what are known as unobtrusive measures. The point of these methods is to evaluate what people think, how they feel, and what they are doing without their knowing they're being assessed.

I love using unobtrusive measures. They strike an appealing balance between creativity, deviousness, and amateur espionage—and are therefore perfect examples of snooping. In a class I teach on personality assessment, I encourage students to think about ways of measuring personality without being seen. I send them out in groups, and I am always impressed by their ingenuity. A few years ago, one group wanted to measure narcissism, the personality trait based on the classical myth of Narcissus, the beautiful youth who starved to death because he could not tear himself away from his reflection in a pool. Personality psychologists use the term *narcissism* to refer to a grandiose sense of self-importance, a need for constant attention and admiration, and a preoccupation with fantasies of unlimited success, power, and beauty.

My students designed a study that echoed the myth of Narcissus. Some of the campus buildings have mirrored glass to combat the fierce Texas heat. A group of students positioned themselves inside one of these buildings and surreptitiously followed people as they walked past. Each time a person looked at his or her reflection, the students put a check mark on their score sheets. They took note of people who slowed down or even stopped to get a particularly good look at themselves. Then another group of students waited for the unwitting passerby and administered a written test that measures narcissism. Although the study was not done as rigorously as it would be for published research, it did show a nice pattern: As expected, the higher the scores on the narcissism test, the more often people checked out their reflections as they sauntered by. The study neatly illustrates one benefit of unobtrusive measurement—the possibility of assessing traits that might be difficult to measure directly. People are usually reluctant to provide honest answers about traits, such as narcissism, that they perceive to be negative. More generally, the design allowed my students to assess people who were unaware of being assessed and without interfering with their behavior (until the end when they used the conventional narcissism measure to evaluate the validity of their cunning checking-out-oneself-in-the-window test).

People can also be measured unobtrusively when we induce them into making a response but they don't know that their behavior is being observed and measured. Several student groups used such methods. One—the street-theater strategy—involves staging an event in the presence of a target person and then secretly observing that person's response. My students "accidentally" dropped their books, stood in front of a closed door with arms full of boxes, or even "stole" a bag from a café table. They wanted to know whether or not the targeted bystander would help pick up the books, open the door, or intervene in the theft. Again, this wasn't top-notch science, but the students found that people who helped in one context were likely to help in another. Other classic unobtrusive measures include figuring out which museum exhibits are the most popular by counting how often the floor tiles in front of each one must be replaced, or by estimating the number of visitors from the number of nose prints on the glass in front of each exhibit—perhaps even estimating the ages of the viewers from the height of the prints.

Behavioral residue is a type of unobtrusive measure. But rather than use it to assess general patterns of behavior (do museum-goers prefer the Egyptian mummy to the Civil War letters?), my research focuses on the repeated behavior of one person (does Alfie ever fold his laundry?). Snoopers are looking for contexts where there is clear evidence of particular identifiable individuals affecting the world. This is best done in places where people spend a lot of time (and therefore have many opportunities to leave their marks) and where we investigators have a reasonable chance of assigning the residue to the right perpetrator. These considerations led us to study personal environments, like bedrooms and offices, and to look at modes of expression, such as music preferences and clothing styles.

To understand why behavioral residue is so essential to our work, consider one useful definition of personality: *An individual's unique pattern of thinking, feeling, and behaving that is consistent over time.* If you alphabetize your book collection just once, that does not make you an organized person. If you try a new dish on a menu once, that does not suggest that broadmindedness is a part of your personality. For a behavior to be part of your personality, it should be something that you do repeatedly. To be truly organized, you must systematically shelve your books and keep putting them back in their proper places. Moreover, you should also organize your CDs and create folders for your e-mails and keep the corkscrew in the drawer assigned to corkscrews.

To be broadminded, you should try the unknown dish on the menu often, not just as a blip in your typically conservative eating repertoire. You should also prefer unconventional vacations to traditional ones, and you should enjoy risking an evening at an obscure dance performance rather than returning to see *The Nutcracker* year after year. Obviously, repeated behaviors leave more residue than the occasional aberration. Bedrooms and offices are often repositories of evidence for these repeated behaviors; that is, I believe, what makes them such good places to find out what people are like. The accumulated residue in a bedroom distills many more behaviors than could be recorded by an observer in an interview, or even after several meetings.

Traces of personality can be found in the most unlikely (and unsavory) places. When a serious crime hits the news, it is common for the police to remove evidence in large trash bags. In all likelihood, one of those bags contains the occupant's own garbage. Trash is one of the richest places to find behavioral residue. Of course, the FBI is more interested in clues to criminal behaviors than in those related to personality, but the principle is the same. To the chagrin of certain celebrities, scavengers have thrown a spotlight on the scope of information that can be harvested from what we throw away. After rummaging through Cher's garbage in 1973, one such scavenger, Ward Harrison, observed, "It was like I had her whole world in my hands," and he later even proposed that "garbage is a window into the soul."

In the same year that Harrison was going through Cher's trash, a somewhat less sensational project was getting under way at the University of Arizona. William Rathje and his collaborators at the Bureau of Applied Research in Anthropology have for many years been mining the stories told by trash. It's not the most glamorous job in academia, but it is one of the most interesting. The Garbage Project was founded by Rathje on the principle that, just as archaeologists have learned about ancient cultures by exploring ancient refuse, we can learn something about our own society by studying contemporary garbage. More than two decades before I started snooping around rooms and offices, Rathje, who has been called the Indiana Jones of solid waste, began deploying researchers equipped with protective suits, gloves, and masks to uncover clues in city dumps.

Refuse analysis is a serious, scientific methodology that identifies and quantifies what people buy, consume, and discard. Rather than learning about specific people, the Garbage Project documents general trends of consumption and disposal. For example, the researchers tracked patterns of social interaction by looking at how many TV-dinner boxes were discarded in a particular neighborhood.

The Garbage Project's principles and methods could be applied to studies of specific people, but unfortunately in our studies of bedrooms and offices we did not have permission to touch anything. So as much as we would have loved to, we could not up-end the trash cans. Of course, there was nothing to stop our coders from peering into the cans. And should you have a (legitimate) opportunity to snoop into someone's trash, I urge you not to turn it down. It may not be a window into the owner's soul, but it will reveal more than one might think. There you might find personal writings telling you how the person thinks and what he thinks about—five aborted notes to a friend, each peppered with references to auras and the power of crystals not only tell you about his brand of new age spirituality but also about the care he devotes to managing social relations, even if we never get to see the letter that eventually made it to the mailbox. The scrunched-up shopping lists and store receipts will give you an idea not only of what he buys but of how he buys—an impulsive buyer will have items on the receipts that were not on the lists, but a planner will think ahead about buying things in bulk long before they're needed. Discarded art supplies attest to a creative flair. Empty prescription bottles—antidepressants, anti-anxiety meds, and the like—all betray underlying tendencies that could be missed in nearly any other place we might look.

Stuff salvaged from trash cans is particularly useful for two reasons. First, as the items are discarded they are also dismissed from the owner's conscious consideration, so they do not receive the same kind of attention to managing impressions as the items still in play in pretrash life. Second, the contents of a trash can reflect behavior that really happened, not just the kinds of things we think we might do one day. This distinction between what we have done and what we plan to do in the future brings us to a new class of behavioral residue: Not only can you detect past behaviors in physical spaces but you may also discover clues to anticipated behaviors. In one room we found an unopened bottle of wine and a set of floor cushions arranged in a circle, items indicating that the occupant was planning to entertain guests; in another, we saw a new scrapbook, scissors, and glue on a shelf, items suggesting that the woman who lived there planned to attend to some of her sentimental needs.

The metaphor of residue breaks down a bit for activities that have yet to be completed, but the general inference process is the same. Items in a space and their arrangement reflect potential behavior. Just as it is instructive to examine the differences between residue in private and public spaces, it is also useful to look for the discrepancy between signs of anticipated behaviors and signs of past behaviors.

Does this person hope to have friends around for tea, as evidenced by the teapot, tea cups, and numerous packets of tea? But does he never do so, as suggested by a clue only the super snooper would detect—the absence of tea stains in the pot and cups and the ancient sell-by dates on the unopened packets of tea?

People also reveal residue inside their personal spaces of activities they engage in outside those spaces. Frida, one woman in our study, stacked a surfboard, a snowboard, and a skateboard against the wall, suggesting a sensation-seeking occupant. If we'd looked into her garage we might have discovered a bag full of mountain-climbing equipment, water skis, and a sporty car. Stuck to her fridge door we might find a calendar listing upcoming mountain-biking events and a note for her doctor's appointment to attend to the twisted ankle sustained in one of her daredevil pursuits. These examples illustrate the breadth of information we can learn about peoples' broader lives from what we find in their personal spaces—theater-ticket stubs, muddy soccer shoes, and parking tickets can be treated as indoor clues to outside behaviors.

Some of the inferences don't require Sherlock Holmes–like perception. If I find a large DVD library and a sophisticated DVD system in a dorm room, it's not unreasonable to assume that the person who lives there likes to watch movies. Athletic equipment is probably an honest sign that the occupant is athletic. Part of the trick of using trace measures often amounts to turning a natural skill into a research tool.

BECOMING A SHARP SNOOPER

Earlier in this chapter, I talked about the photos and symbols you might display to make self-directed identity claims—a picture of yourself with your spouse and kids or a coffee mug decorated with Harvard's emblem. These self-directed identity claims work because they confirm and support your self-image; they reassure you and make you feel good. That is, objects can simultaneously serve as identity claims and feeling regulators. So as you move through this book and as you snoop through people's personal spaces, ask yourself, not only what particular identity a person is shoring up but also what kinds of thoughts or feelings he or she elicits in doing so. Do the photos on display reflect feelings of success through work (driving a new Jaguar to a high-school reunion), of humility in presence of natural wonders (a campsite in the Atlas Mountains), of power by association (shaking hands with Bill Clinton), of connection with a romantic partner (a shot of the occupant embracing her spouse), or of the companionship conferred by a beloved pet (you and Rover sitting on a jetty looking out over the lake together)?

We have seen in this chapter how people, through identity claims, feeling regulators, and behavioral residue leave traces of themselves in their personal environments. These mechanisms are not mutually exclusive, and it is not always clear which mechanisms are responsible for which clues. A snowboard leaning against a bedroom wall may indeed reflect sensation-seeking behaviors, but the occupant's decision to leave the snowboard in a visible place instead of stowing it in a closet may also reflect a desire to convey to others that she has an active life. You need to keep these distinctions in mind as you form impressions. As you build your snooping skills, stop and look around. Whether you're sitting at home, on the train, in a car, or at a café, it is hard to escape the evidence of deliberate and inadvertent expression. As you consider how each item got to be where it is, you can begin to construct the story of the person responsible for it.

Your guesses about people based on their bedrooms, offices, or Web sites are not different from the other guesses we make about personality in everyday life. They just draw on new forms of information, and your job as a snooper is to learn how to interpret it. For that task, we need to attend some ancient Athenian parties and find out about the "Big Five" model of personality—that is, we need to learn what research has told us about the many ways in which people differ.

TWO

OCEAN's Five

ARE YOU A bacchanalian party kind of person? I'm talking about the real deal here, not those mild modern versions thrown by Jay Z and friends on a yacht moored off an island in the Aegean Sea. I am talking about the parties held two thousand years earlier, not so far from Jay Z's present-day gatherings.

If you were hanging out at the right parties in Athens, you might have noticed an odd character sitting in the corner, furiously scribbling notes as fast as his bone stylus and wax-coated tablets would allow. And if you were on the stingy side when it came to spending your obols, the sort who dominated the discussion of yesterday's chariot races, or, heaven forbid, attempted to dance with someone before he was sufficiently drunk, you might even have been the subject of these scribblings. Many consider the note-taker, Theophrastus, to be the first personality psychologist. As the great chronicler of character types, he spent many hours observing the behavior of his fellow Athenians. And although he didn't have the statistical tools of modern personality research, he did have the next best things: A keen sense of observation combined with an ability to vividly capture how certain behaviors co-occur to yield distinct personality types.

Theophrastus observed that the people who were late in paying back their borrowed obols also drove the hardest bargain when buying an amphora of wine, and that they were the same ones who instructed their servants to make sure the fuller added extra dirt to the cloak so that it could go longer without cleaning. Theophrastus

noticed that the person standing in the square confidently holding
forth on the chariot racing was more likely than others to talk inces-
santly about all manner of topics at any time or place, whether it be
while sitting on a jury, watching a play, or at the dinner table.

ANCIENT CHARACTERS

Theophrastus's realization, which is at once straightforward and pro-
found, was that behaviors are not randomly distributed. If you knew
one thing about a person, you could make a better-than-chance guess
about other things. And this confluence of characteristics resulted in a
personality type. In his great work *The Characters,* Theophrastus
sketched thirty types—from the penurious and the garrulous to the
flatterer and the shamelessly greedy—and illustrated his character
portraits with an astonishing level of detail. Here's an example—the
Unseasonable Man:

> Unseasonableness is an inopportune attitude to those we meet. The Un-
> seasonable Man is the sort of person who comes to confide in you when
> you are busy. He serenades his mistress when she is ill. He asks a man
> to act as his guarantor when the man has just lost by standing surety
> for someone else. He comes to court as a witness when the case is over.
> At a wedding he inveighs against women. He proposes a walk to
> someone who has just arrived after a long journey. He brings a higher
> bidder to a tradesman who has just concluded a bargain. He will get
> up and tell a long story to people who have already heard it and know
> it by heart. He is eager to offer services which are not wanted but
> which cannot be refused with politeness. If he is present at arbitration,
> he stirs up dissension between the two parties. When he begins to
> dance, he catches hold of someone who is not yet drunk.

It's been a long time since Theophrastus plied his trade in Athens,
and a lot has changed in how personality psychologists go about their

work, but the core task has remained the same. Like Theophrastus, we are still interested in finding out about what people are like. But now we also want to discover why they are the way they are. Today's personality psychologists want to know how environment and genetic inheritance combine to shape people's personalities—that is, their relatively stable patterns of thinking, feeling, and behaving— and also how their personal characteristics play out in their lives. Personality psychologists try to understand why some people crave intimacy but smoochy coos of "I love you" have others running for the exits. Or why your local librarian seems intrinsically more suited to that job than to a career as a trial lawyer. Or why some people end up experiencing more than their fair share of health problems.

As a novice snooper, you can take a page from Theophrastus's investigations and observe how individuals differ from one another. And then you can turn to the next landmark in figuring out what people are like: the work of another Greek who also drew inspiration from a popular social scene of his time—gladiatorial combat.

A physician working in a gladiatorial school saw more of the inner workings of the body than the average person. And after peering into enough gory spear gashes and lion-toothed crevasses in the flesh, he might have wondered what all those pipes and tubes were doing underneath. One such Greek physician, Claudius Galen, recognized the medical opportunities afforded by these wounds; he regarded them as windows into the body. Living about four centuries after Theophrastus and later to become one of the most influential physicians in Western medicine, Galen took an audacious leap forward by proposing theories about the physiological bases for character traits. He postulated four basic personality types, each one associated with an imbalance of one of four bodily humors (or fluids): An excess of blood resulted in the sanguine personality, too much black bile rendered you melancholic, too much yellow bile made you choleric, and phlegmatic individuals were thought to have an excess of, well, phlegm.

The idea that there are basic styles of temperament became entrenched in the theories of personality that were put forth later. Although the biological mechanisms that Galen proposed have not stood up to scientific scrutiny, his idea that there is a small number of basic temperaments has survived remarkably well, and has allowed later scientists to map out those basic dimensions. With that map in hand, you can enter a bedroom or browse a music collection, not with a vague question about what the person is like but with a set of questions about the known ways in which people tend to differ. When you are snooping, these questions will not only help ensure that you don't miss any important aspects of personality but also provide a ready-made framework for comparing yourself to others.

THE BIG FIVE

By the late twentieth century, several decades of research had indeed confirmed what our ancient forebears intuited: that certain traits tend to go together. For example, we now know that talkative people tend to be more energetic than quiet people but no more or less dependable. We know that creative people tend to be more philosophical but no more or less anxious than other types. And our understanding of such patterns helps us make sense of the information we gather from people's behavior. We can organize what we learn from how people shake hands or how they decorate their bedrooms into likely personality configurations that serve as working hypotheses until we can gather more information. But keep in mind that figuring out someone's personality, getting to know him or her, is more like solving a puzzle than adding up character traits. Thus, as with a jigsaw puzzle, where we start by sorting the red pieces from the green pieces, we can approach the puzzle of personality by grouping the pieces of personality that tend to go together.

By far the most extensively examined—and firmly established—system for grouping personality traits is the framework known as the

Big Five. (Other systems, such as the Myers-Briggs test—or MBTI, as it is also known—are less widely used in academic psychology.) The Big Five traits are openness, conscientiousness, extraversion, agreeableness, and neuroticism, which when arranged in that order, conveniently spell out OCEAN. I'll be talking about personality in terms of the Big Five throughout this book, and you'll no doubt want to think about your own personality traits as you read about other people's. So before I go into the traits themselves, I suggest you take a quick Big Five test.

Below I have listed traits that may or may not apply to you. Write a number next to each statement to indicate the extent to which you agree or disagree with that statement. You should rate the extent to which the pair of traits applies to you, even if one characteristic applies more strongly than the other. Remember, this is for your own information, so answer as honestly as possible.

Chart 2.1

Disagree strongly	Disagree moderately	Disagree a little	Neither agree nor disagree	Agree a little	Agree moderately	Agree strongly
1	2	3	4	5	6	7

I see myself as:

1. ___6___ Extraverted, enthusiastic
2. ___6___ Critical, quarrelsome
3. ___4___ Dependable, self-disciplined
4. ___5___ Anxious, easily upset
5. ___5___ Open to new experiences, complex
6. ___1___ Reserved, quiet
7. ___4___ Sympathetic, warm
8. ___4___ Disorganized, careless
9. ___4___ Calm, emotionally stable
10. ___2___ Conventional, uncreative

Here is a quick and simple way to figure out your Big Five score.

Chart 2.2

Openness	=	(8 – your score on item 10) + your score on item 5
Conscientiousness	=	(8 – your score on item 8) + your score on item 3
Extraversion	=	(8 – your score on item 6) + your score on item 1
Agreeableness	=	(8 – your score on item 2) + your score on item 7
Neuroticism	=	(8 – your score on item 9) + your score on item 4

This should give you five scores, one for each of the Big Five dimensions. But as isolated numbers they don't mean much. To find out where you stand, you can compare your scores to those of many thousands of people who have taken this test. In our research we have found the following averages:

Chart 2.3

Big Five Domain	Females	Males
Openness	10.8	10.7
Conscientiousness	11.0	10.4
Extraversion	9.1	8.5
Agreeableness	10.6	10.1
Neuroticism	6.7	5.7

If you want a more precise estimate of your score, turn to the notes section at the end of the book, which will show you how to calculate that.

In a moment, I'll describe each of the Big Five traits in more detail, but before I do so there are a few things you need to know. First, we all have scores on all five traits. This means our Big Five scores can be presented as a profile, like the ones in figure 2.1.

Fig. 2.1   Big Five Personality Profiles for Rudy and Mimi

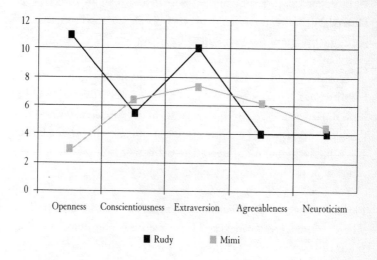

Here we can see that Rudy is relatively high on openness and extraversion, medium on conscientiousness, and relatively low on agreeableness and neuroticism. Mimi has medium levels of conscientiousness, extraversion, and agreeableness, and low levels of openness and neuroticism.

There are two ways of thinking about these personality profiles. First, we can compare a person's trait level to another person's trait level; thus, we could say that Mimi is relatively low on extraversion because her extraversion score is lower than Rudy's. Talking about personality this way is useful when you want to choose between individuals—if, for example, you wanted to know who would be best suited for the position of salesperson (where extraverts do well) or long-distance truck driver (a job that suits introverts).

The second way of thinking compares a person's trait level to his or her other traits; so we can conclude that Mimi is higher on extraversion than she is on the other traits. This approach is useful if we want to characterize a whole individual, as we might if we were describing one friend to another. If I told you about Mimi, I would mention her extraversion because she's higher on that trait than any others, even though she's less extraverted than other people (such as Rudy).

In practice, most of us end up using both ways to characterize others. While snooping around an office, a trait might stick out from other traits—a "Bush/Cheney in 2004" button stuck on a bulletin board would clearly signal the occupant's conservative political beliefs. But given this relatively modest form of expression, we may still think the person is not as conservative as others—that is, the button guy could be higher on conservatism than other traits but at the same time not be the most conservative guy around.

Fig. 2.2   Generation of Personality "Types" by Combining
the Agreeableness and Neuroticism Dimensions

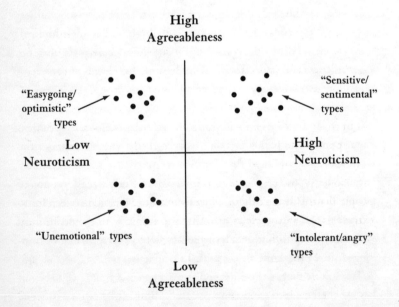

This approach to personality is different from "types" systems, where being placed in one type is at the expense of being placed in another. In the Myers-Briggs system, there are sixteen possible types and you fall into one, and only one, type—if you are an ESTP type (that is, you are classified as a combination of extraversion, sensing, thinking, and perceiving), you cannot be an ISFP type (the combination of introversion, sensing, feeling, and perceiving). The Big Five is distinctive because everyone has a score on all five dimensions.

You can still create "types" from the Big Five by creating groups of people who exemplify combinations of traits. So imagine that we crossed the last two dimensions of the OCEAN model and then plotted the positions of a group of people according to their agreeableness and neuroticism dimensions. As shown in figure 2.2, we could classify people according to the quadrants into which they fall. A person falling in the top-right quadrant (high agreeableness and high neuroticism) could be called a sensitive/sentimental type. Anyone falling in the top-left quadrant (high agreeableness and low neuroticism), could be called an easygoing/optimistic type. Those low on agreeableness but high on neuroticism could be called intolerant/angry types; those low on both dimensions could be called unemotional types. Essentially, this is how systems like the Myers-Briggs test create types.

But there is a problem with splitting people up this way. In reality, the types tend to blend together, with most people falling near the middle of the graph and a few at the extremes (as in fig. 2.3). So talking about "types" of people implies a separation between groups of people that really isn't there. Nonetheless, it can be useful to refer to extraverts and introverts as people at the extremes of the continuum because most of us find that a compelling way to think about personality. We do the same thing with height when we talk about "tall people" and "short people"; when you say a person is tall you are not saying she falls into an entirely different category from short people, just that she falls toward one end of the scale.

Fig. 2.3   A More Realistic Distribution of Individuals'
          Agreeableness and Neuroticism Scores

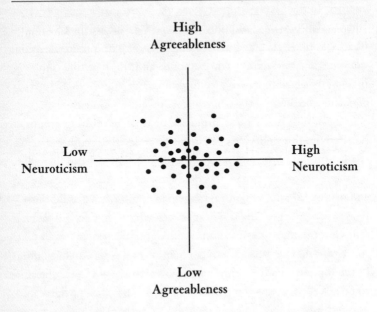

The second thing to remember about the Big Five categories is that they are tremendously broad. Each of the dimensions includes several narrower "facets," which themselves include some even narrower traits. Figure 2.4 shows the hierarchical structure of the Big Five dimension "extraversion." As you can see, extraversion subsumes six lower-order facets: friendliness, gregariousness, assertiveness, activity level, excitement seeking, and cheerfulness. In turn, these subsume narrower traits; gregariousness would be associated with enjoying social activities, and assertiveness with taking charge in group contexts. (To get a better idea of your Big Five scores at the facet level, check out John Johnson's excellent Web site, where you can take a much more extensive 120-question test online and get feedback at the facet level. You can find it at http://www.drj.virtualave.net/IPIP/ipipneo120.htm.)

Fig. 2.4   The Hierarchical Structure of Extraversion and its Facets

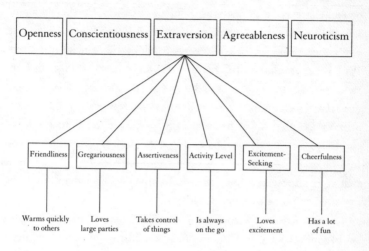

Research has shown that these traits tend to be correlated. But not all the time. So although people who get high scores on gregariousness also tend to get high scores on assertiveness, this is not always so. My own Big Five scores show just such a pattern for the openness dimension. Overall, I am at the high end of the openness dimension and I have high scores on all the facets except one—I am high on the imagination, artistic interests, adventurousness, intellect, and liberalism facets but low on the emotionality facet. So although emotionality generally goes along with the other facets in the population as a whole, for me it does not.

Despite the generalizations that scientists must make, keep in mind that many people have idiosyncratic patterns that don't fit easily into categorical molds—just as I don't in openness. For example, your first look at a prospective roommate's organized bedroom might show that she's high on conscientiousness, which probably means she is high on all the conscientiousness facets. But she is likely to be higher on some facets of conscientiousness than on others. Further snooping will help you find out which ones. Next to the well-organized desk you notice a carton labeled "projects" that is full of marked folders. With the roommate-to-be's permission you have a look. You find stories, art projects, photograph albums (all of which signal high openness). But on closer inspection you notice that few of the projects were actually completed. The first few pages of the photo album are full of carefully labeled photographs, but soon the project peters out and you find random groups of photos stuffed into the back page. You realize that your otherwise conscientious roommate is lower than should be expected on the self-discipline facet.

The third feature of the Big Five that you should keep in mind when you are snooping follows from the last point. The categories can be misleading if they are not interpreted carefully. Some of the labels developed by the Big Fivers (as Big Five researchers are called) correspond more closely than others with how they are understood in everyday parlance. Extraversion does well—what you mean and what the Big Fivers mean correspond closely. But others can be confusing: For example, when you describe a friend as "neurotic" you probably mean that he worries so much that he is unable to function effectively in his daily life. The Big Five dimension of neuroticism does include an anxiety component, but it's much wider than that; it also refers to other negative emotions such as anger and feeling low. People high on this trait tend to react to events more intensely than other people, seeing even minor frustrations as major challenges.

So it's important not to become distracted by the labels themselves; focus instead on the broad array of behaviors associated with each of the dimensions. The Big Five traits, along with representative behaviors and icons exemplifying each trait, are shown in tables 2.1 to 2.5 below. In those tables, I draw heavily from Big Fiver John Johnson's well-researched characterizations of the dimensions and facets. I sug-

gest you fold the corner of these pages so that you can refe
the tables as you read about the results in the rest of the book. (T
of you high on the orderliness facet of conscientiousness have probably already done so!)

The Leonardo Factor—Openness

The dimension known as *openness to experiences*, or just *openness* for
short, is summarized in table 2.1. People at the high end of the scale
enjoy questioning norms and conventions; they like to play with ideas
and they have vivid imaginations. In contrast, the relatively conventional people at the other end of the scale prefer the concrete to the
abstract and the known to the unknown. An icon of openness is
Leonardo da Vinci, the Italian painter, draftsman, scientist, engineer,
architect, sculptor, musician, mathematician, anatomist, astronomer,
geologist, biologist, and philosopher. The painter of the *Mona Lisa*
and the far-sighted inventor of submarines, air-cooling systems, tele-
scopes, and flying machines, Leonardo epitomizes the creativity,
imaginativeness, inventiveness, curiosity, and unconventionality associated with the Renaissance. He's the perfect exemplar of openness.

The high-openness person can be found browsing in the philosophy section of a bookstore, trekking through Bhutan, and driving
past the Olive Garden to Fondue Selassie, an innovative new restaurant that fuses the culinary traditions of Ethiopia and Switzerland. In
contrast, the idea of an "edgy" vacation for someone low on openness
would be forgoing the usual cruise in the Bahamas for a week on a
beach in Florida.

The Robocop Factor—Conscientiousness

My icon of conscientiousness is "half man, half machine, all cop"—
Robocop, the central character from the film by that name. Robocop
is efficient, rule-oriented, and duty-bound. People like Robocop, who

...end to be:
...stract, curious, deep thinkers, inventive,
...etic experiences

People low on op... ss tend to be:
Conventional, concrete, traditional, preferring the known to the unknown

Facets:

- *Imagination:* High scorers tend to engage in fantasy to create a more interesting world.

- *Artistic Interests:* High scorers appreciate beauty in art and nature and are involved and absorbed in aesthetics.

- *Emotionality:* High scorers tend to have good access to and awareness of their feelings.

- *Adventurousness:* High scorers are eager to try new activities, travel to foreign lands, and have different experiences.

- *Intellect:* High scorers love to play with ideas; they are open-minded to new and unusual ideas, and they enjoy debating intellectual issues.

- *Psychological Liberalism:* High scorers are ready to challenge authority, convention, and traditional values.

High Scorers:
Where you might find them:
Browsing in the philosophy section of a bookstore

What they might do:
Take a new route home just because it's different

What they might say:
"Hey, don't throw away that clothes washer—I want to make it into a lamp."

SOURCE: Descriptions adapted from Johnson 2007.

Table 2.2   Big Five Dimension: Conscientiousness

Icon: Robocop

People high on conscientiousness tend to be:
Thorough, dependable, reliable, hardworking, task focused, efficient, good planners

People low on conscientiousness tend to be:
Disorganized, late, careless, impulsive

Facets:
- *Self-Efficacy:* High scorers believe they have the intelligence, drive, and self-control necessary for achieving success.

- *Orderliness:* High scorers are well-organized people who like to live according to routines and schedules; they keep lists and make plans.

- *Dutifulness:* High scorers tend to have a strong sense of moral obligation.

- *Achievement-Striving:* High scorers strive hard to achieve excellence; they often have a strong sense of direction.

- *Self-Discipline:* High scorers have the ability to persist at difficult or unpleasant tasks until they are completed. They are able to overcome reluctance to begin tasks and they stay on track despite distractions.

- *Cautiousness:* High scorers take their time when making decisions.

High Scorers:
Where you might find them:
In the aisle of Office Depot where they sell color-coordinated filing supplies

What they might do:
Buy stamps before the ones they already carry in their wallets run out

What they might say:
"I just checked and I noticed that the meeting we have planned for three months from now is going to clash with a cycling event in the city that day. So I have printed out some maps and highlighted the best alternative routes. In case you need to contact me, you'll find my phone number in the list of useful numbers that I've typed on the back of the map. I'll e-mail you a week before the meeting to make sure everything is still on track."

SOURCE: Descriptions adapted from Johnson 2007.

are high on the trait of conscientiousness, plan ahead. They like order. They buy computer paper before it runs out. They keep their pencils sharp, and they store spare stamps in their wallets. They fold over the corner of the page when it is suggested they do so to help them refer back to a useful table. So although a sense of duty is part of this construct, the dimension is not as dominated by conscience as the Big Five label *conscientiousness* might suggest. Conscientious people tend not to become distracted, and they are not reckless. This is the trait I hope is maxed out in the air-traffic controllers directing a plane I happen to be on; I want that control tower to be entirely populated by people pushing the limits of the conscientiousness dimension—people who are not going to become distracted and overlook the 747 on its way in from Karachi.

When I was in graduate school I had a roommate, Eric, who was training to be a pilot. I'm not very high on conscientiousness myself, so occasionally I would be running late for classes. Sometimes my pilot-to-be roommate offered me a ride to school so that I wouldn't have to go by bike and miss the beginning of class. In great haste I would rush down the stairs from our apartment to the parking lot, jump into the car, and as soon as Eric had turned the key in the ignition, I would brace myself ready to speed away to school. But no bracing was needed. I was forgetting that Eric, quite sensibly, always liked to wait for the car to warm up. Although this level of impulse control might be irksome for those of us lower on the conscientiousness scale, this is exactly the kind of person I want flying a plane—someone who meticulously does things by the book. In a car on a cold morning this means making sure the engine has had time to warm up properly before you hit the streets; and in a plane this means checking all those things that are meant to be checked before hitting the runway.

You might think that conscientiousness is always desirable in ourselves and in the people we are attracted to. Who wouldn't want to be organized, reliable, and persistent? As John Johnson has pointed out: "The benefits of high conscientiousness are obvious—

conscientious individuals avoid trouble and achieve high levels of success through purposeful planning and persistence. And they are also positively regarded by others as intelligent and reliable." However, notes Johnson, there is a down side. "They can be compulsive perfectionists and workaholics. Furthermore, extremely conscientious individuals might be regarded as stuffy and boring."

THE BEVERLY HILLS COP FACTOR—EXTRAVERSION

My extraversion icon is Axel Foley, Eddie Murphy's character in the *Beverly Hills Cop* movies—and, it seems, just about any other character played by Murphy. Foley is talkative, enthusiastic, cheerful, energetic, and gregarious, just the kind of person you want at a party. But, surprisingly, extraversion includes some traits you might not expect to be associated with the dimension. For example, although you might expect that extraverts would be higher than introverts on friendliness and gregariousness, most people would not expect assertiveness to be part of extraversion (it is easy to imagine that assertiveness would instead be associated with low agreeableness or low neuroticism). Of all the Big Five dimensions, extraversion has been studied the most because it is easy to spot in social interactions, the kinds of situations psychologists like to study.

THE MR. ROGERS FACTOR—AGREEABLENESS

For an icon of agreeableness I turn to television. Fred Rogers's gentle and thoughtful manner was so renowned that when thieves realized it was his car they had just stolen, they returned it to the parking spot from which they had taken it. Rogers, the Presbyterian minister who from 1968 until 2001 hosted *Mister Rogers' Neighborhood,* the television program that teaches children about important life issues, was deeply committed to promoting kids' confidence. Rogers anticipated and addressed their fears with great sensitivity, and he

Table 2.3   Big Five Dimension: Extraversion

Icon: Axel Foley *(Beverly Hills Cop)*

People high on extraversion tend to be:
Talkative, energetic, enthusiastic, assertive, outgoing, sociable

People low on extraversion tend to be:
Reserved, quiet, shy

Facets:

- *Friendliness:* High scorers genuinely like other people and openly demonstrate positive feelings toward others; they make friends quickly and it is easy for them to form close, intimate relationships.

- *Gregariousness:* High scorers find the company of others pleasantly stimulating and rewarding; they enjoy the excitement of crowds.

- *Assertiveness:* High scorers like to speak out, take charge, and direct the activities of others.

- *Activity Level:* High scorers lead fast-paced, busy lives; they move about quickly, energetically, and vigorously, and they are involved in many activities.

- *Excitement-Seeking:* High scorers are easily bored without high levels of stimulation. They love bright lights and hustle and bustle and like to take risks and seek thrills.

- *Cheerfulness:* High scorers typically experience a range of positive feelings, including happiness, enthusiasm, optimism, and joy.

High Scorers:
Where you might find them:
At the very center of a party

What they might do:
Rack up a lot of cell phone minutes

What they might say:
"Ha ha ha." (They laugh a lot)

SOURCE: Descriptions adapted from Johnson 2007.

Table 2.4   Big Five Dimension: Agreeableness

Icon: Fred Rogers

People high on agreeableness tend to be:
Helpful, selfless, sympathetic, kind, forgiving, trusting, considerate, cooperative

People low on agreeableness tend to be:
Fault finding, quarrelsome, critical, harsh, aloof, blunt

Facets:
- *Trust:* High scorers assume that most people are fair, honest, and have good intentions.

- *Morality:* High scorers see no need for pretense or manipulation when dealing with others; they are candid, frank, and sincere.

- *Altruism:* High scorers find that doing things for others is a form of self-fulfillment rather than self-sacrifice.

- *Cooperation:* High scorers dislike confrontations; to get along with others, they are willing to compromise or to deny their own needs.

- *Modesty:* High scorers do not like to claim that they are better than other people.

- *Sympathy:* High scorers are tenderhearted and compassionate. They feel the pain of others vicariously and are easily moved to pity.

High Scorers:
Where you might find them:
Saving the baby seals

What they might do:
Console an acquaintance

What they might say:
"Really? They've taken 'gullible' out of the dictionary? I didn't know that."

SOURCE: Descriptions adapted from Johnson 2007.

encouraged them to become happy, productive citizens. He is a good representative for the positive pole of agreeableness because he embodied generosity, compassion, warmth, and kindness. So despite the name, agreeableness does not really refer to people who are pushovers. It's more about interpersonal warmth. People low on this trait are frank in their opinions, and blunt, and not particularly concerned with protecting others' feelings. *American Idol*'s Simon Cowell (or at least the way he portrays himself on the show), who is known for his cruel putdowns, exemplifies the low end of this pole. If after a really tough week you were feeling sorry for yourself and looking for comfort, Simon would not top the list of people you'd call.

THE WOODY ALLEN FACTOR—NEUROTICISM

Neuroticism is another of the traits beset with an unfortunate label. The Big Five brand is far broader than our use of the term in everyday speech. Neuroticism refers to people who are easily stressed and find it hard to remain calm in tense situations. They worry a lot, often ruminating about what lies ahead or what has just happened. I like to think of the dimension as reflecting how easily ruffled someone is. The icon of high neuroticism is the chronically ruffled, perpetually anxious Woody Allen. At the other end of the neuroticism spectrum, reclines "The Dude" from *The Big Lebowski,* the 1998 Coen brothers movie. In a scholarly essay, Scott F. Kiesling, a linguist from the University of Pittsburgh, notes that dude-ness is characterized by nonchalance. Indeed, "El Duderino" is not easily fazed; despite having his carpet urinated on and engaging in altercations with the police, gangsters, nihilists, and pornographers, he remains essentially unruffled.

Grasping the Big Five dimensions is essential for learning what people are like and for discerning the differences among them—as a snooper you are well advised to keep this valuable tool close at hand.

TABLE 2.5   Big Five Dimension: Neuroticism

Icon: Woody Allen

People high on neuroticism tend to be:
Anxious, easily ruffled or upset, worried, moody

People low on neuroticism tend to be:
Calm, relaxed, able to handle stress well, emotionally stable

Facets:
- *Anxiety:* High scorers often feel as if something dangerous were about to happen; they tend to feel tense, jittery, and nervous.

- *Anger:* High scorers are inclined to feel angry; they are sensitive about being treated fairly and feel resentful and bitter when they feel they are being cheated.

- *Depression:* High scorers tend to feel sad, dejected, and discouraged; they lack energy and have difficulty initiating activities.

- *Self-Consciousness:* High scorers are sensitive about what others think of them; they are easily embarrassed and often feel ashamed.

- *Immoderation:* High scorers have difficulty resisting strong cravings and urges and tend to be oriented toward short-term pleasures and rewards rather than long-term consequences.

- *Vulnerability:* High scorers experience panic, confusion, and helplessness when under pressure or stress.

High Scorers:
Where you might find them:
Awake, tossing and turning in bed the night before an important meeting

What they might do:
Think again and again and again what his friend really meant by that remark

What they might say:
"Why are you always criticizing me? . . . Yes, you are."

SOURCE: Descriptions adapted from Johnson 2007.

But the Big Fivers never intended these descriptors to tell the whole story. To gain a richer understanding of a person, you need to move beyond (or below) the level of traits to discover the more deeply rooted elements of personality—goals and needs, hopes and dreams, and perceptions of ourselves as part of a personal story that started long ago. I explore these richer aspects of personality in the next chapter.

~m~

Getting to Know You

ARE YOU READING this book in a public place? If so, sneak a peek over the cover and take a look at a stranger. By definition you don't know much about this person. But some people do. To someone he is a cherished father, a loving husband, a devoted friend. What does it mean to know someone? What does it take to go from being a stranger to becoming a friend?

My colleague Jack was once a stranger to me. Should you meet him, he would strike you as affable and thoughtful. And you'd probably find him generous too; when I was first introduced to him, he invited me to lunch to hear about my latest research projects. I soon discovered that he's talkative and intelligent. After a few more lunches I learned a bit about his scholarly ambitions and how he felt about being a parent and a professor. However, as I continued to hang out with Jack, I began to notice that the stories all seemed familiar, even though they described different events. Then one day it struck me why this was so. Whether he was telling me about a presentation at an academic conference, a squabble with a neighbor, or how he fixed his car last week, the narrative was always a variation on the same story line: *Despite the odds against me and the expectations by others that I would fail, I persevered and succeeded and showed everyone else that I was right all along.* The recurring theme resonated with the way Jack saw the world around him and how he saw his place in that world. And this view of himself was an important part of his personality. After figuring out his theme, I felt I knew Jack better. I had gone to a deeper level.

Getting to know a person requires that we find ways to jump from one level to another, not just travel extensively at the same plane. The psychologist who knows the most about the different levels of personality is one of my academic heroes, Dan McAdams. He's a brilliant and exceptionally creative professor at Northwestern University's School of Education and Social Policy and the author of the influential book *The Stories We Live By: Personal Myths and the Making of the Self*.

I was pleased to bump into McAdams at a recent conference because I had been hoping to ask him something. As soon as it seemed polite, I hit him with my question: "Does Lynn exist?" A knowing smile materialized on his face. Apparently he gets this question a lot because he immediately knew what I was talking about.

PERSONALITY THE LONG WAY

One of the things I have long admired about McAdams is his refusal to shy away from the kind of deep issues that make life complicated. McAdams loves to play in the sticky stuff. His forays off the beaten track have yielded some of the most interesting discoveries in contemporary personality research. His goal is to understand people, in all their richness, from a systematic scientific perspective. He studies personality "the long way," meaning that he is interested in learning not only what people are like now but also how they became one way rather than another and, ultimately, how their past and present play into their future.

In a much admired article, McAdams explores a question at the very heart of what personality psychologists most care about: What does it really mean to know someone? He begins by inviting the reader to imagine him and his wife driving home from a dinner party. Before long, their conversation turns to the other guests. One of them, a widely traveled freelance writer, stood out from the others. At first she intimidated McAdams: "I felt I couldn't keep up with the fast tempo of her account, how she moved quickly from one exotic tale to another. Add to this the fact that she is a strikingly attractive woman, about forty years old, with jet black hair, dark eyes, seemingly flawless complexion, clothing both flamboyant and tasteful." This was Lynn.

As the evening wore on, McAdams and his wife found themselves warming up to Lynn as she revealed more about her life and history, her values and feelings; they realized they both wanted to know Lynn better. This is the point at which McAdams poses his fundamental question. What would he need to know in order to know Lynn better?

This is a powerful question because although we can all bring to mind people we know well and people we know superficially, when we are forced to articulate what exactly distinguishes these two groups of people, the veil of simplicity falls away. Beyond miscellaneous facts (he has a large collection of butterflies) and historical details (she went to school in Guyana), it is hard to put your finger on what more you know about your inner circle of friends than about your acquaintances. What is it, in concrete terms, that we know after a thousand days of knowing someone that we did not know on day one?

McAdams provides a good answer to this question. Getting to know someone, he says, means progressing through three distinct levels of intimacy. When he first met Lynn, he thought about her in broad descriptors—she seemed socially dominant, extraverted, entertaining, dramatic, moody, slightly anxious, intelligent, and introspective. These descriptors are *traits* and they constitute the first level of knowing a person. The Big Five dimensions—openness, conscientiousness, extraversion, agreeableness, and neuroticism—describe people at the level of traits.

Traits come first in McAdams's scheme because they provide an efficient "first read" on someone. When describing ourselves and others, traits are the words we reach for first. They can often be found at the beginning of personal ads. "Kind, vivacious, tolerant, honest, and spunky." "I'm fun, smart, sexy, and open." "I'm honest, crass, a little bit trashy, a lot naughty, and never, ever dull."

Think about the words you might use to describe someone you have just met. There's a good chance that your description will feature traits heavily—terms such as *curious, friendly, extraverted, anxious,* and *moody* arise easily in the language of personality. One study found that the most common words people used to describe themselves or others were *friendly, lazy, helpful, easygoing, honest, happy, moody, selfish,* and *shy.* Words at the bottom of the list—that is, rarely used words—included *jittery, dramatic, reluctant,* and *two-faced.* (And we're not species-ist in our use of trait terms. In one of my studies of dog personality, some of the same traits came up, though of course there were important differences. The equivalent canine top ten descriptors are *friendly, playful, loyal, cute, loud, loving, energetic, protective, affectionate,* and *smelly.* Other rarer items in the dog domain included *wrinkly, vivacious, tender, ragged, skittish,* and *obstinate.*)

Trait terms are common in our language. One classic study set out to find out exactly how common. In 1936, the eminent Harvard personality psychologist Gordon Allport and his hapless assistant, Henry Odbert, published a monograph that has become famous not just for what the authors found but also for what they did. Allport and Odbert must have been short of entertainment because they set themselves a gargantuan task: to go through every entry in Webster's unabridged dictionary and write down each instance of a word that could be used to describe someone's personality. They found 17,953 such words—which ranged from common terms such as *shy, friendly, calm, quiet,* and *wise,* to obscure descriptors like *dubitative, acaroid, bevering,* and *davered.* However, many of these descriptors were not traits; they were evaluative terms, such as *insignificant* and *worthy,* or descriptors of temporary states of mind or mood, such as *gibbering* and *rejoicing,* or physical qualities that are sometimes associated with personality, like *roly-poly* and *red-headed.* So Allport and Odbert whittled away the terms they considered insufficiently observable or trait-like and ended up with a mere 4,500 trait terms. This mammoth undertaking proved that we have an enormous vocabulary for describing consistent behaviors, and it also showed, by implication, that traits are a crucial piece of what people are like.

But, as McAdams notes, traits only take us a short distance toward the goal of knowing someone well. They take us only as far as acquaintanceship. For making weighty decisions, are traits enough? Would you be prepared to choose a spouse on the basis of a description of his or her traits? McAdams would bet not. With a hint of derision, he says that traits provide "a psychology of the stranger." They paint a portrait in broad brushstrokes but leave out much of the finer detail. There are many ways to be extraverted or nervous or entertaining or dramatic or moody. What can traits tell us about Lynn's values and political beliefs, or her goals and roles? We want to know more. What does she hope to achieve during the next five years? What are her regrets? What makes her weak in the knees? Answers to questions like these give us the kind of details we'd have to know to feel that Lynn is no longer a stranger. So to understand the unique way in which Lynn expresses her extraversion (and her other traits), we must step up a level in the McAdams hierarchy to level two: "personal concerns."

Personal concerns provide the contextual details that are missing from traits. They include roles—Lynn is a wife, a mother, and a writer. They include goals—Lynn wants to read more contemporary fiction, win a writing award, make a greater effort to express what's on her mind, and she wants to go to Venice. They include skills—Lynn can climb rocks; she tells good stories, and she writes well. They could include values, too, such as seeking a comfortable or an exciting life, a world at peace, a world of beauty, ambition, courage, family security, forgiveness, imagination, inner harmony, intellect, love, national security, salvation, self-respect, social recognition, true friendship, and wisdom.

These are the kinds of details snoopers dig for when they want to know someone better. Contrary to what you might expect, though, getting to know someone won't inevitably bring you closer to that person. Reading a biography of Winston Churchill might give you insights into his personality at all three of McAdams's levels, but it won't foster a relationship with the great leader. That said, learning about someone often does increase intimacy. That's why research on relationships, romantic or otherwise, can help us understand the getting-to-know-you phenomenon.

Arthur Aron, a psychologist at the State University of New York at Stony Brook, is interested in how people form romantic relationships, and he's come up with an ingenious way of taking men and women who have never met before and making them feel close to one another. Given that he has just an hour or so to create the intimacy levels that typically take weeks, months, or years to form, he accelerated the getting-to-know-you process through a set of thirty-six questions crafted to take the participants rapidly from level one in McAdams's system to level two. The questions are part of an hour-long "sharing game" in which each member of a pair reads a question out loud and then they both answer it before moving on to the next question.

A sampling of questions from Aron's "Sharing Game" appears below. Try answering them in your head and then consider what they reveal about you. You'll see how sharing the answers could make you think you know someone and feel closer to that person, too.

- Given the choice of anyone in the world, whom would you want as a dinner guest?
- Before making a telephone call, do you ever rehearse what you are going to say? Why?
- What would constitute a "perfect" day for you?
- When did you last sing to yourself? To someone else?
- If you were able to live to the age of 90 and retain either the mind or body of a 30-year-old for the last 60 years of your life, which would you want?
- Do you have a secret hunch about how you will die?
- If you could change anything about the way you were raised, what would it be?

- If you could wake up tomorrow having gained any one quality or ability, what would it be?
- Is there something that you've dreamed of doing for a long time? Why haven't you done it?
- What is your most treasured memory?
- If you knew that in one year you would die suddenly, would you change anything about the way you are living now? Why?
- What roles do love and affection play in your life?
- Share with the others an embarrassing moment in your life.
- When did you last cry in front of another person? By yourself?
- What, if anything, is too serious to be joked about?

In just an hour, Aron's subjects learned things about each other that would typically never emerge in a face-to-face meeting with a stranger. Some of these questions look at values and goals. Others are designed to break down the barriers we erect in ordinary formal or superficial relationships. For example, if we admit to others that we rehearse what we are going to say before making a phone call, we have essentially already let others peek behind our public mask; we are now free to talk about other stuff not typically authorized for broad consumption. These may seem like tough topics to share with a stranger, but Aron says he has encountered very few negative reactions from participants; virtually everyone enjoys the experience and finds it meaningful. The one exception was a study he did with police officers for whom the questions about death were too intense (so new questions were developed). Richard Slatcher, a relationships researcher at UCLA who has used the procedure, believes that people can deal comfortably with the personal questions because they slowly escalate their levels of disclosure, in essence giving people the opportunity to get used to the idea (albeit quickly) of sharing their deepest and sometimes darkest secrets.

How do we know it is really the content of the questions that's driving the closeness, not just the camaraderie the subjects share while chitchatting together? To tease this out, Aron also created a small-talk questionnaire that included questions such as these:

- When was the last time you walked for more than an hour? Describe where you went and what you saw.
- Describe the last time you went to the zoo.
- Tell the names and ages of your family members, include grandparents, aunts and uncles, and where they were born (to the extent you know this information).
- One of you say a word, the next say a word that starts with the last letter of the word just said. Do this until you have said fifty words. Any words will do—you aren't making a sentence.
- Where are you from? Name all the places you've lived.
- Do you prefer digital watches and clocks or the kind with hands? Why?
- What are the advantages and disadvantages of artificial Christmas trees?

Yuccch! Digital clocks and artificial Christmas trees?! What a snoozer this session would be. UCLA's Slatcher reports huge differences in the reactions of groups using the "closeness" and "small talk" questions. In fact those participants in the closeness conversations didn't want to part company afterwards; many were seen exchanging cell phone numbers so they could stay in contact. In contrast, Slatcher described participants emerging from the small-talk session as looking as if they had just come out of a tiring committee meeting; he saw no evidence whatsoever that they had any interest in staying in touch with one another.

Aron's procedure has worked well in the lab. But can these questions be used to get to know people in ordinary life? Aron thinks they can, but with one caveat: You should not jump too fast. The procedure is based on long-standing research showing that the best way to build a friendship is to escalate self-disclosure gradually, essentially moving through McAdams's levels. So you should begin with the relatively tame questions—say, "Who would you invite to dinner if you could pick anyone at all?—and take time to work up to the more intense ones, such as "If you knew you were going to die in a year, what would you change about how you are living now?" When a conversation becomes boring or superficial, Aron himself uses questions from his test to spark interesting discussions and deepen friendships.

Of course, even without Aron's clever questioning, most of us develop our own informal conversational ploys to move beyond McAdams's first level of acquaintanceship. But how do we accomplish this? How do we communicate our thoughts, preferences, feelings, and values? And how does what we talk about influence our impressions of one another? My collaborator Jason Rentfrow and I decided to learn more about these conversations. We were particularly interested in seeing which topics came up, because that would tell us where people believed they could acquire useful information about others. We devised a six-week study to track conversations among strangers, all young adults, as they got to know each other. Instead of allowing our subjects to engage in face-to-face interactions, we arranged for them to communicate on an online bulletin board system. This setup excluded all the extraneous information— what people look like or who their friends are—that gets conveyed in face-to-face conversations, and it allowed us to monitor exactly what was said.

In the fall of 2002, we enrolled sixty young men and women in our study. We gave the participants no restrictions; we just told them to talk about anything they thought would enable them to get to know one another. Over the next six weeks, as the strangers took the first steps down the path to friendship, we recorded and coded every word that passed between them.

We knew from our previous research that our subjects would be likely to discuss their preferences for books, clothing, movies, sports, music, and television shows. We conducted this study during football season at the University of Texas, where students take their football seriously, so we added a special "football" category. In the end, we identified and coded seven topics: books, clothing, movies,

Fig. 3.1   Percentage of Students Who Talked About Music vs.
Other Topics in Six-Week Online Getting-Acquainted
Conversations

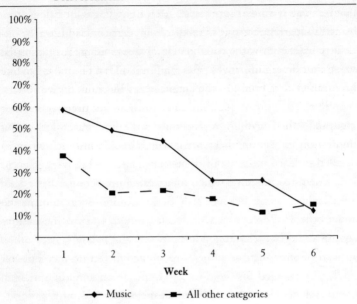

music, television shows, football, and sports other than football. We used a computer program to measure how frequently each of these topics cropped up in conversation.

The results were striking. As you can see in figure 3.1, music was by far the most commonly discussed of the topics. During the first week, 58 percent of participants talked about music; movies (41 percent) and football (41 percent) were next. As the weeks wore on, people began to move beyond the assigned categories, but music continued to be among the most commonly discussed topics; only once in the first six weeks was it not the most discussed topic. It is a testament to the perceived informative value of music that even when people were free to discuss anything they considered relevant to the task of becoming acquainted, the majority chose to talk about music.

Of course, not all groups would use music preferences as a rapid form of communication; music is particularly salient to young people who are struggling to discover and define who they really are. For them, music is an extraordinarily useful language—it can express many different messages (I'm rebellious or angry or traditional or bitter or wholesome, or any combination of these), there are no external constraints determining what you can like (you can't be too tall to like Jazz music), and, crucially, the language is widely understood by the people you're trying to communicate with. At other times, or in other groups, another medium might jump to the fore: Parents of young children might communicate their values and identity in conversations about playgroups and pediatricians, about where they plan to send their daughters to school or what videos they let their sons watch. There again, the language would be widely understood by the group members. But even this medium would not offer the flexibility and versatility of music preferences.

Carefully controlled research projects like our getting-to-know-you study need to be backed up with evidence from the messy difficult-to-control, but real, world. In modern Western societies, this evidence is best found on Internet dating Web sites, such as e-harmony or match.com. Here, someone who wants a platonic or an intimate relationship can search thousands of user profiles for potential matches; with this information in hand, the lonely hearts must decide whether to move on to the next stage of e-intimacy. Dating companies compete fiercely to win your business, so user profiles feature the categories that are believed to be rich in personal information. When we visited the ten most popular online dating Web sites (purely for research purposes, of course), we found that 90 percent of them asked users questions about their music preferences. This was entirely consistent with our snooping research, which has shown that music consistently trumps books, clothing, food, movies, and television shows in helping people get to know each other. And we'll come to see in chapter 7 what can be learned from different music tastes.

IDENTITY

Once you've dug through the traits and personal concerns of McAdams's first two levels, you strike the bedrock of personality—identity. McAdams describes his third level, identity, as "an inner story of the self that integrates the reconstructed past, perceived present, and anticipated future to provide a life with unity, purpose, and meaning." Thus, identity brings coherence to the different elements of our lives; it is the thread that ties the experiences of our past, present, and future into one narrative. I wouldn't be a bit surprised if my colleague Jack—the one who was constantly beating the odds against him to prove others wrong—held a memory from an early experience, like being ridiculed by a critical and unsupportive parent, that served to drive his narrative, perhaps with the theme-making appearances later in adolescence and during his early career. Now that theme of fighting those who don't believe in him drives and guides his future behaviors. And it may work in good ways, too, perhaps motivating him to show them all by writing a book and also making up for the harsh parenting he suffered by building close relationships with his children and grandchildren. These kinds of events are what the psychologist Jefferson Singer, of Connecticut College, calls "self-defining memories" because they help explain who you are as an individual.

Our identities have many parts, and it is amazing how easily we can integrate new pieces into our coherent sense of self. I remember driving to work several years ago, having recently made the decision to write this book. I was listening to a radio interview with Tom Clancy. He started a sentence with the phrase "We writers . . ." and then went on to explain the challenges and pleasures of the writing life. Without realizing what I was doing, I found myself nodding knowingly, saying to myself, "Yes, we do encounter those challenges, don't we?" At that point, I still hadn't written a word of text, yet I had somehow begun to integrate the role of "writer" into my identity. It was preposterous behavior and I was grateful there was nobody there to witness it.

Elements of identity can wax and wane with the circumstances; I am English, but this had never been a central component to how I saw myself until I moved to the United States, where my Englishness suddenly became much more salient. My accent stands out much more in Austin than it does in London, and in the eyes of others (and hence myself), I have become the ambassador of all things English. How you define yourself is influenced to a large degree by your context. For example, when I lived in England, I didn't think of myself as European because that term mainly referred to the continental Europeans over there across the English Channel. But from over here, that tiny sliver of water between us and the French seems so very irrelevant; I've been integrated into Europe, even in my own mind.

Identity is deeply rooted in all of us but—my instant-writer self-image notwithstanding—it typically isn't articulated explicitly. Rarely is someone able to describe his or her identity on demand. It needs to be drawn out. As part of his research program, McAdams has developed an interview explicitly tailored to elicit the elements of identity. Learning the intimate details about someone can bring you closer—perhaps closer than you want to be, as we saw from Arthur Aron's research—so the interview comes with a whole set of warnings. McAdams urges both the interviewer and interviewee to think carefully about whether their relationship is prepared for the increase in intensity that such an interaction nearly always produces.

Based on the idea that identities involve developing stories, not snapshots of single instances, McAdams's interview starts by asking you to break your life up into chapters. People vary in how they do this—some use chronological eras, such as grade-school, high school, college, work; others use critical incidents, like their parents' divorce, the accident, their first kiss; some use thematic systems, such as work, education, romance, play. The interview continues to ask questions about the very good and very bad experiences in your life, about your heroes and your turning points.

As you might expect, McAdams's interview yields a wonderfully rich harvest of personal information; typically, even people who believe they know you well will learn a lot more about you from such an intimate encounter. But from a research perspective the challenge lies in bringing the information together to form a coherent picture of a person. Unlike information on traits, which can be collected in minutes and readily compared, the differences between these portraits are difficult to quantify. However, identity lies at the core of who we are, so really getting to know someone means locating this core.

Most of us don't have access to McAdams's formal method of eliciting information about identity. But, happily, snooping is a good shortcut to this key component of personality because much of our everyday stuff holds clues to identity. As I noted in chapter 1, a good place to find these clues is in the photos of themselves that people choose to display. When I was last in New York City I visited John, a good friend of mine, who is a faculty member at NYU. He is the quintessential academic intellectual—widely read, cultured, philosophical, and sophisticated—and he has long been politically active. These are genuine features of his personality and they are, I believe, also central components of his identity. As I was waiting for John to finish a phone call, my eyes wandered to an old photograph from a college newspaper that he had framed and placed on top of a filing cabinet. The photograph depicts a student protest and, there at the front of the march, was John back in his days as a student activist. Near the news story were a couple of posters—one advertised a play inspired by the works of Kafka and the other was a print commemorating a Salvador Dali exhibition. Although he genuinely liked how the images looked, they resonated with John's sense of who he was, reminding him of interests and episodes consistent with his self-views as a cultured person (I subsequently learned that the print also reminded him of a childhood visit with his grandfather to the Dali Museum in St. Petersburg, Florida). Later, I had a chance to stay in John's apartment in Budapest. There on the bookshelf was a framed photo of John as a boy deeply engrossed in a game of chess with his father, a professor of philosophy. It was not a photo of John playing soccer (which he had done) or on an adventure with his high-school friends or drinking beer in a ski chalet in Utah. It seemed to me that the photo that had made it all the way to the bookshelf helped John connect with his deeply rooted intellectual leanings and that this element of his personality reflected his close bond with his father.

McAdams makes an important point about identity: It is a story you tell about yourself to make sense out of what has happened in the past and the kind of person you are now. From this perspective, it is not essential that the story be true. I see myself as culturally adventurous (that is, high on openness). I happen to believe this is also true—that is, compared with others, I would be relatively open to trying new things on a menu, taking up new activities, visiting new places, and so on. But, from McAdams's perspective, when we're talking about identity, whether our beliefs about ourselves are true or not is pretty much irrelevant.

This is why McAdams brilliantly invokes the concept of a myth when talking about the stories we tell ourselves about ourselves—like ancient myths, they're coherent narratives that may or may not be true. So how can I tell whether being open is part of my identity (irrespective of whether it's true)? One way is to see how I react when my openness is challenged. If someone accuses me of being closed-minded, it's remarkable to watch myself leap into action to protect my identity. "Oh, yes, you think I'm closed-minded, do you?. . . Excuse me one moment. . . . Waiter, I've changed my mind about the crème brulee. I'll have the seared tripe ice cream with the lawn-grass reduction." My reaction would show that being open is central to how I see myself—just as my colleague Jack envisions himself locked in struggle against imaginary oppressors who seek to hold him back. How I feel about my openness is different from how I feel about my other traits. Should you accuse me of being too talkative or too quiet or too messy or too neat, I would be just fine with that because those traits are not tied so tightly to how I see myself.

An interesting source of clues about identity are the signature quotations at the foot of e-mails, where people display phrases that connect to a particularly salient piece of their identity. Below are eight quotations pasted from the signature sections of e-mails I have collected in the past few years:

A. "An individual has not started living until he can rise above the narrow confines of his individualistic concerns to the broader concerns of all humanity." —MLK, Jr.

B. "Solutions that ignore causation solve nothing."

C. "There are two primary choices in life: to accept conditions as they exist, or accept the responsibility for changing them."
—Denis Waitley

D. "You know, it's a small world . . . but I wouldn't want to have to paint it." —Steven Wright

E. "There may be times when we are powerless to prevent injustice, but there must never be a time when we fail to protest."
—Elie Wiesel

F. "Basic psychology is one of my subroutines."
—A. Schwarzenegger as T3

G. "The future belongs to those who believe in the beauty of their dreams." —Eleanor Roosevelt

H. "I'll play it first and tell you what it is later." —Miles Davis

See if you can match these to the people who sent the e-mails:

1. A police officer
2. A graduate student interested in evolutionary explanations for human behavior
3. A nerdy computer technician
4. The director of an Hispanic research center
5. A professor of animal behavior known for taking giant imaginative intellectual leaps
6. An undergraduate student hoping to be admitted to our Ph.D. program
7. A psychology professor

8. A low-ranking person in an organization who had just taken the plunge and sent out an e-mail to the whole organization detailing a superior's sexual misconduct

So how did you do matching the e-mail signature quotations to the people who sent them? Here are the answers:

Table 3.1   Signature Quotations Matched with their Originators

This quote	was in an email from
A. "An individual has not started living until he can rise above the narrow confines of his individualistic concerns to the broader concerns of all humanity." —MLK, Jr.	4. The director of an Hispanic research center
B. "Solutions that ignore causation solve nothing."	2. A graduate student interested in evolutionary explanations for human behavior
C. "There are two primary choices in life: to accept conditions as they exist, or accept the responsibility for changing them." —Denis Waitley	1. A police officer
D. "You know, it's a small world . . . but I wouldn't want to have to paint it." —Steven Wright	3. A nerdy computer technician
E. "There may be times when we are powerless to prevent injustice, but there must never be a time when we fail to protest." — Elie Wiesel	8. A low-ranking person in an organization who had just taken the plunge and sent out an e-mail to the whole organization detailing a superior's sexual misconduct
F. "Basic psychology is one of my subroutines." —A. Schwarzenegger as T3	7. A psychology professor
G. "The future belongs to those who believe in the beauty of their dreams." —Eleanor Roosevelt	6. An undergraduate student hoping to be admitted to our Ph.D. program
H. "I'll play it first and tell you what it is later." —Miles Davis	5. A professor of animal behavior known for taking giant imaginative intellectual leaps

Even if you only got a few right (getting more than one is beating chance), that's a pretty impressive feat when you consider the task: to match a few words pasted at the end of an e-mail to an exceptionally brief description of a person you had not even heard of just minutes ago. Each of the quotations resonated with the person who sent it. For some of them, the connection is clearer than for others: that the psychology professor chose the Terminator quotation about psychology being one of his subroutines is not surprising; nor is the choice of the MLK quotation by the director of a center focused on an ethnic minority. But the "Solutions that ignore causation solve nothing" quotation could have belonged to several people on that list; perhaps most likely was the animal behavior professor. However, even when we don't know exactly why the person chose that particular quotation, we still learn something about the sender, and in doing so we have collected another piece of the personality puzzle. We may not know the full story connecting the animal behavior professor to the "I'll play it first and tell you what it is later" quotation, but merely knowing they are associated may tell us about his approach to life and science— one that is whimsical and playful and embraces the (as yet) unknown.

Your e-mail signature quotations may change over time, especially when you go through a major transition, such as leaving home to go to college, getting your first job, becoming a parent, or getting divorced. I saw an interesting e-mail example of this when I accepted an undergraduate to work with me as a Ph.D. student. Here's what appeared at the foot of her e-mail when she was still attending a small liberal arts college:

> Never doubt that a small group of thoughtful committed citizens can change the world. Indeed, it is the only thing that ever has.
> —Margaret Mead

Only a matter of days later, just after she had been accepted into our program where she would soon embark on her career as a scientist, the quotation had changed:

Everything should be made as simple as possible, but not simpler.
—Albert Einstein

Several years later when I showed my student the quotations, she confirmed the shift in identity. The first reflected her self-image as an activist idealist college student. Later, although she still believed in the quotation's message, it had become less central to her identity, which had become wrapped up in the challenges of doing good science.

Other e-mail signatures illustrate continuity. Consider the three quotations below, all received in e-mail correspondences over the course of a year from a student I never met:

Sed Omnia Praeclara Tam Difficilia Quam Rara Sunt (but everything great is just as difficult to realize as it is rare to find).
—Spinoza, *Ethics*

But the one who feels no distaste in sampling every study, and who attacks his task of learning and cannot get enough of it, him we shall rightly pronounce the lover of wisdom, the philosopher, shall we not?
—Plato's *Republic*

Creativity is not merely the innocent spontaneity of youth and childhood; it must also be married to a passion of the adult being, which is a passion to live beyond one's death.
—Rollo May

Each of these conveys a similar high-minded, almost pretentious, message about the noble but demanding journey toward achieving greatness, wisdom, or creativity. It seems the student has internalized the identity of an intellectual—one who sees himself as part of a rich tradition. If I had the task of buying him a gift, I'd head straight to the used bookstore and buy him a first edition of William James's 1890 classic, *The Principles of Psychology.*

THE PUZZLE OF PERSONALITY

I was not the only one intrigued by McAdams's characterization of Lynn; indeed, it was at the urging of my graduate students that I stalked him at the conference and asked him whether Lynn existed. The answer was yes and no. It turns out that Lynn was a composite of several real people. I have to admit that I was disappointed to learn that this character McAdams had portrayed so vividly wasn't out there in the world—though I surely wasn't as disappointed as the man who, according to McAdams, claimed to have fallen in love with her!

But McAdams's contribution goes far beyond clever portraiture. The crucial lesson from his work is that getting to know someone is not just a matter of knowing more about the person; that "more" must be a different kind of information. You have to go beyond traits, such as how kind the person is or how talkative; you have to begin understanding the person's goals and values: what she hopes to accomplish in her career, how she feels about being a parent, whether she believes in a higher power, whether she strives for excitement in her life, or craves family security, or covets success in her career. And to know someone really well, you must go even deeper, ultimately learning about the person's identity, a concept that, as we shall see, is crucial to the snooping I have done in bedrooms, offices, Web sites, and music collections.

FOUR

Belgian Sleuths and Scandinavian Seabirds

I N MAY 1942, five months after the United States entered World War II, the newly created Office of Strategic Services instituted a program to identify candidates suitable for work behind enemy lines—essentially they were looking for spies. The hastily recruited staff developed tests that would distinguish good spies from bad ones. One task, the "Belongings Test" required candidates to describe people based solely from information gleaned by assessing items they had left in their bedrooms—among them clothing, a timetable, and a ticket receipt. The assumption underlying this test was the same one that drives my own research—much can be learned about people from the spaces they inhabit.

I thought about the OSS spy tests one summer not long ago when I spent a few weeks working in New York City with a research collaborator. A colleague of his at the business school where he teaches—I'll call her Stephanie—had kindly made her office available to me. As soon as I opened the door, I couldn't help but notice the large wooden seagull mobile hanging from the ceiling. It was hard to miss because it was in the center of the room, near her desk, about six feet up from the floor. Soon after I arrived, people started dropping by to say hello; when they heard about the kind of research I do, they quizzed me about the seagull hanging between us. Did I think it had a special meaning? What did it say about Stephanie's personality?

I wasn't surprised by these questions—I get them all the time. When I enter someone's office or home, my host will point to an item and ask me with great anticipation what it means. At times like this, I wish I had a codebook. For Stephanie's mobile, I'd find the section on suspended seabirds, then the paragraph on seagulls, and look up the answers. But, of course, no such codebook exists. Snooping is so fascinating because the relationship between clues and personality is imperfect. Unlike those dream dictionaries you find at the supermarket checkout counter, which would have you believe that a blue rabbit means one thing and a juggling bear means another, the conclusions we reach from real-world snooping are more difficult to come by— and are therefore much more interesting.

Consider my own office. If you had stopped by last fall and were an astute observer, you would have seen on the desk, right next to my computer, a CD containing a compilation of religious music. You would also have spotted an impeccably maintained plant—the soil contained just the right level of moisture, there were no dead leaves, and there wasn't even one of those brown crusty stains on the dish under the pot. If you had looked at the windowsill, you would have seen a box that contained a metal cable for securing a computer to a desk and a device that can be attached to a laptop that emits a piercing screech if it's moved.

Does the CD suggest that I'm a spiritual person? It could, but I'm not. Does the vibrant plant say that I'm meticulous? I hope not, because I'm not like that either. Nor am I a worrier, as the computer security devices might suggest. The CD was in my office for just one day; the owner had lent it to me for a class demonstration and she was going to pick it up later. Three weeks later (indeed, three months later) the beautiful plant had become dry and wizened because I had neglected to take care of it. The day after I was given the computer alarm, I passed it on to someone else because I knew I would never get around to using it.

So although clues such as the religious CD, the healthy plant, and the computer alarms could suggest that I'm spiritual, or meticulous, or anxious, they could also be irrelevant to figuring out what I'm like. That's because these objects were in my office for reasons unrelated to my personality. And that's why expert room readers have little use for codebooks. Instead, snoopers need a broad flexible strategy that can be applied in many situations. For that strategy, we find our inspiration in Belgium.

THE BELGIAN SOLUTION

As my colleagues and I proceeded with our research—moving from offices and bedrooms to Web sites and music collections—we learned how to build portraits of our snoopees in much the same way that Agatha Christie's legendary Belgian detective, Hercule Poirot, built his cases from disparate clues and circumstantial evidence. I'm calling this method the "Belgian Solution," and mastering it is the first step in becoming a successful snooper.

By looking for consistent patterns across domains, this solution allows you to tie clues with unknown provenance (like the seagull) to clues for which you're sure of the source. If you're in doubt about who owns a certain piece of evidence, you should look for other clues that you can confidently attribute to your snoopee. E-mail "signature quotations"—the pithy one-liners I talked about in the last chapter, serve this purpose well. As we saw, whether a writer chooses the wisdom of Thomas Hobbes or the wit of Calvin and Hobbes can tell you a lot about that person.

I had the Belgian Solution in mind when I considered Stephanie and her seagull. I had assumed that she was the mobile's owner, but when you're snooping you can never be sure; you must find out whether your snoopee is really responsible for the items you're trying to interpret. When the guy your best friend fixed you up with picks you up for a date, you immediately begin drawing inferences from his car. You notice the dings in the door (is he reckless?), the dance CDs tossed on the back seat (is he energetic?), the political stickers on the bumper (is he progressive?). But can you safely attribute all these clues to your date? Perhaps the dings and bumper stickers were already there when he purchased the vehicle. If so, they may not tell you much (although if a bumper sticker conveys something directly contrary to the driver's attitudes he may go to the trouble of removing it). The same challenge crops up when we are looking for clues in shared houses. To whom should we attribute the décor in a couple's living room? One person? The person who spends the most time at home? An amalgam of both people?

Poirot would also be careful not to be caught out by these issues of diagnosticity. Suppose I discover that Stephanie's office was located in the building of a seagull-mobile manufacturer. Or maybe I learn that it's hang-a-seagull-in-your-office week. Or perhaps I notice that all the offices have seagulls in them. If one of these scenarios is correct, the seagull in my borrowed office tells me much less about Stephanie than I had first thought. When I was looking around the office of my book editor, I discounted the diagnosticity of the rubber chicken hanging from her lamp when it emerged that everyone in the publishing company kept a rubber chicken somewhere in their workspace (they were freebies to publicize a book the company had published). Similarly, Poirot would dismiss a misleading clue pointed out by his slow-witted sidekick, Arthur Hastings: "*Non*, Captain Hastings, the sword in Reverend Craddock's trunk is not nearly as suspicious as it may at first seem because he belongs to a special civic society whose members traditionally keep swords in their trunks."

I don't get many questions about swords in trunks, but I'm often asked what we can learn about a person from his or her refrigerator. The answer: "Not much . . . 95 percent of the time. Sure you can pick up something from how clean and organized it is: If it's immaculate, you might infer that the person is slightly neurotic, overly fearful of all the nasty things that evil germs might do to her; but the pristine state might also mean that the owner is away on vacation and tidied up before she left. Or that she's so busy at the office she never eats at home. Interestingly, refrigerators don't differ much from owner to owner—they tend to have the same kinds of items organized in more or less the same ways. That said, sometimes I do come across a startling example that screams volumes about its owner—the fridge that contains only six-packs of pomegranate juice, or the one with the items stacked alphabetically, or the fridge filled with birdseed or other things you would not ordinarily expect to find in a fridge.

Refrigerators fall into a class of items that can tell you something about a person, but only in extreme circumstances. The same is true for e-mail usernames. The names most of us choose or have assigned to us are surprisingly unimaginative and say little; only a small subset offers a window into personality. Eating styles are also revealing only at the extremes. However, other domains, such as bedrooms, almost always tell you something because even the failure to make a bedroom distinctive is itself a sign of what a person is like.

Poirot's procedure is useful for the snooper because it is so flexible. It applies not only to physical clues but also to behaviors. If your job candidate has a firm handshake, you should not immediately and irrevocably conclude from that isolated clue that she is more open-minded or creative than the previous candidate with the weak handshake (I'll have more to say about handshakes in chapter 5). What the firm shake should do is raise in your mind the likelihood that she is open-minded and creative but then send you on a search for other clues to confirm or disconfirm this hunch. So when you usher your candidate into your office and begin the interview, you may want to pay special attention to her clothing or ask her about the kind of music she likes. The slightly conventional Gap outfit and her comments about her extensive collection of Garth Brooks hits would immediately cause you to temper your initial handshake impression of open-mindedness.

THE GULL IS MINE

I knew I would have to use the Belgian Solution to figure out the significance of Stephanie's seagull. The gull alone couldn't tell me anything for certain, but that doesn't mean it couldn't tell me anything at all. I would just have to be systematic and cautious about what I took from it. I knew from my snooping experiences that the item's provenance was a sensible place to begin. Who was responsible for doing something (or failing to do something) that resulted in the gull's being in this office in its present location and condition? Investigators must ask what caused the "trace" (the presence of a seagull), what the intentions of the person who left the trace were, and what sequence of events led to the trace. If I could deduce something about this path, there would be a good chance that I'd find out something about the person responsible. Did the previous occupant leave the gull? Was it still hanging there because Stephanie had neglected to take it down? No, the office was devastatingly well-organized, neat, and clean, showing very little sign of neglect, all of which suggested that no seabird was left behind.

Another possibility was that the gull was a gift. If so, did the gift reflect an interest in seabirds? I saw no evidence to support this idea; no hints at interests in ornithology or animal behavior. Perhaps the seagull referred to Stephanie's name—was it Seagull, Segal, or Seigel? Or Petrel, Gannet, or Albatross? With a name like Gosling, I can relate to this possibility because people are always sending me goose-, gosling-, and gander-related gifts. But no, I knew her last name and there was no seagull connection there. Or perhaps the gift came from someone in an emergency gift-buying situation who hastily bought whatever was closest when she ran into the store in a panic. This last path was possible but unlikely because a close inspection of the solid screw from which the seagull dangled from the ceiling revealed that Stephanie (or her minion) had made an effort to hang it properly; a randomly selected item is not likely to strike an emotional chord that will result in someone going to all this effort to hang it properly.

Thus, regardless of how it was acquired, the seagull's prominence in the room suggested to me that it served an important psychological purpose. It probably elicited a fond memory—a time in her life or an occasion or incident that was meaningful to her. And at the same time, her choice of this kind of memento suggested something more. She had chosen an elegant mobile, a seagull whose ponderous movement was calming. She had not chosen a bird made from seashells glued together; nor had she chosen a bobbing executive desk ornament equipped with furiously flapping wings or an enormous bright wall poster depicting a soaring seabird. After considering the seagull along with the relaxing CDs on the bookshelf and the absence of a highly stimulating décor, I postulated that the bird helped Stephanie regulate her emotions; it helped her to stay calm, collected, and focused in a difficult and demanding work environment. Of course, she wouldn't describe the seagull's function in those terms; she might claim that it makes her feel good or, even more simply, that she "just likes it."

I met Stephanie several weeks later, and she told me she had bought the seagull when she attended a conference in Stockholm (seagulls are a symbol of Sweden, I learned). It did indeed remind her of a happy time in that city. When I asked her why she'd placed the gull right next to the desk, she said, somewhat mysteriously, that it was there to stop tall people from standing too close to her (I would have liked to get to the bottom of that story!). Over the years, she had become attached to her companionable bird. She was about to change jobs and I was not surprised to hear that the gull would join her westward migration.

So I learned a little bit from the gull, but not enough to paint a full portrait of Stephanie. Keep in mind, though, that knowing every single intimate detail about someone's personality is an unreasonably high standard with which to measure the success or failure of a snooping venture—after all, we might not figure these details out even after years of being someone's friend. Often, finding out just something—a general tendency or an area of particular importance—is useful. Knowing whether someone is a Republican or a Democrat could be crucial for some decisions—if, for example, you're thinking of that person as a potential mate—even if you don't know his precise position on immigration policy or estate taxes.

Keep in mind, too, that trying to form an impression when you have no information other than a seagull or a fridge or a bedroom or an iPod Top-25 list is an unrealistic scenario. Only rarely do you know absolutely nothing about a person, especially a person whose room or office or music collection you're snooping around. So often the idea is to look for clues that can lead you to further information. Once you know where to look, you can continue your investigations by more conventional means. Snooping into where Stephanie had placed the gull led me to ask questions that took me to her intriguing statement about tall people standing too close, a topic I'd never have discovered without the seagull's guidance.

A FEASTFUL OF CLUES

Not long after I met a new friend, Lisa, she found out what I did and invited me back to her place for coffee, cookies, and a snoop. While she ground the coffee beans, I excused myself to make a trip to the bathroom; en route I took a quick look around the bedroom. I noticed that the small neat bookshelf next to her bed contained well-worn volumes by authors such as J. D. Salinger, Jon Kabat-Zinn, Chuck Klosterman, and Simon Wiesenthal, and the like—together pointing to a broad-minded, thoughtful person. But one book, *A Moveable Feast,* Ernest Hemingway's classic evocation of life in 1920s Paris, had a special place; it sat on its own little platform, a kind of mini-shrine on top of the bookshelf. Like Stephanie's seagull, it had not just been left in that spot. It had been placed there deliberately.

I didn't know what Hemingway's slim volume meant to Lisa but I could see from its placement that it was important to her. So I decided to follow this clue and ask her about it directly. It turns out that the book was recommended by a former boyfriend of hers. She read it and loved it, she told me, and she thought it especially moving that Hemingway had written *A Moveable Feast* about the time when he was still an unknown writer living in France. She was captivated, she added, by the idea that Hemingway's brilliant and still unrecognized circle of writers and artists, which included F. Scott Fitzgerald, Gertrude Stein, and Ezra Pound, would soon, like Hemingway, become world famous.

What did this explanation tell me about Lisa? I'd already found out, from the books on the shelves and the music-related décor on the walls (including posters promoting concerts in Los Angeles by Bob Dylan at the El Rey Theatre and by Joni Mitchell and Van Morrison at the Pauley Pavilion) that she valued the arts, literature, and music more than, say, the work of scientists, explorers, athletes, or captains of industry. But how she described her reaction to *A Moveable Feast* conveyed even more about her. Again, she would probably not use these terms herself, but I learned that she had been inspired and heartened to realize that even if brilliant achievements go unrecognized early on they can be acclaimed and rewarded much later, sometimes only after a person's death. Further support for this interpretation came later when Lisa and I began an e-mail correspondence. At the foot of one of her e-mails I noticed a quotation attributed to Albert Einstein: "Great spirits have always found violent opposition from mediocrities. The latter cannot understand it when a man does not thoughtlessly submit to hereditary prejudices but honestly and courageously uses his intelligence." The quotation echoes the sentiment underlying the Hemingway shrine. Here we see the Belgian Solution in action—supporting the Hemingway hunch with the Einstein e-mail. If I had any remaining doubt about Lisa's central identity, it was dispelled when I saw the name she had given herself on MySpace—it wasn't just "Lisa," it was "Lisa is a VERY important person." Picking up a theme yet?

Realizing how strongly she resonated with this theme made me wonder about Lisa's own talents and dreams. It seemed that she might be worrying about the value of her contributions to the world, and that she took comfort from knowing that a current failure to "succeed" in conventional terms does not signal the absence of meaningful achievements, and it does not mean that those achievements will never be recognized more widely. The book was also a meaningful reminder of the connection with her former boyfriend—it reflected a special bond because he had known her well enough to recommend a book that spoke to her at such a fundamental level.

Simply noticing the enshrined Hemingway volume gave me a shortcut to important information about Lisa. It prompted me to ask her a question I would have been unlikely to ask otherwise. And this points to another important piece of the snooper job description: Besides being a detective, you must also become a bit of a psychologist. Snooping turns you into the keenest of observers when you poke and probe beneath the surface of personality.

BEYOND INTUITION

Good detective work provides a solid foundation for snooping, but it will take you only so far because only some of the connections you might reasonably make turn out to be right. Imagine you're visiting a friend, and he steps out of the room for a few moments. You happen to be sitting at his desk, and while he's gone you casually look around. You notice that the computer is switched on. You are not really snooping but it's hard to avoid looking at the screen. There your eyes settle on the record of his latest IM (Internet Messaging) chat session with his girlfriend. You see his short messages to her and the notes she has written back to him. As it happens, you've been wondering how these guys are getting along, so now you can't resist combing their Internet interactions for clues.

What would you look for? In this situation, most people hone in on clues to emotions. Research by Richard Slatcher at UCLA and Simine Vazire at Washington University has shown that observers who have examined romantic couples' IM chat sessions base their predictions of relationship stability on words that refer to positive feelings (such as *love* and *glad*) and words related to anger (such as *furious* and *pissed*). Would you do the same? If you did, you would be half right and half wrong. It turns out that the quantity of words related to positive feelings really does predict long-term (by young adults' standards at least!) relationship stability. Young lovers who constantly refer to their happiness and joy were more likely to be together six months later than those who used fewer such words. But what's especially interesting about this finding is that the number of times these words were used predicted how long the relationships would last even more accurately than what the couples actually say about how happy they are in that relationship.

And what about the couples whose messages are peppered with negative or angry words? Contrary to what most people suppose, couples who used a lot of anger-related words were not more or less likely to be together than the couples using fewer anger words. This study underscores how important it is to go beyond what our intuitions tell us. True, our intuitions are often right—positive words do predict relationship longevity, as one might expect; but, as the prediction based on negative words shows, they are also often wrong. The crucial point is that without looking at the research, we would never know which intuitions are right and which are wrong. In the next chapter we'll begin to find out what researchers have discovered across a broad array of snooping domains.

—ᴟᴟ—

Jumpers, Bumpers, Groovers, and Shakers

I F YOU WERE around in the 1960s and had a coffee table in your liv-ing room, there's a good chance that Philippe Halsman's *Jump Book* was sitting on it. The book contains nearly two hundred photo-graphs of leading socialites and entertainers, political figures and judges, captains of industry and scientists, with each one performing a jump. Liberace "floats like a cherub," Marilyn Monroe jumps with "childlike playfulness," and Professor Stanley Hyman leaps with "ex-plosive joy." The book is fascinating because, as the famed photogra-pher Halsman was well aware, each subject's character is betrayed by the way he or she jumps. Indeed, a few of his famous subjects refused to jump because they were concerned about divulging too much about themselves.

At its core, the *Jump Book* is based on the idea that our personalities seep out in almost everything we do. (So enamored was Halsman of jumping as a portal into personality that he coined the term *jumpology*.)

Personality seepage doesn't stop with jumps. A friend of mine be-lieves that how we laugh reflects what we are like. How long do you laugh? How loudly? And how guardedly? Are you a circumspect chuckler or the type to unleash an exuberant guffaw? It's a theory that hasn't been tested, but I bet there's something to it. It wouldn't be surprising to find that an exuberant laugher is high on extraversion. What is surprising, though, is that scientists have only recently begun to develop the methods and do the studies on the countless contexts in which our personalities leak out. My bedroom-snooping study was one such investigation but, as we shall see, there are many more.

Seepage and Leakage

When I talk about seeping or leaking, I mean that many elements of personality find their ways into our behaviors without our being conscious of it. When told to jump, few of us would strategize about the kind of jump we wanted to execute. We probably wouldn't even consider that there are many different ways to jump—a jump is a jump, right? We would just jump in a way that came naturally. But in doing so, we would inadvertently give away clues about our personality. You could signal your reticence with a controlled jump, head stiff and arms by your side. Maybe you'd give away your ebullience with a yelling and waving leap toward the sky. Or betray your creativity with an unusual interpretation of the instructions (the famous Halsman photo of Salvador Dali's jump, complete with cats and buckets of water flying through the air, comes to mind).

Projective tests such as the famous Rorschach "ink-blot" test are one of the most familiar means by which seepage and leakage are captured. In the Rorschach, the tester looks for personality patterns revealed by the person's "free associations" about the meaning of ink-blot images. Enormous efforts were devoted to developing coding systems to figure out what the various responses mean, but, with a few exceptions, most researchers now agree that the ink-blot tests have almost no value for diagnosing mental illness, assessing personality, predicting behavior, or uncovering early trauma.

One projective test that has gained support from researchers, however, is the Picture Story Exercise (or PSE), which has been used in research for more than fifty years. It requires the person being assessed to tell a story about a series of pictures. The psychologist uses the drama the person creates—and the wishes, thoughts, and feelings of the characters—to interpret the signals of personality that leak out.

The PSE is used to measure motives, needs, and other aspects of personality that drive our behavior but are so deeply rooted that we cannot access them simply through introspection.

In a series of fascinating studies, Oliver Schultheiss and his collaborators at Friedrich-Alexander University, in Erlangen, Germany, used the PSE to measure the motivations for power (a concern with having impact on others), achievement (a concern for doing well according to a standard of excellence), and affiliation (a concern for establishing, maintaining, or restoring close, friendly relationships). He showed that American students scored higher on implicit needs for achievement but lower on needs for power than German students and that there were no differences between the two student populations in their needs for affiliation. Past research has linked the need for achievement to innovation and economic growth so, the researchers suggest, such deep-seated differences at the individual level could be at the root of the economic differences between the two countries.

Schultheiss's research also showed that people high on these story-based measures of power respond poorly to defeat in a competitive game. They secrete high levels of cortisol, a hormone associated with stress. But people low on this motive for power are actually more stressed out by winning! So the fanciful stories that people construct on this projective test can shed light on some basic features of how they approach the world in which they live.

Motives can also be gleaned from various other forms of writing. In the spring of 2001, less than six months before September 11, University of Michigan's David Winter published an article analyzing the power, achievement, and affiliation motives present in George W. Bush's inaugural address. Using a system identical to the one used by Schultheiss, Winter concluded that, compared to previous presidents, Bush was high on affiliation and power motivations but a little below average on achievement motivation. Going by these scores alone, Winter made some surprisingly prescient predictions about the forthcoming Bush presidency.

He predicted that Bush would be more politically effective than some might expect, and that he would enjoy being president. However, Winter cautioned, in making his decisions Bush might rely on small secluded groups of close friends and advisors who are similar to himself, a strategy that might alienate people who have different views and experience. Winter further predicted that Bush could be vulnerable to scandals arising from the excessive influence of advisors and friends. Winter suggested that in foreign affairs Bush would endorse "aggressive policies (for example, on Iraq)" and that his decisions would depend on which faction of his foreign policy advisors, hawk or dove, influenced him the most. These predictions are particularly striking because they were based on one speech and were made many months before the events of 9/11 and the subsequent conflicts in Afghanistan and Iraq.

HIP READING

What's the connection between Halsman's jumping celebrities and projective tests such as the PSE? The idea behind them is similar; that is, a person is given a task that could elicit a wide range of responses—whether it be floating like a cherub, spinning a creative tale about two people in a picture, or setting out foreign policy objectives—and the responses give us clues to what that person is like. Nobody has developed a scheme for interpreting jumps, but some scientists are conducting research that is not dissimilar. One of them is the ethologist Karl Grammer at the Ludwig-Boltzmann Institute for Urban Ethology at the Institute for Anthropology in Vienna, Austria.

Like snoopers, ethologists study behavior in its natural habitat. Usually, you'll find them standing in icy pools watching stickleback fish send signals to potential mates, or dangling from the Amazonian canopy hoping to learn something about how frogs forage. So you could be forgiven for not expecting to find an ethologist standing next to the subwoofer under the stroboscopic lights of a nightclub. Yet,

Grammer is interested in how primates (in this case, human primates) interpret the signals people send out about themselves, so a nightclub turns out to be a sensible venue for his research. By studying how people express themselves, he is essentially doing what many personality psychologists do. But Grammer takes a perspective rooted in evolutionary theory. This means he tries to understand our modern-day traits and preferences by considering the pressures—such as the need to find a good mate or quickly detect a dangerous foe—that have shaped our ancestors over the millennia.

Deception is a topic that interests ethologists like Grammer. Just like humans, most species seek to win mates by making themselves appear as attractive as is humanly (well, not always humanly) possible. Creatures who are good at looking (or smelling or sounding or tasting or feeling) good will be more likely to pass on their genes. To the extent the motive to look attractive succeeds in improving our attractiveness, this motive will be passed on to subsequent generations.

While trying to appear attractive to others, we are also trying to get a good read on what others are like. Ideally, we want to find mates who will enhance the survival prospects of our genes in the next generation. Thus, we look for mates who appear to provide good physical material (being healthy and vital) or good behavioral material (being a good parent) for our genes. Of course, most of these calculations are not conscious; we do not actually think a certain person will maximize our genetic prospects, we simply find the person attractive. So a conflict of evolutionary interests underlies the mating game. On one hand we are trying to fool others by appearing as appealing as possible, regardless of the honesty of the signals we're sending; but on the other hand we're trying to get an accurate read on what others are like, hoping to slice through their low-down, sneaky deceptive strategies designed to fool us. It is in the service of this second task that scientists (or snoopers) search for clues that are hard to fake.

Grammer proposes that body movements are one such clue. This is the idea that has led him to study what people reveal when they shake their thang. Like Halsman, Grammer bases his work on the idea that our body movements hold clues to our deeper selves. His research, much of which he conducted in nightclubs, suggests we sometimes say more with our hips than with our lips. In one study, Grammer looked at the tightness of women's clothing and the amount of skin they showed as a reflection of where they were in their reproductive cycles (determined by estrogen levels obtained from saliva samples). And, by having women volunteers turn around in front of a video camera, he showed that the "explosiveness" of movement (defined by the amount of change between consecutive video frames) was also related to estrogen levels; even in the simple act of turning around, women may give off signals that reveal their fertility levels—and thus their attractiveness, in basic evolutionary terms, to potential mates.

The trouble with nightclub clues is that you can't simply go up to someone and ask her to dance for you or to twirl in front of a camera. If we want to use body expression to determine what people are like, we need a movement common to just about everybody. Walking fits the bill. You may have noticed that you can often recognize a person you know well purely from the way he or she walks, even when you're too far away to detect individual features. According to Aaron Bobick and his collaborators at Georgia Tech in Atlanta, where they have developed computer systems to recognize individuals from gait, people have unique walking signatures. And research by Peter Borkenau and Anette Liebler, then both at Bielefeld University, Germany, identified connections between walking style and personality. In two studies, each with a hundred people, participants were videotaped as they walked across a room, sat down at a desk to read a short standard statement (actually an old weather report), and then as they got up and left the room. Using the videotapes, Borkenau and Liebler looked for clues to personality in how the participants moved from place to place and how they spoke. For example, they found that a sprightly gait—in which the volunteer lifted his feet and swung his arms—was a clue to extraversion.

This finding may seem obvious now that you know it. But the researchers' data show that in practice it's not. The observers in Borkenau's study saw arm swinging as a sign of extraversion and low neuroticism, but only the first inference was correct. Similarly, people perceived others with a pleasant, calm reading style as being low on neuroticism and high on openness, but neither inference was correct. So, if you're sitting in a café and you see someone walk across the room to pick up a newspaper, what, according to these researchers' data, should you look for? Here's a brief Snooping Field Guide derived from the results of Borkenau's two studies. Bold type indicates the cues that were both valid and used by the observers to make their inferences.

Table 5.1   Snooping Field Guide

When judging . . .	Observers actually relied on . . .	When they should have relied on . . .
Openness	Refined appearance Made-up face Fashionable dress Slim physique Friendly expression Self-assured expression Extensive smiling Pleasant voice Fluent speech Easy to understand Calm speaking Does not avoid the camera	None in this context!
Conscientiousness	Refined appearance Plain (non-showy) dress **Formal dress** Controlled sitting posture Touches own body infrequently Fluent speech Easy to understand Calm speaking	**Formal dress**

(continues)

Table 5.1   Snooping Field Guide *(continued)*

When judging . . .	Observers actually relied on . . .	When they should have relied on . . .
Extraversion	Made-up face	
	Showy dress	
	Refined appearance	**Refined appearance**
	Friendly expression	**Friendly expression**
	Self-assured expression	**Self-assured expression**
	Extensive smiling	**Extensive smiling**
		Lifts feet when walking (vs. shuffling)
	Fast movements	
	Frequent head movements	
	Relaxed walking	**Relaxed walking**
	Swings arms when walking	**Swings arms when walking**
	Loud voice	**Loud voice**
	Powerful voice	**Powerful voice**
	Pleasant voice	
	Easy to understand	
	Does not avoid camera	**Does not avoid camera**
Agreeableness	**Soft facial lineaments**	**Soft facial lineaments**
	Friendly expression	**Friendly expression**
	Extensive smiling	
	Pleasant voice	
	Does not avoid camera	
Neuroticism	Less muscular physique	Dark garments
	Grumpy expression	
	Timid expression	
	Little smiling	
	Lack of arm swinging when walking	
	Stiff walking style	
	Weak voice	
	Unpleasant voice	
	Halting speech	
	Difficult to understand	
	Hectic speech	
	Avoids the camera	

You'll notice that for traits such as extraversion, there are a lot of clues; extraversion is a visible trait. But other traits, such as agreeableness, neuroticism, and openness, are harder to spot in this context; people are all too willing to draw inferences from walking and talking style, but this snippet provided virtually no information about these traits.

It's easy to see where a lot of the inferences come from—judging the weedy, camera-shy person with the timid expression, the stiff walk, and the hectic, halting speaking style to be high on neuroticism seems so intuitive. But in these studies, it just happened to be wrong. It's also understandable that the self-assured, slim, smiling, fashionable camera-darlings with the calm, fluent speaking style were seen as high on openness. But, again, our intuitions would have led us astray. The field guide also shows how changing your appearance might influence how you're seen—Borkenau's findings suggest that creating a refined appearance for yourself will tend to make people see you as extraverted, conscientious, and open.

Borkenau's data suggest that formality of dress was the key to judging conscientiousness. With the benefit of knowing the findings, you can see how the two things are connected (although you would not have guessed beforehand that dress was the one valid cue). It was the responsible, motivated (that is, conscientious) people who took their task seriously and planned for their appointment at the psychology laboratory in a professional manner. But suppose that instead of being recruited for a short experimental session in a psychology department the subjects had been recruited to paint an old warehouse. In that case, it would be the organized on-the-ball conscientious types who would leave themselves time to find some painting clothes (perhaps they'd have a special drawer full of old shirts and trousers ready for messy activities like this) and they'd have their act together and remember to bring them. In this situation, I would expect the conscientious people to be the *least* formally dressed.

This example is a practical reminder to use this field guide (and all the others in this book) with a broad snooper's perspective—as a rule of thumb, not a codebook that rigidly links one clue, such as formality of dress, to conscientiousness. The correlations in these tables are individually weak—even in Borkenau's study there were plenty of informally dressed conscientious people. But our job as snoopers, in the tradition of detective Hercule Poirot, is to build a case that draws conclusions based on the preponderance of evidence and so become more and more confident as the clues accrue.

One of Borkenau's most surprising findings is that soft facial lineaments (that is, the contours of the face) are a key to spotting agreeableness; consistent with this result and with some earlier research from the 1980s, he found that a "baby face" look (a round face, large eyes, small nose, high forehead, and small chin) is associated with agreeableness. It would be imprudent to draw too many firm conclusions from this research alone. But the discovery is provocative because, unlike the other findings, which draw on different styles of behaving, this one seems to rest on immutable physical features of the face. It's an intriguing possibility partly because it echoes the ancient practice of physiognomy—the idea that character traits are revealed in physical features, especially the face. In one of its most famous cases, physiognomy came close to derailing the theory of evolution when Charles Darwin was almost barred from traveling on the *Beagle* because Captain Fitzroy believed his bulbous nose indicated a lack of determination!

The practice of physiognomy has long been considered quackery, but some recent research suggests there could actually be something to it. Anthony Little of the University of Stirling and David Perrett of the University of St. Andrews did something that all such previous studies had failed to do: They isolated the targets' facial features by excluding clues to behavior, clothing, and hairstyle. For men and women, they created ten composite images, each one being created through merging the photos of people selected from the high and low poles of each of the Big Five dimensions. For example, the fifteen most extraverted women's faces were merged into one image that reflected what was common to all of them. When judges rated these combined images they were surprisingly good at picking up the correct personality traits, especially for the images of women; the findings suggest, as the physiognomists had argued long ago, that certain personality traits are reflected in our facial features. How can this be?

There are several likely causes, and they probably combine to drive these personality-face connections. The first is biological. Hormones such as testosterone are known to influence facial features as well as personality characteristics like dominance; this could be why the image combining fifteen male extraverts (the Big Five dimension associated with assertiveness; see table 2.3) has more masculine facial features than the image made up of fifteen male introverts. The second link between appearance and personality is behavior: Attractive people may be treated differently in social interaction, a phenomena that actually leads to differences in how they behave and how they see themselves. Consistent with this idea, Borkenau found that attractive people saw themselves more positively than unattractive people across four of the Big Five dimensions.

Finally, it's possible that personality leaves a behavioral residue on the face; some personalities might use grooming aids or follow a diet that, over time, results in minor facial differences, such as better skin. More interesting is the possibility that momentary facial expressions eventually leave permanent traces in the shape and lines of the face— that a lifetime of frowning, or glowering, or smiling, leaves its mark. On the assumption that over many years characteristic expressions would reveal themselves in the lines etched in people's faces, Carol Malatesta at the New School for Social Research in New York City and her colleagues examined the judgments of older people (about seventy years old); her findings showed that, indeed, people generally inclined to feel angry were thought to be expressing anger regardless of their expressions; the same was true for other habitual emotional expressions, such as sadness, contempt, and guilt. Little and Perrett's targets were on average half a century younger than Malatesta's, raising the possibility that they would have found even stronger connections between personality and facial features had they used older participants.

Another of Borkenau's intriguing findings is the connection between neuroticism and dark clothing. One element of neuroticism is expressing negative emotions, so perhaps the dark clothing is a reflection of the darkness inside. Again, although the association is pretty weak, it's captivating because it recalls one particular subculture known for its dark clothing.

GOTH OR NOT

A few years back, one of the most popular locations on the Web was a site called hotornot.com, where people could post photos of themselves and get brutally honest ratings, ranging from hot to not, on their sexual appeal. Soon a flurry of similar sites appeared, riffing on the hot-or-not theme. One of my favorites was gothornot.com in which users rated photos submitted by various eye-linered, pallid, scowling, black-clad hopefuls vying for the best "Goth" look. One of the top-rated Goths, Trashstar, is dressed all in black; she has marble-white skin, long jet-black hair, and dark makeup on her eyes and lips. She kneels with surly disdain by a stream. Another user high on the Gothometer, Lament of Innocence, is ashen-skinned, and her clothes, hair, and makeup are dark; she looks at the camera with her own smoldering brand of surly disdain. There's more on the surly disdain front from Blackenedsoul666 (there's not much smiling on this Web site).

The impression of the personalities conveyed by these photos is certainly not the same as the impressions one might expect to find at peppycheerleaderornot.com (if it existed). It seems likely that our personalities might lead us to look a certain way—a shy person might be less likely to make direct eye contact than a bold person. And we might also use our appearance, as the Goths do, to associate ourselves with certain values, goals, and ideas, such as a fascination with death and all things macabre.

There haven't been any studies of the personalities of Goths alone, but Craig Nathanson and his colleagues at the University of British Columbia included Goths in their research on tattoos, body piercings, and provocative dressing. They found that people exhibiting these culturally deviant markers have a slight tendency to be high on the Big Five trait of openness, low on self-esteem, or high on both impulsive thrill-seeking and callousness.

Even in the mundane non-Goth world, appearance provides clues to personality. In our own research we have asked volunteers to rate people's personalities just from looking at photographs of them. Considering they have nothing more than a still photo to go on, our observers (who were just ordinary students) were surprisingly accurate at judging others' levels of extraversion, agreeableness, and openness. The field guide below shows you some of the cues our judges used to form their impressions and which ones turned out to be correct. Of course, observers rely on other cues, too, that we did not assess in this study.

Table 5.2   Snooping Field Guide

When judging . . .	Observers actually relied on people who look . . .	When they should have relied on people who look . . .
Openness	Unattractive Messy Disorganized Unhealthy Creative Unconventional	Unattractive Messy Disorganized Unhealthy Creative Unconventional
Conscientiousness	Attractive Neat Organized Healthy Relaxed Conventional	

(continues)

Table 5.2   Snooping Field Guide *(continued)*

When judging . . .	Observers actually relied on people who look. . .	When they should have relied on people who look . . .
Extraversion	Attractive Cheerful Relaxed Conventional	Attractive Cheerful Relaxed
Agreeableness	Cheerful Organized Relaxed	Cheerful Relaxed
Neuroticism	Unhealthy	Unhealthy
Narcissism	Stylish Wearing expensive clothes Fraternity/sorority types Cheerful	Stylish Wearing expensive clothes
	Have spent time preparing how they look Feminine (fem. only) Makeup (fem. only) Plucked eyebrows (fem. only) Cleavage showing (fem. only) Masculine (males only) Muscular	Have spent time preparing how they look Feminine (fem. only) Makeup (fem. only) Plucked eyebrows (fem. only) Cleavage showing (fem. only)

The observers were pretty good at picking up on the right clues to narcissism and the Big Five domains of openness and, to a lesser extent, extraversion. As in Borkenau's studies, we see that the stereotypical views of conscientious people were not borne out as valid. And we also see a pattern that I'll return to later, where organized-looking people are viewed as both agreeable and conscientious.

In addition to giving us ideas about which cues the observers should and should not have used, our data yielded another important finding. Even though there was very little accuracy in judgments about people's levels of conscientiousness and neuroticism, the judges agreed with each other about the targets' standing on these traits as much as they did for agreeableness and openness, for which their judgments were more accurate. As snoopers, we should take notice of this finding because it shows that the consensus among observers bears little relation to their accuracy; in other words, just because everybody agrees about an appearance-based judgment of someone else, that doesn't make the assessment correct.

SHAKE 'N' BRAKE

One of the pleasures of working in the field of personality is that many people can relate to what I do. When I tell someone I study how personality is expressed in everyday life and that I find clues by snooping in bedrooms and offices, I sometimes get lucky and learn about new places where clues may be lurking. Occasionally, someone will tell me they can distill personality from an entirely unexpected source.

An experienced mechanic once told me that anxious, fearful people wear out their brake pads more quickly than calm, relaxed people do. Anxious people constantly ride the brakes; the slightest disturbance or distraction is enough to bring the car to a screeching halt. And after enough screeching halts, the wear on the brake pads begins to show. Of course, you can't jack up a prospective date's car, take off the wheels, and inspect the brake pads. But the mechanic's observations reminded me of the importance of exercising creativity and thinking broadly as we snoop for signs of personality. I like to turn on the radio and look at pre-set stations, as well as examine the CDs or iPod, for further clues to the kind of environment the driver is trying to create—Metallica or John Coltrane?

Going beyond brake pads to the cars themselves can tell us something about their owners in terms of our three broad personality mechanisms. The style of vehicle—a high-status car or a hybrid—and the ornaments, such as the bumper stickers, could serve as identity claims directed at others and at the drivers themselves. The kind of car—say, sporty for driving fast—and other features, such as a photo of a loved pet hanging from the mirror, could act as feeling regulators and thus communicate something about the driver's characteristic ways of thinking and feeling.We could learn something about a driver via behavioral residue—damage on the bumpers and body could reflect past recklessness (ever notice that the car that narrowly misses sideswiping yours usually has dings and dents all over it?). The state of the car's interior also provides information: Has the ashtray been emptied and polished clean? Are cookie crumbs falling from the folds of the seats?

Drawing on this kind of snooping, Georg Alpers and Antje Gerdes, researchers at the Julius-Maximilians University in Wurzburg, wanted to see whether, based solely on appearance, judges could match drivers to their vehicles. The duo spent four days hanging out in a tollroad rest area nabbing drivers and asking their permission to photograph them and their cars separately. The researchers then showed the photos to a bunch of strangers to see whether they could guess who drove which car.

The judges didn't always get it right, but they were right far more often than one would predict on the basis of chance alone. That they could do this is impressive. After all, they had to make two sets of judgments—what the driver was like from the personal photograph and then what kind of person would be driving which kind of car. And then they had to match the two bits of information. If either of the judgments failed, the matching would not be possible. Consider, too, that the judges' guesses were based on slim data—one waist-up photo of the driver and one profile view of the car. They couldn't search under the seats, rummage through the trunk, or listen to the radio stations on the pre-sets.

The judges probably drew on direct inferences to make generalizations about the effects of traits (for example, tidiness)—so they may have inferred that people who are meticulous about maintaining their physical appearance are also meticulous about the appearance of their cars. And they may also have used indirect inferences; perhaps they drew on stereotypes (in all likelihood valid ones) that older people tend to be wealthier and that expensive-looking cars tend to be, well, expensive, allowing them to connect older people to expensive-looking cars.

Of course, you can also learn things from personal contact with your snoopee. At the University of Texas, I am part of a mentoring program that pairs professors with groups of students to encourage them to hang out together. One year, before I had gotten to know any students, I arranged to have dinner with some of them. At the end of the dinner, we said good-bye and shook hands. With so many shakes in quick succession, I couldn't help but notice the differences in style. Some shakes were stiff, others were limp. Some were firm, others weak. The woman with the firmest handshake, Ritz, whose hair was dyed bright red, had been chattering away the whole time, smiling a lot, full of positive energy, endlessly waving or nodding recognition at others across the dining hall without interrupting her conversation, and getting in and out of her seat to organize where people sat. Could I have predicted her energetic, socially buzzing behavior, I wondered, from her handshake alone? The hunch that you can learn something about a person from the way they shake your hand is widespread and, it turns out, has been the subject of psychological research.

Handshaking as key to personality must have interested shakers ever since shaking began, but it was first investigated by psychologists in the 1930s. More recently, in the 1990s, Swedish researchers conducted a number of complex studies of handshakes. Unfortunately, the results have not been particularly useful. One study involved only psychiatric inpatients, hardly representative of the general population. The other suffered so many flaws that it was impossible to answer important questions: Do people shake hands the same way from shaker to shaker? And do they shake hands with members of their own sex differently than with opposite-sex shakers?

What was needed was a study that measured a wide variety of handshake features, that used a well-established method to assess the shaker's personality, assessed the consistency of handshakes across shakers, examined gender differences in the characteristics of handshakes, and systematically assessed the impressions people give when they shake hands. In 2000, a study published in the *Journal of Personality and Social Psychology,* the field's most prestigious journal, did just that. Today, this paper still stands as the most rigorous examination of the links between personality and handshaking.

William Chaplin and his students at the University of Alabama in Tuscaloosa examined the shakes and personalities of more than one hundred shakers. They measured eight handshaking qualities (such as temperature, dryness, strength, and duration) and related these to the Big Five as well as the traits shyness and emotional expressiveness.

What would you predict they found? For example, which of the traits just listed would you expect to find in a person who shakes your hand firmly? And would you expect to find the same traits in men and women? Chaplin and his team assessed each shaker's shake eight times, twice with two female experimenters and twice with two male experimenters. And, crucially, as we shall see, they managed to do this without the shakers realizing the study had anything to do with handshakes.

To ensure consistent assessment, the experimenters were trained extensively to shake hands in a neutral way and to do it exactly the same way each time. This is not easy. As an experimenter, you have to extend your hand to a shaker subject straight out from the waist with the thumb raised at a forty-five-degree angle. It's important not to influence the shaking in any way, so upon contact, you have to wait for the shaker to initiate the strength of the grip and the upward and downward shaking. In addition, you must release your grip only when the shaker begins to relax his or her grip or shows other signs of wishing to end the handshake. Once you get your standard handshake down, you need to learn the eight handshaking dimensions, which include temperature, strength, duration, and texture. In the Alabama study, this training took a month.

At the appointed time, subject shakers showed up for the experiment. A clever cover story was concocted to get them to shake hands twice with four trained shakers without raising suspicions that the study was examining handshaking. The subjects were told they were part of a study on whether four personality tests taken all at once would yield findings different from those of the same tests taken separately. They were asked to fill out four questionnaires and then were given these instructions: "To emphasize the separateness [of the questionnaire sessions], each experimenter will greet you as though you were coming to them for an individual experiment." The instructions provided a plausible explanation for all the shaking going on, and they allowed the experimenters to collect all the personality questionnaires at the same time. A cunning example of snoopology in action.

Most shakers fell somewhere in the middle; they were neither steely-vise-like firm grippers nor droopy dead-haddock danglers. But the study showed that some aspects of personality can be inferred from the way people shake hands, and it also showed that certain handshaking attributes seem to go together. In other words, just as people may combine several personality traits (the stereotypical nerd combines introversion, studiousness, and social ineptitude), handshakes typically combine several shaking qualities.

It turns out that the typology of shakers is simpler than the typology of people, with just two main types—firm shakers and weak shakers. Firm shakers tend to have a complete grip, be strong and vigorous, shake longer, and include eye contact. As might be expected, overall, males had firmer handshakes than females. And according to Chaplin's findings, firm shakers tend to be more extraverted and less neurotic and shy. In women only, firm shakers also tend to be higher on openness to new experiences. People who drape a limp palm into another's hand tend to be introverted, neurotic, and unexpressive. And, confirming some exploratory research by the Swedish group, in which they canvassed the opinions of such experienced hand-shakers as therapists, clergymen, and salespeople, Chaplin's group also showed we form impressions of others from their handshakes. In support of the many etiquette books on the subject, the firm hand-shakers elicited much more positive first impressions from the coders than did the weak ones.

PERSONALITY 24/7

The conviction that everyday activities like walking and handshaking can reveal things about what we're like drove an extraordinary study about a seven-year-old boy now known only by his pseudonym, Raymond Birch. One warm but overcast Tuesday in April 1949, just before seven in the morning, Raymond's mother went into his room. She pulled a light cord and turned toward the bed at exactly 7:00 A.M. "Raymond, wake up." Not much doing. She gently roused the sleeping boy, who sat up and rubbed his eyes. At 7:01, he pulled on his left sock. At 7:03, he pulled on his right sock. At 7:04, he put on his right shoe. His mother asked him whether he wanted an egg for breakfast. Sleepily, but without irritation or resentment, he said no.

How, you might ask, do we know all this? Raymond was the subject of a unique scientific project spearheaded by Roger Barker and Herbert Wright, directors of the Midwest Field Station in Oskaloosa, Kansas. They decided to follow one person for an entire day, meticulously documenting minute-by-minute what he did. On that day, everything Raymond did, from the moment he rubbed his eyes in the morning until he drifted off to sleep at 8:33 P.M., was meticulously recorded by a team of eight observers, one taking over from another every half an hour. Raymond's quotidian activities, pulling on socks and all, were immortalized as the now classic case study *One Boy's Day*.

Just as my colleagues and I did in our snooping studies, Barker and Wright escaped the confines and constraints of the psychological laboratory and put everyday behaviors front and center. Their massive undertaking, a milestone in naturalistic observation, yielded more than four hundred pages of information. But even though their ideas resonated strongly in the field, a surprisingly long time passed before their work was taken even a step further.

Some forty years later, Kenneth Craik at the University of California at Berkeley developed what he called Lived Day Analysis, an observational method that uses a handheld video camera to capture people in the natural pursuit of their ordinary lives. It is based on the realization that ultimately "lives are lived day by day, one day at a time, from day to day, day after day, day in day out."

In creating permanent audiovisual records, Craik's method constituted a major improvement over Barker and Wright's written record. But it was still tremendously time consuming and cumbersome. And, of course, traveling with a full team of videographers and researchers is a conspicuous and ungainly way to move about. Would you want the whole team there as you snagged a quick nap between classes or snuck off for a furtive cigarette behind the bike sheds? Wouldn't this kind of snooping interfere with the very behaviors the psychologists wanted to study? A method was needed that didn't impinge so obtrusively on ordinary, everyday activities.

One such method was developed by James Pennebaker, a colleague of mine at the University of Texas, and Matthias Mehl at the University of Arizona. As part of an ingenious foray into moment-to-moment snooping they adapted microrecorders so that the devices could be carried around all day; they were controlled by a chip that turned the recorder on for thirty seconds every twelve minutes. Subjects carried these Electronically Activated Recorders, or EARs for short, in little pouches attached to their belts (microphones were attached to their lapels), usually for two to four days. They were thus spared the intrusion of an entourage of scientists. If researchers had been standing around with video cameras and note pads it is unlikely that Subject 439 would have talked so earnestly about the "well-proportioned girl" with "breasts that were large, but not too large, which fit the body JUST right." And although Subject 363 provided a moment full of psychological richness for the inconspicuous EAR to hear, I suspect she would not have reached the end of her tether and broken up with her boyfriend in front of a full research team.

Mehl thinks the EAR gains such prime access to moments beyond the reach of most psychological research because people are inherently inclined to believe that what they are doing is "normal" and therefore doesn't need to be censored. It helps, too, that the participants are specifically told that the researchers are interested in "everyday lives" and that they can delete snippets later if they feel censorship is needed. In one of the rare occasions that a participant did delete recordings, he excised nothing more salacious than off-key singing. (Sadly, for the sake of the researchers who had to code the samples, not all the singing participants were considerate enough to keep their songs from science.) Participants in Mehl's studies typically report that they are hyperconscious of the device during the first couple of hours, but after that they forget about it most of the time. In fact, Mehl himself almost destroyed one of his own expensive recorders when he forgot he was wearing it and pulled off his sweater, ripping the microphone out of the unit.

The EAR yielded a wealth of interesting facts about the ways people live their lives. It showed that, despite the variety of things each of us do, we are unmistakably creatures of habit. When people wore the EAR for two days and then for two more days four weeks later, they were remarkably consistent in how they interacted with others, in the kinds of things they did, and in the places they frequented. People who spent a lot of time alone or talking on the phone at first were still alone or yakking on the phone four weeks later. The same patterns held for talking with others, laughing, watching television, playing music, using the computer, reading, working, and attending lectures. How much time participants spent in their apartments, outdoors, in transit, or in a restaurant or other public places did not change. EAR wearers were even consistent in the kinds of words they used, especially for swear words and fillers such as *um, uh,* and *like.*

Swear words and fillers, and, in fact, all the words we use reflect our personalities. In another venture into personality snooping, James Pennebaker and Laura King used a computer program to dissect the elements of language in eight hundred people's writing samples. They found that extraverts tend to use language about social events and positive emotions and to avoid words that express negative emotion; they also tend to make distinctions through exclusive words *(but, without, except),* tentative words *(perhaps, maybe),* and negations *(no, not, never).* People high on openness tend to have a different pattern—they use fewer first-person singular pronouns *(I, me, my)* and more articles *(a, an, the)* and long words while avoiding verbs in the present tense than people low on this trait. People high on neuroticism tend to use a lot of first-person singular pronouns, fewer articles, and fewer words expressing positive emotion than negative emotion. In fact, differences in the use of first-person singular pronouns show up in many of Pennebaker's findings. Who would you think uses *I, me,* and *my* more often in the following groups: high- versus low-status people; suicidal vs. nonsuicidal poets; women or men; depressed or nondepressed people. Pennebaker sees *I, me,* and *my* as a linguistic marker of self-focus and has found higher rates of usage in women (vs. men), low-status (vs. high-status) people, suicidal (vs. nonsuicidal) poets, and depressed (vs. nondepressed) people.

Without specialized software, it's just about impossible to detect these differences in everyday speech, and it's even difficult to pick them up by reading your snoopee's writing. To show how hard it is to estimate the frequencies of words, think back to two conversations you have had over the past day or so. Although you could probably take a guess as to which one had more words in various content categories (such as words related to work or travel or certain people or activities)—that is, you have some idea what the conversations were about—you probably are clueless about the relative frequencies of what Pennebaker calls "junk" words (pronouns, prepositions, articles, conjunctions, and auxiliary verbs). Do you have any idea which of the two conversations used the words *the, of, in, that, but,* and *me* more? Yet it's precisely these junk words that mark our style of speaking, and that's why they are the best markers of personality and particular social circumstances. For example, Pennebaker has found that when people are telling the truth, they tend to use a relatively high frequency of first-person singular pronouns *(I, me, my)* and exclusive words (such as *but, except,* and *without),* which tend to mark complex thinking. So, when explaining something honestly, they are more likely to "own" it by making it more personal and describe the story in a more cognitively complex way.

Understandably, to do this very deep kind of snooping properly you really need to look at the frequencies of various elements of speech; the easiest way to do this is to use specially designed text-analysis software such as that developed by Pennebaker (and available on his Web site). The downside of these kinds of language analyses is that it requires specialized software. The upside is that since people have no idea about their own language style it's exceedingly hard for them to use language to present a deliberately false impression of their personalities. This is true even when they write rather than speak.

Not surprisingly, e-mail is a good conveyer of personality clues. And sometimes you don't even need to open the message. Christine Chang-Schneider is a graduate student at the University of Texas whose keen sensitivity to everyday expressions of personality led her down a path of research she didn't expect to follow. As part of a study that examined how people choose romantic partners, she needed to select female participants who liked themselves a lot as well as those who did not (determined by self-liking scores collected earlier). To invite both groups—the likers and the nonlikers—to show up for the study, she collected their e-mail addresses. Immediately she noticed differences between the two groups. Participants with high self-liking scores tended to have usernames to match, such as redhotjenni or princess_suzy. But the participants low on self-liking chose names like sadeyesagain and nothingmuchinside. When Chang-Schneider looked to see whether this was part of a broader pattern, she found that indeed in certain cases—and especially when people create their own monikers—usernames can give us clues about how people see themselves.

Here are some usernames from Chang-Schneider's study (slightly modified to protect the anonymity of the participants): naomiprincess, kingtony23, emotional_void82, Fatneckendra03, gorgeouschic, empty_heart, and strangelittleboypeter. You don't have to be Hercule Poirot to figure out which were high and which were low on self-liking. Christine also found that people's sense of competence shone through in the names they chose for themselves. Again, no awards for guessing who was high and who was low on self-perceived competence in this collection of names: stevethetennisace, spaceystacy, longtimeprodigy, smartguy, thatotherboy, sloppycrazyandweird, brainmissing, and julessavestheday.

Even when you have the opportunity to create your own e-mail name there are limitations in what you can communicate because the names are so short, and when you are using them in professional interactions you need to avoid anything too wacky. In Japan, in addition to regular e-mail accounts, many people have special e-mail addresses for their cell phones. There, the e-mail accounts on computers and cell phones serve different functions, especially for young people. Although they use their regular e-mail accounts for public purposes, such as sending a paper to a professor, they use their cell-phone e-mails purely for private purposes, such as making a date or chatting with friends.

Tsutako Mori of Konan Women's University in Japan told me that when young people meet for the first time and find they like each other, the first thing they do is exchange phone e-mail addresses. In these circles, phone e-mail addresses are the equivalent of swapping business cards. Mori reports that the first topic of their conversation is often about the origins of your e-mail address, so young people take considerable time to create unique phone addresses. And from a snooping perspective, it's amazing how much can be picked up just from these addresses. Mori found that observers who had nothing more than an e-mail to go on (and their gender, because that affects the meaning of the words) were surprisingly accurate at judging the owner's extraversion and, to a lesser extent, openness.

One feature that distinguished the addresses of outgoing positive extraverts from those of the low-key serious introverts was the former's playful and happy tone—one extravert's address was a riff on the name of an energetic, exciting video game. Extravert addresses included cute-rabbit, sunshine-go-go, love-and-smile. Many of the addresses incorporated smiley emoticons. Introverts often stuck with assigned meaningless numerical addresses; they did not personalize them, reflecting perhaps the lack of action and absence of interest in connection with others that is characteristic of this trait. Some introvert addresses referred to somber subjects like "setting sun" and "distortional addict."

Since we live in a society that puts few restraints on self-expression, it's a snooper's paradise when you know which clues to look for. But I'm often asked these two questions: What is the likelihood that someone can completely fool you about who they are simply by manipulating clues that reveal personality? Or would you be able to construct an entirely false personality if you knew what clues to manipulate? I'll address these provocative matters in the next chapter.

SIX

Space Doctoring

I TAKE MY RESPONSIBILITIES as a research mentor very seriously. When I train undergraduate students I typically insist they read several basic research papers, even though these tend to be dry and full of statistics. But one year, I departed from standard practice and assigned *The Rachel Papers,* a novel by the British writer Martin Amis. It's a psychologically vivid chronicle of several months in the life of a devious character, Charles Highway, a young man who goes to extraordinary lengths to lure women into his bed. In one episode, he watches a movie the day before he plans to see it with a woman named Rachel. This gives him time to prepare witty "impromptu" remarks to impress her. In another episode, he carefully arranges the items in his room:

> Not knowing her views on music I decided to play it safe; I stacked the records upright in two parallel rows; at the head of the first I put *2001: A Space Odyssey* (can't be wrong); at the head of the second I put, after some thought, a selection of Dylan Thomas's verse, read by the poet. . . . The coffee-table featured a couple of Shakespeare texts and a copy of *Time Out*—an intriguing dichotomy, perhaps, but I was afraid that, no, it wouldn't quite do . . . I replaced them with the Thames and Hudson *Blake* (again, can't be wrong) and *The Poetry of Meditation,* in fact a scholarly American work on the Metaphysicals, although from the cover it could have been a collection of beatnik verse: Rachel could interpret it as she wished.

So extensive and intricate are Highway's plans that he maintains files on each woman whom he hopes to seduce. The book's title, *The Rachel Papers,* refers to the file he keeps on Rachel's likes and dislikes to help him create an image of himself that will appeal to her. (Ironically, when I was rereading *The Rachel Papers* in preparation for writing this book, a visitor saw it on my bedside table and accused me of leaving it there to impress guests.)

I assign *The Rachel Papers* because it captures in a compelling and entertaining fashion how someone might use faux identity claims and fabricated behavioral residue to create a false impression. When people first come across my work, they often pick up on this idea: "Can't I just arrange my room to give you the wrong idea of what I'm like?" As we shall see, the answer is "Yes . . . but with limits."

DOWN WITH OCQ

To begin, let's do a quick exercise called the Test of Familiarity. From the following list of fifteen people, who vary from the famous to the obscure, rate your familiarity with each. If you are familiar with the name, write a 10 next to it. For most people, a 10 will come in handy with the first name on the list—Princess Diana. If you've never even heard of the person—as I'd never heard of Leo Hendrik Baekeland before I took a version of this test (he patented Bakelite)—then write a 0. If you're slightly familiar with the person, choose an intermediate number. Thus, I might give a 5 to Susilo Bambang Yudhoyono because I know he is the president of Indonesia, but that's about all I know. Enough preliminaries. Let's see how much you know:

1. Princess Diana
2. Dennis Hardcastle
3. Hermann Helmholtz
4. Quentin Tarantino
5. Mario Testino
6. Amelia Earhart

7. Angelina Jolie
8. Susie Gray-Putnam
9. Q-bert
10. Walt Whitman
11. T. C. Flutie
12. Kofi Annan
13. Apple Blythe Alison Martin
14. Frank Muir
15. Dan Rather

A survey similar to the one you've just taken was conducted in December 1966 in Tampa and Orlando, Florida. The topic was not famous people but television programs. The woman conducting the interviews stopped passersby to ask their opinions about various shows. Most people were only too happy to cooperate. When asked what in particular she liked about the program *Space Doctor*, for example, one woman pointed to all the "scientific work" in it, adding that her little boy loved it. She thought science shows were so good for children that this one should be extended to an hour. Some of the questions probed more specifically. When asked to express a preference for the episode about "getting stuck on the moon" versus "the wedding on Venus," the latter was one man's clear favorite. He wasn't bothered by the "space baby" or the men and women with antennas coming out of their heads. In fact, *Space Doctor* was one of his favorite shows. Another respondent highlighted the leading woman's voice and appearance as reasons for keeping Faith Harper in that role. But not everyone was enthusiastic. One woman pointed to the difficulty of explaining all the details about space science to her twelve-year-old daughter.

Another show listed on the survey was *Candid Camera*, the television program that contrives elaborate practical jokes and films people falling victim to them. Had the people of Tampa heard of *Candid Camera*? They sure had. Did they know that in one episode an interviewer stops people on the street and asks them to comment on programs that don't exist? Yes, but, on that day, rather too late. As you've probably guessed, *Candid Camera* had set up the survey and *Space Doctor* was entirely fabricated. So, when they were quizzed about that program, why didn't the respondents simply say they had no idea what the interviewer was talking about? Were they trying to help the interviewer? Or trying to look good? Or perhaps they somehow believed that they had seen the show.

Teasing apart the motives for what psychologists call "socially desirable responding" can be a challenge. Researchers have developed instruments to assess the degree to which people prevaricate to make themselves look good. Actually, you've just taken one such test. The Test of Familiarity is not what it claims to be. In reality, it assesses your propensity to claim to have heard of people who don't exist. Some of the names, rather like *Space Doctor,* are foils. Don't go back and change your answers! The test, developed so cunningly by Del Paulhus of the University of British Columbia, has proven to be remarkably good at pinpointing people who try to manage the impression they make.

Paulhus's Over-Claiming Questionnaire (or OCQ for short) is scored by evaluating how likely people are to say they have heard of nonexistent names. Did you give a 2 or more for Dennis Hardcastle, Susie Gray-Putnam, and T. C. Flutie? If you did, you were "over-claiming." (For references to the full scoring method, which is much more complex, see the note section at the end of the book.)

Maybe you didn't over-claim. Not everybody does, but rest assured that plenty of people reading this book do; some people generally over-claim much more than others. And how much you over-claim varies from one situation to another. When your boss is deciding who should get a special assignment you would be more likely than usual to paint yourself in a positive light.

Part of wanting to look good is concealing your efforts at *trying* to look good. If, like Charles Highway, you're trying to impress a date, you want to make it clear that the act is not an act. Highway's knowledge of the film he saw with Rachel would not be the slightest bit impressive if, when she asked him how he knew so much about it he said he'd seen the film the day before to prepare himself for the date. Unsurprisingly then, when you warn people before they take the Test of Familiarity (or OCQ) that there are some ringers on the list, their claims diminish, and they suddenly become much more honest—that is, their "familiarity scores" plummet. But there is one exception to this rule: Narcissists are relatively unaffected by warnings. Even when warned about the foils, the narcissists still over-claimed significantly more than the non-narcissists. One would expect them to back off to the level of non-narcissists, but they don't. For anyone who wants to look good—and narcissists certainly fall into that category—this would seem to expose them as frauds. So what's going on? Somehow, narcissists convince themselves that they really are familiar with these nonexistent people. It's not an act they're putting on for others; they actually come to believe it.

To understand the process of self-deception so common in narcissists and which many of us share to some degree, Professor Paulhus makes a useful distinction between two types of socially desirable responding. The most obvious type, Impression Management, refers to deliberate attempts to present oneself in a way that makes a favorable (socially desirable) impression on others. To do this we can inflate or enhance our positive attributes or we can deny or repudiate our negative attributes. The second, less obvious, type of desirable responding is known as Self-Deceptive Enhancement, which is a tendency to give positively biased but honest self-descriptions. People high on this trait are not saying one thing but thinking another—they really believe all the wonderful things they say about themselves. They're deluded. So when you instruct people to paint themselves in a positive light, their Impression Management scores skyrocket (because this is something we do deliberately), but their Self-Deceptive Enhancement scores hardly change (because this is something we're not conscious of). As you might guess, people high on the trait of narcissism have unusually high scores on Self-Deceptive Enhancement but are the same as other people on Impression Management.

The research on the differences between the two types of socially desirable responding sheds light on why narcissists—who are especially concerned about how they are viewed—don't worry that their over-claiming will be discovered. They don't heed the warnings that some of the names are fake; they hear a fictitious name such as T. C. Flutie and convince themselves that they know it. Del Paulhus, the inventor of the over-claiming questionnaire, told me that narcissists will argue aggressively with you when challenged with the fact that the names are made up—even when they hear that you invented the names, they will trust their own sense of knowing more than what you are telling them and continue to argue with you about the existence of the people behind the names. Paulhus believes that this defensive behavior is what allows them to maintain their self-deception. By making it unpleasant to challenge them, narcissists can reassure themselves that they must be right because their opponents have backed down. Of course, not everyone arguing with a narcissist can be so sure about their position; unlike Paulhus, few of us have had the luxury of making up names out of thin air and then tricking people into claiming they've heard of them.

Narcissists are a fascinating group. Unlike many people with extreme personalities—those who are paranoid or excessively emotional and attention-seeking—narcissists often function well in positions of power and responsibility. My colleague Daniel Ames at Columbia University's School of Business allows his MBA students, all of whom are exceptionally high-functioning, to take various personality questionnaires, and he offers the students feedback on the scores. A few years back, one student got the maximum possible score on the narcissism test. Given that most people view narcissism negatively, Ames was concerned that the feedback might come as a shock to the student. But he need not have worried. The student's high levels of narcissism swung into action to construe this troubling information in a positive light. Ames later overheard the student telling another, "I aced the narcissism test—I got every single question right."

Another feature of narcissists is their unlimited ability to absorb compliments. A few years back, some colleagues and I were meeting with an incredibly gifted but narcissistic collaborator. We set a goal in advance of seeing how excessive we could be with our compliments before he figured out that we were exaggerating. During that meeting, and several others, our collaborator's reaction was not the incredulity we had expected to elicit but one of flattered modesty. Indeed, by the end we were saying such things as "I think that comment may be the most brilliant thing I have *ever* heard." But no matter what we said, our collaborator kept lapping it up.

To illustrate further how narcissists see themselves, consider how some of them responded to a managerial exercise in a study conducted at UC Berkeley some years ago. Researchers seated six people at a round table and later queried them about where they had sat. Narcissists were more likely than others to report they had been seated at the head of the table.

Of course, it's normal to want to be seen in a positive light. For example, I have an admission to make: As I was picking the examples for the introduction to the OCQ, I forgot the name of the Indonesian president. So I looked it up on Google and then casually tossed it into the text to give the impression that my grip on world affairs is better than it actually is.

But how far could I go in establishing my reputation as an expert on global matters? With enough time, and full access to Google, I could create and maintain the subterfuge. I might have casually referred to lesser Indonesian ministers, offhandedly drawing on my detailed knowledge of the country's parliamentary and judicial system and throwing in an anecdote or two about political incidents. But if you and I met, it would be harder for me to keep up the pretense. I might prepare myself with all kinds of facts to drop into the conversation, but when you hit me with a question about Muhammad Yusuf Kalla, the vice president of Indonesia (okay, okay, I admit it, I just looked that up on Google, too), the ruse would soon unravel. So in some circumstances we can make ourselves look good, but in other situations—in many day-to-day interactions—it's harder. Where do the everyday contexts that I've studied—bedrooms, offices, and the like—fit on the continuum of allowing us to look good?

WAITING FOR GOFFMAN

I did my first snooping studies of bedrooms when I was a graduate student at UC Berkeley. So several years later, when I was asked to give a talk there on my latest work, I was pleased but also a bit nervous at the prospect of embarrassing myself in front of my former teachers. The material seemed to generate a great deal of interest because, when we moved into the discussion period, a lot of people asked questions. First with his hand in the air was a well-known Berkeley psychology professor who posed this question: "What would Goffman say?" He was referring to Erving Goffman, the eminent sociologist famed for his influential work on how people present themselves to the world. Although the question had never been posed in exactly that way before, it reflected a common concern: Do the signs we let others see reflect valid information about us, or are they all part of an elaborate act aimed at portraying ourselves as we wish to be seen?

In his classic book, *The Presentation of Self in Everyday Life,* Goffman suggests that in our daily lives we are like characters in a play: We take on roles and present a front. Accordingly, what we say and do during a social interaction is like a script. Goffman says that it is easier to stay in character than to react authentically. When we act and react, we can draw on a well-known and rehearsed script associated with the character we play. Role-playing makes it easier to understand other people's behaviors, but it also makes our actions less authentic.

As in theatrical plays, the roles we play can be enhanced with props and costumes that increase the audience's belief in the role. When I teach undergraduate classes, I dress the part—collared shirt, nice trousers, and proper shoes—making it easier both for me and my students to negotiate the classroom situation. When you visit your lawyer, you expect him or her to be dressed "professionally" and that his office will be adorned with framed certificates and degrees, thick volumes of unreadable books, and a sturdy desk with one of those reassuring brass-finished bankers' lamps on it. When interviewing a juggler or a clown for your kid's birthday party, you'd hope to find something a little less austere in his office. Presumably you could juggle in a business suit and you could try a case wearing a cherry-red nose, but that's not part of the script. Clearly, appearances are important to the presentation of self. So when the Berkeley professor asked me what Goffman would say about my research, he was essentially questioning whether the props found in bedrooms and offices, in music collections and on Web pages aren't just Goffman-esque aids to the roles we play rather than authentic expressions of ourselves.

On the face of it, he had a point. There's no reason why bedroom occupants couldn't strategically manipulate their spaces to make a good impression. With a little bit of effort, it would seem that occupants, like Charles Highway in *The Rachel Papers,* could craft their environments to project whatever impressions they deemed appealing to others. They could display socially desirable symbols (for example, an award for public service), they could fabricate behavioral residue (a made-up bed), and they could deceivingly display objects they had no intention of using (a snowboard). And hiding evidence of less socially sanctioned behaviors—the bondage equipment perhaps—could also count as impression management. When I began snooping in bedrooms, I was worried that the occupants might project entirely false impressions.

Since they knew when the assessment team would arrive they could easily have tidied their rooms before the team got there, thus projecting a false impression, rendering the research data less valid.

If all of the bedroom occupants were trying to look good (and had the ability to do so), then all the rooms should have been immaculate. But we did not find eighty-three uniformly clean, tidy, organized dorm rooms. Instead there was a staggering amount of variation: In some, observers had to pick their way between dirty socks and half-finished take-out meals strewn across the floor; in others, our judges encountered freshly washed socks rolled and filed neatly in a specially dedicated section of the drawers and without a speck of dust in sight. Even if the participants did engage in some anticipatory tidying, it wasn't enough to cover up real differences. And we soon discovered an important distinction: that between a *tidy* room and a *tidied* room.

If you do not generally live a tidy life—putting things back in place when you're done with them, implementing an underwear organizational system, stocking up on supplies long before they run out—then in all likelihood you won't have a deeply tidy room, and there is only so much you can do about it in the short term. Granted, you could hide the socks (although even this didn't evade our observers, who got down on their hands and knees to look under the beds) and dust your bookcase. But it takes more than an afternoon to color-code your paper clips, to install and arrange a shoe organizer, and to sort and file all your papers. It takes consistent and persistent behavior to have a deeply tidy room. But a hurried hour, or even a day or two of tidying, can produce, at best, only a tidied room. No matter how hard we try, many parts of our personalities are simply irrepressible. Research suggests that we cannot simply play any role we choose—sadly, we can't all be James Bond or Lara Croft. Not convincingly, at least.

Clearly, the things we do consciously are easier to fake than what we do outside our own awareness. Thus, identity claims have the greatest potential for deception. If I want to fake it as a conservative or a liberal or a feminist or a devoutly religious person, it's pretty clear what I would need to do. To signal political affiliation, I could praise political icons such as Ronald Reagan or one of the Kennedys. A T-shirt displaying "Well-Behaved Women Seldom Make History" (a quotation from the feminist Laurel Thatcher Ulrich) or the Christian symbol of a fish on the bumper of my car would unambiguously signal the intended message. But it's harder to manipulate behavioral residue because it is the *inadvertent* consequence of your actions and thus usually escapes your conscious awareness. If I open my window shades in haste before dashing out the door in the morning, I would not attend to the unevenness of the shades because my focus was directed on the task itself (letting light into the room and heading out to work), not its unintended consequences (uneven blinds).

Projecting a false identity is difficult because our real personalities persistently try to express themselves. Some things we do automatically. In the film *The Great Escape,* the English-speaking inmates of a POW camp in World War II make plans to merge into German society once they have sprung themselves. They attempt to learn German but they also prepare for a trick the Germans used to detect foreigners (according to the movie, at least). The clever Germans would speak to suspects in English to see whether they answered in English; the trick relied on people's impulse to respond in their native language. In principle, an appealing aspect of snooping around people's bedrooms or offices is that so much of the evidence— a collection of books about crafts or well-used camping equipment— is so hard to fake. This helps explain why so much variation remained in the dorm rooms, even though the occupants knew we'd be coming and could have fixed things up before the snooping got underway. Much of what we saw resulted from unreflective behavior.

What if an occupant resolves to create an image of order and high-mindedness—tidying up the room, hiding the parking ticket, and replacing *People* with the *New York Times?* In fact, it's not so easy to fabricate a good impression. It takes many years to build up a book collection; it is expensive to buy mountaineering equipment, and the equipment needs to be used if it is to look used; having photos of oneself hiking in Nepal requires that one actually goes to Nepal and hike; having an honors society award upon the wall requires winning the award in the first place; and having a well-thumbed personal organizer requires that one does a great deal of thumbing through that organizer. Contrast the effort required to create a false impression in one's living space with what you'd need to do to look good in an interview or on a personality questionnaire. If you're just answering questions, it's all too easy to claim that you enjoy reading, that you love adventurous travel to exotic locations, that you're an excellent student, and that you are fabulously well organized. So of all the contexts in which we can learn about people—meetings, interviews, behavioral tests, personality questionnaires—bedrooms are the ones that give the most reliable information.

A Towel's Rightful Place

Another reason why it is difficult to create a false impression is that people's standards vary. What may seem noticeable to one person could be missed by another. Personality is expressed not just in our behaviors but also in the way we perceive the world; that is, anxious people not only fidget when under stress but they see more dangers, threats, and things to worry about than their laid-back neighbors, who see no good reason to get their knickers in a twist. The same goes for the trait of conscientiousness.

People high on this trait have different standards from the rest of us. This point was brought home to me recently when I visited the home of Lisa (of *Moveable Feast* fame from chapter 4) whom I knew only slightly at the time. She insisted that I look around her house, and it quickly became clear from the organization and lack of stuff lying about that she was high on conscientiousness. I shared my analysis with her. Lisa appeared confused and asked how I had come to such a conclusion. I pointed out that just about everything in the house seemed to be where it should be, the place was clean, and there was little clutter. She countered that with so much stuff in such a small place she was forced to be organized, right?

Wrong! If you are high on conscientiousness, it seems self-evident that you need to control the clutter, so getting organized is a high priority. But I have been in plenty of spaces where that apparently self-evident point has been lost somewhere amongst the flotsam scattered across the floor. I pointed out to Lisa that not everyone would have two matched towels, folded in exactly the same way on the towel rack, hanging to exactly the same length, and spaced just far enough apart to allow access to the tissues below (in an immaculate tissue box holder, of course). I predicted that if I had moved one of the towels it would not have taken long before it was returned to its rightful place. She agreed. I pointed out that the fact that she could make sense of the idea of a towel having a rightful place was a good sign that she was pretty high on conscientiousness.

A similar point was driven home to me a couple of years ago when a colleague whom I had always considered organized, punctual, and careful lamented that she had started behaving like a slacker, showing up late to work and not doing much preparation for her classes. I was surprised, but not for long. As soon as she described what she actually did, I realized that her definition of a slacker came from a world view that was entirely different from mine. By her definition, she was slacking because she was recklessly arriving at work at 8:45 A.M. instead of 8:15 A.M. for her 9:00 A.M. classes. Not only that, but (in her mind) she had really let things go because she was preparing for classes three days ahead instead of the usual week or two. To those of us who pull things together the night before they are due and wouldn't dream of scheduling a class at an hour as uncivilized as 9:00 A.M., her behavior seems highly responsible. After our conversation, it dawned on me that we see the world very differently.

More recently, I was teaching a class of Ph.D. students about my research and noted in passing that my desk was a complete mess. My fellow teacher objected: "No, it's not." The students now wanted to know—was it tidy or was it messy? No point bickering; to settle the matter all eighteen of us got up and went upstairs to my office. My colleague and I stood by, both of us happy in the knowledge we were about to be vindicated in our tidiness assessment. Of course, no such vindication came. Five of the students were impressed with my powers of organization; six were appalled by the conditions, surprised that anyone could get anything done there at all; and the rest were somewhere in between. Shouldn't I be concerned about this astonishing lack of agreement about a rather simple judgment? If we can't even agree which offices are tidy and which are messy, how can we possibly be in a position to say tidiness (or any other feature of the space) reflects personality? Fortunately, the judges in my research showed considerably more agreement about whether spaces were messy (or decorated, clean, cheerful). The secret to their strong consensus was that they had so many offices to compare; instead of just thinking is this place messier than my own place, they were comparing the offices to the last twenty offices they saw. This is why, as we shall see in chapter 9, it is important to snoop in as many comparison spaces as possible when you make your assessments.

This issue of different standards has implications for how we go about evaluating the effectiveness of our snooping. Consider my "slacker" colleague who had fallen into a downward spiral of delinquency, now showing up only fifteen minutes before her classes. If I had looked around her (immaculate) office and shared with her my diagnosis that she was a responsible and punctual person, she might have objected, reminding me that she often shows up late for appointments. But if Tiger Woods told me he had just played a bad round of golf, I would not think his round was "bad" by mortal standards; similarly, I should not judge my colleague's self-assessment by her unusually high standards of conscientiousness.

So where should I turn for an accurate reading? For the traits and behaviors associated with conscientiousness I ask a person's friends; to make sure Amber shows up to the movie on time, does she have to be told that it starts twenty minutes earlier than it really does? Do Courtney's friends know that she's a good bet when they're looking for a spare stamp? Indeed, our insight into our own levels of conscientiousness often comes from our interactions with friends and colleagues. Do we constantly find ourselves being the first person to show up for a meeting? Or the last?

To illustrate how various personalities see the world differently, imagine that you have arrived for a meeting with a few people who don't know each other. One key person is late, so you kill fifteen minutes while you wait. In all likelihood, someone, almost certainly an extravert, will start chatting, and then others will join in. But the introverts might remain quiet. How would you view the people jabbering away and the people sitting quietly? According to new research by Daniel Ames (the same guy who studied narcissism in MBA students), your response would largely be determined by your own personality. Elegantly demonstrating how people with different personalities see the world, Ames has shown that extraverts and introverts have radically different takes on people's behavior. When I run Ames's study in my own classroom, I find the same thing: The extraverts don't disguise their disdain for the uncommunicative introverts, who selfishly refuse to keep the discussion alive; they cannot fathom why their mute colleagues don't do their bit to carry some of the conversational load. At the same time, the introverts have nothing but contempt for their garrulous counterparts; why not, they wonder, wait until you've got something worth saying before opening your mouth.

What all this shows is that different personalities perceive the world differently, and it is hard to fake this difference. A truly organized person finds it difficult to focus on other tasks when his office is disorganized, but the person who is only pretending to be organized would probably not even notice that the books on the shelf are out of alphabetical order. These basic differences in perception have clear implications for our ability to create false impressions. To fake it as a highly conscientious person, I would do all the obvious things, such as tidying up my desk, organizing my books, sharpening my pencils, and taming the jumble of cables under and over my desk. But I would miss all kinds of things—I wouldn't even notice that the ordering system for the books on the shelf next to the door doesn't parallel the system in the bookshelf under the window. Or that I hadn't closed the box of staples properly, or that the appointments on my desk calendar were not consistent in the coloring system I had created—one birthday would be in green ink, another in red. To prove to yourself that people at one end of the conscientiousness pole see the world differently from those at the other, you need only ask a group of people whether they carry spare postage stamps. When I pose this question to my classes, those at the high end are puzzled that I would ask such a question because of course they do. The people at the low end are equally puzzled: Why on earth would anyone carry spare stamps?

LOOKING GOOD VS. LOOKING REAL

As we've seen, spaces generally give an accurate view of the people who occupy them. But is this because the occupants are trying to create a false impression and failing or because they are not even trying? This question cuts to the heart of one of the most fundamental questions in social psychology—do people want to be known? Ultimately, would you rather be seen as you'd like to be? Or would you rather someone saw you as you see yourself, warts and all?

The obvious answer is that we generally want to be seen in a positive light, but one idea—known as Self-Verification Theory—suggests that such a desire is not always true. It suggests that we would prefer to be seen as we see ourselves, regardless of whether those self-views are positive or negative. So if someone sees herself as uncreative, she will try to present herself as uncreative even if she thinks that's a negative quality.

The inventor of Self-Verification Theory, Bill Swann (whose office is down the corridor from mine), and his colleagues have conducted numerous studies that suggest people seek self-verifying feedback across a wide range of situations. The most powerful studies show how even people with negative opinions of themselves seem to want these confirmed. In a huge study of employees' reactions to pay increases, those employees with positive self-views were happy to receive a pay raise; but low self-esteem employees found it hard to make sense of a pay increase because the idea that they were valuable was discordant with their own views. They were actually more likely to leave the company after a pay raise than without one!

Down a different corridor, another couple of colleagues, Bob Josephs and his collaborator Pranj Mehta, found something similar in their studies of how dominant and submissive people react to wins and losses in a rigged competition. They invited pairs of participants to their laboratory and asked them to trace a line through consecutive numbers in a huge grid. To make the task more meaningful, they told the subjects that the studies measured spatial intelligence, an important component of general intelligence. Both participants were given the puzzle at the same time in a competitive situation. This task can easily be tweaked by altering the pattern of the grid; in this way, the experimenters can secretly determine who "wins."

Mehta and Josephs predicted that men and women with high levels of testosterone would desire high status, and that those with low levels would desire low status. According to this "mismatch" hypothesis, people would become stressed, feel bad, and do poorly on tests when their performance was inconsistent with where they thought they belonged on the status hierarchy. In a study that used the rigged number-searching competition, high-testosterone participants were more stressed (as indicated by increased levels of the stress hormone cortisol in their bodies) after losing than when they won. But for those with low testosterone, winning was more disturbing than losing—the low-testosterone winners subsequently performed less well than the losers on a series of logic questions. They were more troubled by winning than by losing! These findings converge to suggest that people would rather get feedback that is consistent with their self-views even if it comes at the expense of seeing themselves in a positive light. This is another reason why snooping can be so effective.

WORLD WIDE WEB OF DECEIT?

One especially interesting snooping adventure gave further credence to the idea that people want to project a realistic picture of themselves. My former graduate student Simine Vazire and I were interested in whether people, when given the opportunity, would use identity claims to project an honest image of their personalities or whether they would try to portray themselves as they'd like to be in an ideal world. To test this idea, we needed a context where the easy-to-fake identity claims were not constrained by the difficult-to-manipulate effects of behavioral residue. We realized that personal Web pages would be ideal—just about every element on a Web site is put there deliberately and only rarely do items show up by accident or neglect.

Web sites that are explicitly made for others to view are more obviously about identity claims than those made for fun or for an inner circle of friends. So for our research we chose only those pages listed in a directory requiring people to submit their pages for inclusion. We soon saw that Web pages allow identity claims to be made about values, interests, and goals through all kinds of media. They included simple text statements about the user's political beliefs; videos of the owner surfing, an activity of obvious importance to her sense of who she was; blogs railing about the latest tweaks in the rules of football; photos of famous movie directors and other heroes; and a huge number of symbols signaling allegiance to religious, ethnic, cultural, and political groups.

If you spend time browsing personal Web sites—and I encourage would-be snoopers to do so—you will be amazed by how much information you find. The Web site of a woman named Christina, for example, included information about her leisure interests, her political beliefs, her poetry, an ongoing record of her moods, and an assortment of personal essays on current and personal events. It included photos of her family (several generations), her vacations, her pets, her garden, her kitchen, her car, as well as images of people, places, and events she admired. It listed the movies, books, musicians, and television shows she had seen along with her rankings of them.

The second thing that will strike you is the tremendous variety. Whereas Elise's site primarily conveyed her caustic views on the shortcomings of certain religious movements, Sven's was a mundane account of his daily life for the benefit of his friends and family. The black opening page of William's site was sparse and simple with just three artfully arranged symbols pointing the way to other pages labeled "Art," "Mind," and "Self." Laura's opening page was completely different—a jumbled colorful confusion of bright words and symbols arranged higgledy-piggledy over a hastily drawn house.

We randomly chose a number of Web sites and saved them on a computer. (We saved the sites before contacting people because we didn't want them to alter their sites when they learned they were going to be in a study.) Then we contacted the site owners and asked whether they'd like to be included. (If they did not, we deleted the saved Web site.) We then asked them to tell us how they saw themselves and how they would like to be seen ideally.

Next, we essentially repeated the procedures from our snooping studies of bedrooms and offices. But instead of physical places, the targets of perception this time were virtual environments. We recruited judges and asked them to browse Web sites and form an impression of what the owners were like. Then we compared what they thought with owners' self-reports of actual and ideal selves. We found that the judges' impressions converged more strongly with the actual self-reports than with the ideal self-reports—suggesting once again that people want to be seen as they are, not as they'd like to be. Our study was done before the advent of social-networking Web sites, such as MySpace, Friendster, and Facebook, but on those sites you see the same effects, perhaps even more strongly. Not satisfied with the standard categories, people supplement the basic personal information by creating questionnaires to express an infinitely complex and fine-grained portrait of themselves.

It seems that people are crying out to be known. But even if they were not, it's unlikely they could pull off a convincing ruse. Although it is easy to throw out false clues about what you are like—you might claim, for example, to enjoy classical music when you don't—it is difficult to emit those clues consistently enough to project a false identity. It's hard to replicate the other behaviors of a genuine classical-music lover—the books on their shelves, the stations to which their radios are tuned (not just classical music stations), the art on the walls, the stuff in the trash can. This is why actors spend many weeks getting into a role. To portray someone else convincingly you have to learn how that person thinks, lives, and sees the world.

We have since followed up our original Web-site research with a study of impressions based on Facebook profiles. In this work, we uncovered yet another impediment to creating a false impression. With the exception of their extraversion levels, people are virtually clueless about the impressions their profiles convey. If you have no idea about how you are seen, how can you construct a phony self-portrait?

Another major finding from our research was that Web sites are extraordinarily good places to learn about people—perhaps the best of all places. Our site snooping yielded information that was at least as accurate as what we learned from the bedrooms, offices, and music collections we studied, and accurate across a much broader array of personality variables than most other domains. For example, when it came to the Big Five OCEAN traits, bedrooms were particularly revealing about openness and conscientiousness, and Top-10s were especially useful for learning about openness, extraversion, and emotional stability. But Web sites proved useful for learning about all five traits.

FOOL ME ONCE

We can draw various lessons about the extent to which people can manage how others see them. First, some situations are particularly vulnerable to impression management. In places where you have a great deal of control over the flow of information, such as job interviews or on a date, it may be possible to manage your impression very well. I once interviewed a research assistant who assured me he was a meticulous record keeper, a claim proven false within a week of his first assignment. In contrast, most places that interest snoopers, such as bedrooms and offices, are much harder to fake because they have accumulated a great deal of information deposited over time— it's hard to undo that much information, and it's even harder to create large amounts of false information that suggest personality traits you do not have. So when interpreting clues according to their probability of being manipulated, it is useful to think of them in three categories:

Category 1 clues are the easiest to manipulate—they are deliberate signals, where sending signals is the prime goal of the clues (displaying the gay pride rainbow symbol on your bulletin board).

Category 2 clues are deliberate modifications of the environment, but signaling is unintended (creating a comfortable space).

Category 3 clues, the hardest to manipulate, are the inadvertent signals we send, as byproducts of our behaviors (the neglected dying plant on the windowsill).

The second lesson is that, although it is generally hard to create bogus impressions in physical environments, some traits are harder to fake than others. Guessing a trait based on its residue, such as tidiness indicating conscientiousness, is much harder to forge than those based on identity claims, which are relatively malleable, such as prominently displaying a poster of the Marxist icon Che Guevara to signify left-wing views.

I'll focus in more detail on these topics in later chapters, but for now here are a few quick snooping suggestions to help you see through the smokescreen laid by someone who wants to mislead you. First, look for consistency in the information being transmitted. The poster of Che Guevara is a good starting point, but is it supported by the other evidence of economics texts in the bookshelves and the ticket stub from a Broadway musical found in a jacket pocket? If not, it could be a clue to a forged impression. Second, if you know there is an incentive to appear a certain way, be vigilant. Did the poster of Che appear suspiciously close to the anticipated arrival of a sexy single Marxist? Third, we know that personality seeps out even when we don't want it to; even though the many-tabbed filing system seems to signify a need to keep things in order, look to see whether the organizational system has actually been maintained. Are there bills in the wrong section and one too many folders labeled "miscellaneous"? If so, you may have discovered a faux filing system that cloaks a muddle-minded personality. Fourth, don't allow your snooping to be directed by the occupant or the occupant's expectations. If you sit in the office visitors' chair—as your snoopee no doubt expects you to—you may see only the pristine desk, not the tangle of wires and the twelve pairs of shoes underneath it.

EN GARDE!

Be on your guard. As we've seen, people sometimes do try to paint themselves in a positive light. Whether they're pretending to have seen the space baby on a fictitious television show, to have heard of nonexistent people, or deceptively scooped all the paper clips into the paper-clip holder to make themselves appear more responsible, people are going to try to mess with how you think of them. In addition, some people are more prone to this behavior than others. Narcissists even manage to convince themselves that their subterfuges are true. However, hope is at hand. First, methods such as Paulhus's over-claiming questionnaire can identify these self-aggrandizers. Second, as a snooper, you can pay attention to the signs—such as the discrepancy between easy-to-fake identity claims and difficult-to-fake behavioral residue—that someone is trying to fool you. Third, and most important, as we've seen, the research points directly to the conclusion that people typically don't want to portray themselves in a false light. They may exaggerate a bit, but there's only so much room for positive spin, and it is very difficult to pull off major deceptions. In *The Rachel Papers,* Martin Amis's character Charles Highway was ultimately unable to control people's perceptions of him—in the long run, they were not taken in by his elaborate charade.

As a snooper, you've got to do far more than slice away what's fake— you have to construct what is real. Typically, your initial constructions will rely on ready-made mental armatures. These frameworks are stereotypes. Although they are more commonly known for their pernicious effects, stereotypes give us a starting place from which to sort out the myriad signals that bombard us every day. They are mental shortcuts, usually based on a bit of truth, that we take when we don't have more explicit information. Stereotypes are crucial to our perceptions because they give us known patterns against which to test our experience. Anyone interested in the science of snooping must know something about them. In the next chapter I'll show you why.

SEVEN

In Defense
of Stereotypes

A S A CHILD growing up in England, I was aware of the stereo-types of the people living in the countries nearby. Some of these national images became almost socially acceptable, and even crept into television shows and advertising. These stereotypes included elaborate scripts about the kinds of interactions you could expect to have with a German, an Italian, or a Frenchman should you ever have the misfortune to encounter one.

When I grew up, German vacationers were the subject of one particular stereotype dearly held by many English girls and boys. The stereotypical encounter starts with a hopelessly disorganized English family somewhere on the Mediterranean coast, Greece perhaps. On the first evening, as the kids polish off the *taramasalata* and the parents sip their *ouzo,* the family laments previous vacations when they arrived too late at the beach to secure a pleasant spot to sunbathe and build sandcastles. Spurred by these bitter memories, the family resolves to get up early the next morning and secure a prime spot of sandy real estate. At the crack of dawn, the bleary-eyed parents rouse the kids and bundle them into the back of the rental car. They stuff the trunk with towels, beach balls, buckets, and spades. With grim determination, the parents head beachward. After a wrong turn or two, they finally find the parking lot near the beach. They gather their belongings and rush down to the beach only to discover all the best spots are already occupied by the infuriatingly efficient Germans. As the German children stride across the beach after a wonderfully invigorating swim, their parents complete their morning exercises. Resigned, the English family shuffles to the shady, rocky section of the beach, comforting themselves with the fact that they can get a glimpse of the sea if they climb onto the nearby sewer pipe.

This stereotypical script said about as much about the Brits' ineptitude and their willingness to persevere stoically as it did about the fiercely organized Germans, but it became sufficiently engrained in the culture to make its way into the British advertising campaign for Audi, the German carmaker. After extolling the performance of their sporty model, zipping around Europe, the voiceover said: "If you want to beat the Germans to the beach, you'd better get an Audi."

What's the point of stereotypes? Do they serve a useful function beyond poking fun at the inhabitants of neighboring countries?

THE SHREW THAT ROARED

Imagine you are walking along a path in the jungle and you hear the roar of a tiger. You turn and, behind a nearby bush, you see the tail of the tiger. Although you have yet to see the whole beast, it's a good bet that you're in danger of encountering a tiger, not a hitherto undiscovered species of shrew with the tail and roar of a tiger. You would be wise to make a run for it, or do whatever you are supposed to do when encountering a tiger, (although, of course, if it really *was* a tiger-tailed shrew you might have just missed the biological find of the century). The example shows that we use stereotypes to fill in the gaps when we are unable to gather all the information. And most everyday opportunities for perception are riddled with gaps. If you didn't use stereotypes, you would be overwhelmed, because every item, person, and experience in life would have to be treated as though it were a totally new experience, not part of a broader class.

Thinking about stereotypes this way—as assumptions about things (people or objects) in the absence of direct experience of those particular things—allows us to see how common they are and how often we use them in all manner of impression-formation contexts. Without them, we couldn't take a walk down the street or bite into a sandwich. When you go to a new part of town, what makes you think the sidewalk slab in front of your foot is going to hold up when you put your foot on it? You have never put your foot there before. How do you know it's not going to cave in or catch fire or swim away? Or why should you believe the sandwich you're about to eat is edible? You've never eaten this particular sandwich before. Face the fact that, by making generalizations to guide your interactions, you are using evil oppressive stereotypes about sidewalks and sandwiches, not considering them as individual unique entities in their own right. But if someone accuses you of using a stereotype, it almost certainly means that you are making an assumption about a person based on their membership in a certain group (such as African Americans, Jews, homosexuals, or Germans).

Is there anything to stereotypes like the ones about the German and British vacationers? It's hard to answer that question because people have different standards for judging behavior. Recall from my faux-slacking colleague, who thought she was being negligent by showing up less than half an hour before class, that we can't always take a conscientious person's word for how conscientious she is. Similarly, people in different cultures use different standards to judge behaviors. Arriving one minute past the appointed time could be considered late in Switzerland but quite acceptable in Brazil. The problems caused by shifting standards have led some researchers to adopt a more objective approach to studying national stereotypes by comparing countries according to things you can count or measure.

One of the most noticeable things about traveling from country to country is the apparent difference in the pace of life—in some countries the whole population appears to be on amphetamines, their natives frenetically scurrying around accomplishing tasks and going places with alarming rapidity. Other places, where citizens saunter lackadaisically from one resting spot to the next, seem to have something a little more calming in the water. Peruvians even have the concept of *hora peruana,* or Peruvian time, which translates to about an hour late. So lax is Peruvian punctuality that its government promoted a campaign—*la hora sin demora* or "time without delay"—to improve the nation's reputation.

Robert Levine, a psychologist at the California State University in Fresno, was curious about these apparent differences in pace of life. Does life in some countries move faster than others, or is it just an illusion? To compare the speed at which people do routine activities around the world, Levine trained a team of clandestine researchers. As the denizens of downtown Amsterdam, Dublin, Jakarta, Rio de Janeiro, Sofia, Tokyo, and twenty-five other urban centers, innocently went about their daily lives, the researchers surreptitiously placed themselves at strategic points around the cities.

They measured out a distance of sixty feet on the sidewalk and, from their hiding places, used stopwatches to calculate how fast the locals walked. Next, the undercover researchers went into downtown banks and recorded the accuracy of the clocks. The final test was to measure the time it took to buy a stamp in a local post office. By combining the results of these simple tests, Levine was able to quantify the pace of the various cities. Which countries were at the top of the list? The pace of life was fastest in Switzerland, Ireland, and Germany. It was slowest in Mexico, Indonesia, and Brazil. So if you learn that a new coworker is from Brazil, in the absence of other information, it is reasonable to think that he or she will have a more casual approach to time than your Swiss colleague. The full list of countries in Levine's study—from fastest to slowest—is presented in table 7.1.

Table 7.1   Pace of Life in 31 Countries from Fastest to Slowest

Fastest:			
1.	Switzerland	16.	United States
2.	Ireland	17.	Canada
3.	Germany	18.	South Korea
4.	Japan	19.	Hungary
5.	Italy	20.	Czech Republic
6.	England	21.	Greece
7.	Sweden	22.	Kenya
8.	Austria	23.	China
9.	Netherlands	24.	Bulgaria
10.	Hong Kong	25.	Romania
11.	France	26.	Jordan
12.	Poland	27.	Syria
13.	Costa Rica	28.	El Salvador
14.	Taiwan	29.	Brazil
15.	Singapore	30.	Indonesia
		Slowest: 31.	Mexico

You'll notice some basic patterns in the table. Levine discovered that the pace of life was associated with a slew of other characteristics of the countries. Fast-paced countries tend to have colder climates, are more economically productive, have higher smoking rates, and higher rates of death from coronary heart disease.

THE PERSONALITY OF PLACE

Stereotypes about people from different places can get a lot narrower than the ones based on their countries of origin. Think about the stereotypes we hold about people from cities or states, such as neurotic New Yorkers, laid-back Californians, and whitebread Midwesterners. It seems intuitive that people are different in different places—but why is this so? One reason is that different environments can shape personalities because they offer different opportunities to the people who live there. Physical and cultural environments play a part in shaping the activities and interactions, and hence the personalities, of the people who live there; for example, teenagers growing up in rural neighborhoods will engage in activities quite different from those of youngsters growing up in urban or coastal neighborhoods. With no subways, crowds, or strangers, kids from Hazelton, Idaho, seldom get to ride a subway crowded with strangers, and, the last time I checked, beach parties were still rare in Iowa City. An interest in contemporary art is easier to nurture in a city with a thriving artistic community than it is in a small country town where the only thing thriving is the corn.

Environment explains only part of the truth behind geographic stereotypes because there is a limit to how far people can flex. A liberal in a red state may be able to temper his political views somewhat, but eventually he will reach his limit. And when this happens, the best solution may be a move to a place that better matches his personality. I saw the life-changing effects of relocating when I was on sabbatical in the San Francisco Bay Area. As my caffeine levels waned in the evening, I would often head down to the Stanford University CoHo to get some work done and drink a latte. On one occasion, I was struck by the animated conversation among a group of students at a nearby table. A few days earlier, I had seen something similar in the predominantly gay Castro area of San Francisco. Here were people who had finally discovered a place in which they felt at home. The CoHo students were able to talk with giddy delight about the nerdy intellectual topics that would have elicited disdain in their hometowns. At last they'd found other people (three at this table alone!) who also appreciated the scintillating possibilities of the hexadecimal system. In the Castro, I got the same feeling as I watched gay men and women happily letting their true selves off the leash.

In fact, people do gravitate to their niches as they gain the social and financial freedom to exercise control over where they live. In his influential book *The Rise of the Creative Class,* Richard Florida makes a compelling case that people—especially creative types—are drawn to a place not by mere economic considerations, such as the best-paying job or favorable house prices, but by the idea that they will fit in. In one persuasive example, Florida describes meeting a young man, with body piercings, tattoos, and multicolored hair, on the campus of Carnegie Mellon University in Pittsburgh. The student was in the process of graduating and had just taken a lucrative job in Austin, Texas, after turning down several good offers from high-tech firms in Pittsburgh. Why, Florida wondered, was this guy moving from a major city that was home to numerous museums and cultural venues, professional sports franchises, and many other assets, to a smaller city in the middle of Texas?

The young man's answer boiled down to the fact that Austin was a place where he thought he would feel at home. Sure Pittsburgh had a great symphony and opera, but that wasn't the kind of place where he was comfortable. He wanted to be around similar-minded people and to live where his counterculture look and values were an asset, not a hindrance. And, of course, as soon as the young man arrived at his new job he himself would become part of the landscape, making it ever more appealing to the next generation of people who felt out of step with their hometowns. The appeal of Austin for the spiky-haired man, of Stanford for the nerds, and of San Francisco for new gay arrivals was partly that they expected to be affected by their new homes. Your outlook on life can be shaped by where you live. It really does make sense to be less trusting among strangers in a dangerous Chicago neighborhood than in a small town where everyone you bump into has known you since the day you were born. An environment with a diversity of residents and cultures really does offer more opportunities for others to expand their minds than a locale that's highly homogenous.

Through these two processes—certain people being drawn to certain places and then those places affecting the people who live there—connections will emerge between what people are like and where they live. So if you know nothing else about someone, you can make some initial personality inferences merely by looking at where he or she lives. Although there does appear to be some evidence for the validity of geographic stereotypes, the exact patterns are not always so easy to discern. Take a look at the three maps plotting the relative scores on three of the Big Five personality domains. The darker the shading, the higher people are on that trait. Can you guess which three traits the maps are showing?

With its east-west gradient, the first map is the easiest to identify. It's for neuroticism—showing the differences between Woody Allen–esque New Yorkers and the Dude-some Californians. And these distinctions go a lot further than merely confirming stereotypes. When my collaborator Jason Rentfrow (who commandeered this novel research) dug deeper into the kinds of things that went along with regional personality differences he found some remarkable patterns. For example, the inhabitants of states with high levels of neuroticism tend to smoke more than people in other states, and they have higher incidences of cancer, heart disease, diabetes, and obesity; and the easygoing states, those with low levels of neuroticism, tend to be populated by people who know how to relax, who go jogging, and who exercise at home. Of course, the causal connections are far from clear. We can't know whether high levels of neuroticism lead to the health problems, as would be true if anxious people were more likely to smoke, which in turn could lead to higher rates of cancer and heart disease. Or perhaps something else causes the health issues, which results in people becoming more anxious, stressed, and worried (that is, neurotic in Big Five terms). It's also possible that a "third variable" explanation is at work, that some other factor leads both to higher levels of neuroticism and higher rates of health problems.

Map 2, which plots the average openness of the states, shows that the creative, imaginative, philosophical, abstract thinkers are to be found all down the West Coast and in the Northeast, with other pockets here and there. As with neuroticism, Rentfrow has shown

Map 7.1

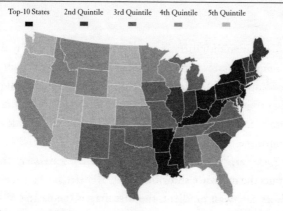

Top-10 States   2nd Quintile   3rd Quintile   4th Quintile   5th Quintile

Map 7.2

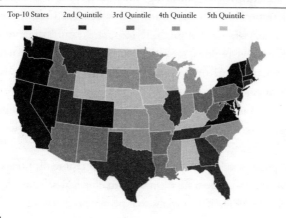

Top-10 States   2nd Quintile   3rd Quintile   4th Quintile   5th Quintile

Map 7.3

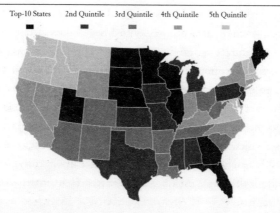

Top-10 States   2nd Quintile   3rd Quintile   4th Quintile   5th Quintile

that these personality differences are played out in the real world. People living in states high on openness have relatively high rates of book reading, going to the library, visiting art galleries, and expressing interest in other cultures. They go to church less than others, take out more patents, and tend to have relatively liberal attitudes toward sex and drugs.

The last map plots extraversion and suggests that this trait blooms most robustly in the Midwest. Rentfrow's research shows that those chirpy and wholesome folks from Illinois and Wisconsin really do enjoy social gatherings more than people living in introverted states (such as Maryland, New Hampshire, and Alaska). They attend club meetings, go to bars, and visit friends more than people in other regions, and religion tends to be an important part of their lives. Rentfrow has reported similar findings for states low in agreeableness (where rates of murder and other violent crime are high) and conscientiousness (where people work long hours and are relatively more religious than those in slacker states, such as Hawaii, Alaska, and Maine).

The processes driving these genuine geographic differences at the national level also operate on much smaller scales. Consider where you work and the different jobs that people do there. Most of us tend to gravitate to positions that suit us. A wild extravert manning the reference desk of the local library would probably go nuts and drive his colleagues and patrons crazy with his inability to stop yakking. And external forces are at play, too. Most people don't want to hang out with socially inept, grumpy, and hostile colleagues, so those people tend to get slowly eased to locations that allow others to avoid them. In fact, our research showed that the disagreeable people tended to end up in low-traffic areas of an office. In one of the offices we visited, the person with the lowest agreeableness score in the whole study had been banished from the office hubbub, so far down a long corridor that some members of our research team even had trouble locating it.

RED STATE, BLUE STATE

Looking at the personality maps of the United States, Jason Rentfrow and I saw similarities to the familiar Red state/Blue state divide. We began to wonder whether there is a relationship between the personality of a state and the ways its citizens voted. After all, political orientation is closely tied to basic values and attitudes. Liberals are more egalitarian and interested in social diversity than conservatives, who are more supportive of traditional institutions (such as the police and government), and they prefer that change be gradual. Recent research by John Jost and David Amodio at New York University has even found evidence for a corresponding difference in the brain. In a region known as the anterior cingulated cortex, response patterns to a task requiring people to change a habitual pattern suggest that conservatives are neurologically more resistant to change than liberals.

In collaboration with John Jost, Dana Carney, and Jeff Potter, Jason and I embarked on a series of studies to look more closely at the connection between politics and place. To our amazement, the number of votes cast in a state for the Democratic or Republican candidates was strongly linked to a state's level of openness, conscientiousness, and, to a lesser extent, extraversion. States that voted for Bill Clinton (rather than Bob Dole), Al Gore (rather than George W. Bush), and John Kerry (rather than Bush) tended to be higher on openness and extraversion and lower on conscientiousness. These findings challenged conventional wisdom, which had generally relied on sociodemographic factors to make predictions. Our findings showed that personality, too, plays a big part in who votes for whom. What we are (educated, African American, wealthy, and living in a city) can tell us no more about who we're likely to vote for than what we are like (open, conscientious, and extraverted).

Our interest was piqued by these findings. If Democrats and Republicans have different personalities, can we find differences in the ways they behave in everyday life and in the evidence they leave in their spaces? To assess how liberals and conservatives might differ in face-to-face interactions, we set up an experiment that masqueraded as a discussion of movies between two people. In reality, one of the discussion partners was a research assistant. What subtle nonverbal behaviors would liberals and conservatives express in this situation? Consistent with what we had found with the voting patterns across the states, analyses of the videotapes showed that liberals were more extraverted—they were more expressive, they smiled more, and they engaged more in conversation with their interaction partners. Conservatives behaved in a more detached and disengaged manner in general, reflecting a somewhat withdrawn, reserved, and inhibited interaction style.

Given the connections between voting patterns and extraversion, it made sense to look for differences between liberals and conservatives in face-to-face interactions. But our findings linking openness and conscientiousness to political attitudes told us we might also find differences in their living spaces. Sure enough, conservatives' rooms tended to include more organizational items, including calendars and postage stamps. They also contained more conventional decorations and items, including sports paraphernalia, flags of various types, American flags in particular, and alcohol bottles and containers. In general, conservative bedrooms had the hallmarks of the high conscientiousness, low openness personality profile—they were neater, cleaner, fresher, better organized, and better lit.

The bedrooms of liberals reflected the residue associated with high openness. They contained a significantly greater number and variety of books—on travel, ethnic issues, feminism, and music, as well as a greater number and variety of music CDs, including world music, folk music, classic and modern rock, and "oldies." Liberal bedrooms also contained a greater number of art supplies, stationery, movie tickets, international maps, and cultural memorabilia.

ADAM'S HUNCH

When I was first trying to figure out how people form accurate impressions of others, I didn't consider stereotypes relevant. But as I began to analyze the data from my study of bedrooms and their occupants, I was forced to reconsider the important role of these mental shortcuts. In the bedroom study, many of the findings made good intuitive sense, at least with the benefit of hindsight. It seemed reasonable that task-focused, time-oriented people kept their rooms stocked with the accoutrements of punctuality—several calendars, multiple clocks, to-do lists, desk organizers.

But many of the findings were puzzling. We discovered that although our judges had done nothing more than snoop around a bedroom they were remarkably good at estimating the occupant's level of neuroticism. We hadn't predicted this finding, and our follow-up analyses did not reveal any features of rooms that consistently differentiated the up-tight from the laid-back. We were stumped.

As we scratched our heads, I remembered a comment made by our most accurate judge, Adam Klinger, as he emerged from evaluating one of the rooms. It was a small and reasonably tidy room, with stuffed animals on the bed and an unremarkable array of trinkets and posters, which he had just rated as high on neuroticism. Handing in his rating form, he shook his head, flummoxed by what seemed to be an over-simplification: "After a while, it feels like you're just rating stereotypes," he said. Could this be the key to the accuracy of the neuroticism ratings? I wondered whether we might learn something from gender stereotypes.

I knew that past research had identified a number of small but consistent sex differences in personality traits, the most consistent of which is that women rank higher than men on the Big Five trait of neuroticism. Women tend to be more anxious, less even-tempered, less laid-back, more emotional, and more easily stressed than men.

So perhaps Adam was right. Perhaps when the judges entered a room they made inferences about the occupant's gender and used them to assess the person's level of neuroticism according to stereotype.

The judges were extremely good at guessing the gender of the bedroom occupants. Males' rooms are different from those belonging to females. The space is usually less decorated, colorful, cheerful, comfortable, and clean. Men's rooms are not as inviting, distinctive, and stylish as women's. Males are less likely to display pictures of babies, friends, and family. Calendars and mirrors are not prominent. Males have fewer fashion magazines and books than females, but more CDs, and they buy more substantial stereo equipment. Males are low on lotion but high on hats and caps. Stuffed animals, candles, and flowers, so prominent in females' rooms, give way to bills, visible laundry baskets, and athletic equipment. Males' closets are usually left open, and men are much more likely to hang stuff on hooks than women.

Our statistical analyses confirmed Adam's hunch. It seems that gender stereotypes, not direct clues gleaned from the contents of the rooms, held the key to detecting occupants' levels of neuroticism. The judges did make some mistakes, and these were revealing about the impact of gender associations. In one room, Fernando (not his real name) had clearly hosted an "overnight guest"; her stilettos were still lying on the bedroom floor. On seeing the shoes, one judge immediately classified the room's occupant female and ignored all the other clues—male jeans and T-shirts on the armchair, the shaving cream and the male-oriented décor. From this simple mistake, our judge presumed a wide variety of traits unrelated to the specific clues in the room. Instead of attending to the information right there, he had relied on gender stereotypes to form his impression.

Although stereotypes seem to drive the accuracy of the neuroticism ratings, they can interfere with the accuracy of personality judgments, too. A common stereotype about women is that they are kinder and more sympathetic than men. In terms of the Big Five dimensions, the stereotype suggests that women will be higher on agreeableness. And, in fact, our judges rated female bedroom occupants higher on agreeableness than men. The problem was that in reality there were no differences; the men and women were equally agreeable. So here the stereotypes diminished the accuracy of the personality judgments.

These observations about gender got us thinking about other kinds of stereotypes. When I sublet an apartment in Detroit a few years ago, I certainly drew on stereotypes to infer from the careful attention to the interior design, the numerous sculptures and paintings of small dogs, and the copious quantities of men's magazines that the occupant was gay, even in the absence of any explicit gay iconography. What about race? Our bedroom study was carried out in the San Francisco Bay Area, which has a large Asian population, and 80 percent of the participants in our bedroom study were evenly split among Asians and whites. A commonly held stereotype about Asians is that they have narrower, more concrete interests than whites—the caricature of the quiet, mousy, hard-working, law abiding Asian engineering student. Such stereotypes suggest, among other things, that Asians would be lower than whites on traits associated with openness. People low on openness like to focus narrowly on concrete concepts rather than play with abstract ideas, and they tend to abide by conventional habits rather than question them. In our sample, the Asians really did score lower than the whites on openness, and the bedroom judges were very good at determining the race of the occupants (although not as good as they were at detecting their gender).

Our analyses again proved Adam right. Race-based stereotypes seemed to account for at least some of the judges' accuracy in how they rated occupants' openness. Despite stereotypes' bad press, our research made it clear that they can play an important role in the way we all form impressions of one another. This is not the conclusion that comes easily to those of us who hope that people will be judged by what they do rather than what they look like.

A STEREOTYPICAL MINEFIELD

No matter how useful or innocuous, stereotypes can be a highly charged topic. Soon after I published my first paper on the links between personality and bedrooms, a colleague in the design department asked me to talk about my work to her undergraduate class. As I began my presentation, the students were attentive, and although few of them had a science background, they seemed to be genuinely engaged. But about halfway through my talk, something changed. Students began to squirm. The looks of receptive interest transformed into skeptical frowns. The shifts in facial expressions marked the point in my presentation where things can turn nasty—I had reached the part about stereotypes. I was arguing, as I did above, that when people make judgments of others on the basis of impoverished information—such as might be found in a bedroom—they often use stereotypes and, more controversially, I added, this can be a good thing to do. As hands shot up around the class, I braced myself for the wave of indignation that I knew would arrive.

The design students' reactions were not unusual. Stereotypes have earned themselves a bad name, so most people are defensive about suggestions that they may be using them. As I soon discovered, just discussing stereotypes can turn a calm crowd volatile. What really rankles is the idea that some stereotypes contain a kernel of truth. So if you're giving a talk and want a smooth ride, the "stereotypes are bad" route is safest. This isn't the most sophisticated approach to what is an inordinately complex phenomenon, but rarely will anyone disagree with your position, and with good reason.

Without doubt, stereotyping has all too frequently resulted in perceptions and decisions that are at best unfair, and at worst deadly. Stereotypes helped keep the vote from women and civil rights from African Americans; they also underwrote a litany of rights withheld, privileges abused, and opportunities denied for numerous groups throughout human history. Our most common media exposure to stereotypes usually involves some unfair decision based on race or nationality or gender, so it is hardly surprising that many people assume they are always bad.

If you browsed through the most prestigious journals in social psychology, you would discover that stereotypes are one of the biggest topics in the field. And you might expect a bunch of studies of how and when people use stereotypes and when, if ever, they are accurate. Instead, most stereotype researchers concentrate on just one side of the process—the ways in which stereotypes interfere with how we perceive others. In one classic study, research subjects were more likely to make use of racial stereotypes while they rehearsed an eight-digit number than when they were not distracted by this task. This and other studies have led to the view that we rely on these snap judgments when we don't have the time or capacity to think things through from every angle. But as we are about to see, some people are reluctant to share even their legitimate perceptions if they think it might lead to accusations of racial prejudice.

Compelling evidence of our super-sensitivity to stereotypes came from an ingenious series of studies by the Harvard Business School's Michael Norton and his colleagues. They observed a curious disparity in how people use certain characteristics to describe other people. Imagine you work in a company where about 10 percent of the employees have red hair and about 10 percent have dark brown skin. Suppose that you want to identify one of these people to a colleague, but you don't know the person by name. For either person, it would make sense to use the characteristic (hair color or race) in your description to narrow the pool of people you could be talking about. However, Norton and his colleagues have shown that people are much less likely to refer to "the black guy" than "the guy with red hair." This reluctance comes even though sidestepping race means that we communicate information much less efficiently.

One of Norton's experiments went something like this: Assume for the moment that you're white. You and a person you've never met before are invited to play a game based on an array of photos arranged on a table. The photos show different faces—male and female, black and white, old and young, and so on. Your partner has a book that only he can see. It contains "target photos" that match some of the photos on the table. The game is played once for each target photo. Your task is to ask as few yes/no questions as possible to identify the target photo. Is the target male? Yes. Is the target photographed in front of a blue background? No. Asking your questions helps narrow the possible photos, making the pool smaller and smaller until you find the match to the "target photo."

The game is set up to make race and gender information equally useful, but most people are far less willing to ask questions about race than about gender. And this reluctance is exacerbated when your partner (really a confederate in cahoots with the experimenter) is black. Moreover, questions about race in this context could be phrased in two directions—you could ask whether the target is black. Or whether the target is white. When the partner in the game is black, and people finally get around to asking about race, they are far more likely to ask whether the target is white. It seems that people resist even mentioning the word *black* for fear that noticing that someone is black could be construed as being racist. They would prefer to appear colorblind. "Oh, he's black? I didn't even notice."

If you add a twist to the game, the story gets even more interesting. What happens if we change the name of the game to "FBI's Most Wanted"? This subtle change has big effects. When the photos are supposedly of criminals, people become even less likely to mention race in their questions. There's an important qualification here. Only white subjects show this super-sensitivity to black/white racial information. When black subjects were tested, they were as likely to use racial information as gender information, and they were unaffected by the conditions that affected whites. Apparently, being black liberates people from the fear of appearing racist.

It's not that whites are unable to discern who is black in this experiment; they simply fear the social stigma of being called racist. If the incentives are high enough, whites are perfectly able to make effective use of racial information. In one set of studies, Norton asked subjects to make a choice between two photos—who would do better in college? Which one is most likely to have a perfect GPA? Who is more likely to commit a violent crime? When the two photos were of the same race (that is, two white males or two black males), subjects were quickly able to pick one of the two in response to the questions—they even reported enjoying expressing these gut reactions. But when Norton's subjects had to choose between a white male and a black male, they started rebelling, refusing to make decisions. Did this mean they couldn't now make the choice or that they just didn't want to? Norton's results suggest it was the latter. When the financial rewards were high enough, subjects were more willing to make a choice between a black and a white target. They would make the choice when they were paid five dollars for accuracy, but not when paid only one dollar. In other words, they would rather forfeit the dollar than make a judgment that could be construed as racist. But for five dollars, it was worth it.

SEX, DRUGS, AND ROCK 'N' ROLL

In my classes I have an exercise in which my students rank their ten favorite songs, with their favorite listed as number 1. I tell them not to discuss their lists and to hand them directly to me. The next week, I randomly divide the class into three groups. As one group stands at the front of the classroom, I read aloud their Top-10 lists. The task for the rest of the class is to match each list to a student. Surprisingly, the class carries out this task with impressive accuracy. But how do they do it? Some of the students pay attention to body language, trying to notice who blushed, looked down, or smiled as a list was read.

But others claim to match people to their music according to the stereotypes associated with the styles of music in the lists, such as pinning the guy wearing cowboy boots as a country music fan.

I have done this exercise many times, and each year the judges who use music stereotypes make more correct matches than those who rely on nonverbal cues. The results of this informal demonstration provide compelling evidence that music preferences convey at least some information about us. But do they offer clues to personality?

One of the most intriguing things about music preferences is that they seem to provide information about us that cannot be detected in ordinary daily interactions. As John Schwarz wrote in a *New York Times* article on iPods, "I like to think I present an innocuous, well-socialized face to the world—nothing for anyone to worry about. But if you know that I like the Canadian band Moxy Fruvous (raucous, four-part, leftist harmonies) then you know a little something else about me. You've gotten a new data point. If you have all of my songs, the points coalesce to form a picture, an intimate one that doesn't quite match the public persona." To see what he's getting at, just consider the following Top-10 lists gathered in our research on music preferences.

OLIVIA'S TOP-10 SONGS
1. Britney Spears—"Oops! I Did It Again"
2. Britney Spears—"I'm a Slave 4 U"
3. Garth Brooks—"The Dance"
4. Dave Matthews Band—"Crash"
5. Dixie Chicks—"Wide Open Spaces"
6. Grease Soundtrack—"Summer Lovin'"
7. N'Sync—"Bye Bye Bye"
8. Faith Hill—"Breathe"
9. Destiny's Child—"Survivor"
10. Chris Rice—"Smell the Color 9"

SADIE'S TOP-10 SONGS

1. Miles Davis—"Kind of Blue"
2. John Coltrane—"Giant Steps"
3. Dave Brubeck—"Take Five"
4. Glenn Gould—"Goldberg Variations"
5. Thelonius Monk—"Straight No Chaser"
6. Nick Drake—"Fly"
7. Ray Charles—"Ray's Blues"
8. Herbie Hancock—"Maiden Voyage"
9. Stevie Ray Vaughn—"Texas Flood"
10. Yo Yo Ma—"Six Suites for Cello—Suite 1"

On the basis of your stereotypes, which of these women would you want to help kick off a raucous party? Would you rather be stuck sitting next to Olivia or Sadie on a long plane ride? When asked to describe the owners of these lists, judges (in this study, a selection of my friends and colleagues) typically perceived Olivia as uncreative and conventional, perhaps because she had mainly mainstream popular artists on her list. And noticing that all her songs are energetic vocals, judges described her as gregarious and sociable. In contrast, Sadie's preponderance of classical and jazz selections suggested to the judges that she was refined and erudite. And perhaps because most of her songs are quiet and instrumental, they concluded that she was reserved and introspective. So it appears that we can readily call stereotypes to mind based on music preferences. But are those impressions accurate?

Presumably dating services ask their clients to list their favorite books, movies, and music because they believe that such categories provide an efficient shortcut to a broad range of interests, values, and dispositions. But as you flick through the list of potential partners on an Internet dating Web site, nixing the punk rocker and bookmarking the country music fan, are you justified in doing so? To find out, Jason Rentfrow and I looked at the stereotypes held by young adults—for whom music is especially important—about fans of various music genres. What assumptions did people make about others on the basis of their music collections and which, if any, are correct?

The following graph plots the stereotypes about the Big Five personality traits for fans of classical, rock, contemporary religious, and rap music. Can you tell which line represents which genre? The answers are in the next paragraph, so make your guess now.

Chart 7.1   Big Five Stereotypes About Fans of Classical, Rock, Religious, and Rap Music

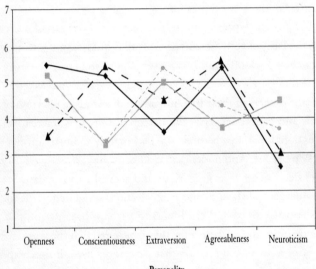

Personality

As charted, students believed that classical fans (represented by the diamonds and solid black line) and religious-music fans (represented by the triangles and the broken black line) had similar personality traits: highly agreeable, conscientious, and not very neurotic. But they saw classical music fans as less extraverted and much more open than religious-music fans. They viewed rock fans (squares and solid gray lines) and rap fans (circles and broken gray lines) somewhat similarly: high in extraversion, moderate in agreeableness, and low in conscientiousness. But they considered rock fans more neurotic and more open than rap fans.

What about other traits—political values, intelligence, religiosity, attractiveness, athleticism, and artistic abilities—that might figure into a decision about whether you want to date someone? Can they be predicted from a music collection? The next graph plots the stereotypes of fans of the same four genres—classical, rock, religious, and rap music—on these traits. Again, see whether you can figure out which traits are associated with which of the four stereotypes before you look at the key below.

Chart 7.2   Stereotypes About the Characteristics of Fans of
             Classical, Rock, Religious, and Rap Music

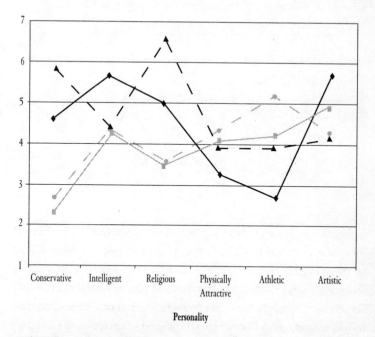

Personality

This chart shows that the stereotypes differ much more for these traits than they did for the Big Five traits. College students think of classical music fans (black diamonds, solid black line) as intelligent, physically unattractive, unathletic, and artistic. They think of religious music fans (black triangles, broken line) as different from the others most clearly in two domains—politically conservative and, of course, religious. The students' stereotypes of rock (grey squares, solid line) and rap (grey circles, broken line) music fans were almost indistinguishable, except that they considered rap fans a little more athletic than rock fans and rock fans a little more artistic than rap fans. How do the stereotypes play out on the deeper characteristics, such as values? Of the four genres, which fans would be considered most likely to value a world at peace? Or friendship? Or wisdom? Or love? The next graph plots stereotypes of the four fans on eighteen values.

Chart 7.3   Stereotypes About the Values of Fans of Classical, Rock, Religious, and Rap Music

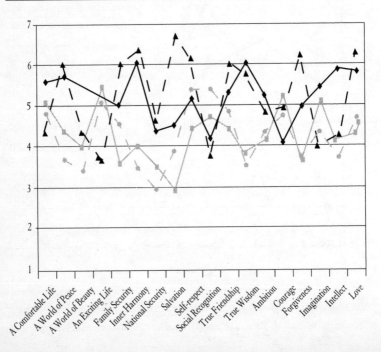

Values

The students believed that classical music fans (black diamonds) valued comfort, beauty, wisdom, imagination, intellect, and love; they thought that religious-music fans (black triangles) valued peace, family security, forgiveness, love, and, not surprisingly, salvation. They believed that rap fans (grey circles) valued self-respect and social recognition, and that rock fans (grey squares) valued excitement and courage. Note that the students considered the fans of religious music to have the highest values—the triangles are often at the top. They ranked rap fans and rock fans the lowest on holding values, generally much lower than fans of religious and classical music.

The final graph plots the stereotypes about the alcohol and drug preferences of the four kinds of fans. Who would drink more wine than beer? Which would be considered the most likely to use drugs overall?

Chart 7.4   Stereotypes About the Alcohol and Drug Preferences
            of Fans of Classical, Rock, Religious, and Rap Music

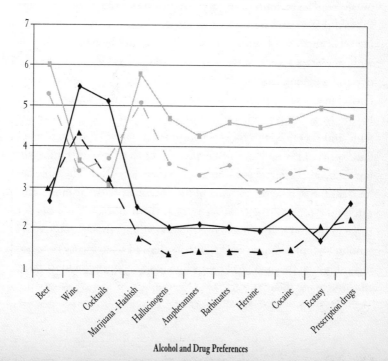

Alcohol and Drug Preferences

The graph reveals some interesting differences among the music stereotypes. College students viewed rock (grey squares) and rap (grey circles) fans as beer drinkers, and they believed classical-music lovers (black diamonds) would imbibe more wine and cocktails than beer. The students considered religious-music fans (black triangles) the least likely to drink alcohol, but if students assumed that they did drink, the preferred beverage would be wine, perhaps for communion. As for drug preferences, students stereotyped rock music fans as abusing all types of drugs. And rap fans were less than a point behind them in their stereotyped drug use. In contrast, students judged classical- and religious-music fans as much less likely to consume illegal drugs.

So when you discuss your music preferences, be careful what you tell people. You may inadvertently communicate all kinds of information about your personality, values, and even your preferences for drugs. But is the information correct? Is it true that fans of religious music really are more agreeable than fans of rap? Our analyses showed that several stereotypes served as effective shortcuts to learning what the fans of certain music genres would be like. Consistent with stereotypes, rock fans really were less agreeable, less conservative and religious, and more artistic and neurotic than religious-music fans. They placed relatively lower values on family security, inner harmony, and salvation, and, although they showed little taste for wine and cocktails, the rockers consumed a whole lot more alcohol and drugs. This may not be surprising, especially with hindsight; however, other stereotypes were considerably less valid. The table below lists the stereotypes in order of their accuracy with the most accurate at the top and the least accurate at the bottom. Thus, only for those in the top half, those above the dotted line, should you pay attention to your stereotypes. The others showed no evidence of validity—although they may feel compelling, as a snooper you must resist the urge to use them.

Table 7.2   Which Music Stereotypes Are More Accurate?

Music Genre	Example Artists/Composers/Movies
Most accurate	
Contemporary Religious	Praise Band, 4Him, Third Day
Country	Clint Black, The Judds, Shania Twain
Classical	Bach, Debussy, Wagner
Jazz	Duke Ellington, John Coltrane, Miles Davis
Rock	Rolling Stones, Jimi Hendrix, Aerosmith
Folk	Nick Drake, Indigo Girls, Bob Dylan
Blues	B. B. King, Muddy Waters, Robert Cray
Heavy Metal	Slayer, Marilyn Manson, Black Sabbath
Electronic	Paul Oakenfold, Moby, Kraftwerk
Sound Tracks	Pulp Fiction, Dreamgirls, Walk the Line
Alternative	Blur, Smashing Pumpkins, Jane's Addiction
Pop	Britney Spears, N'Sync, The Cheetah Girls
Rap	50 Cent, Public Enemy, Timbaland
Soul	Al Green, Eryka Badu, Marvin Gaye
Least accurate	

KENNELS OF TRUTH

Much of this chapter can be read as a response to researchers' overemphasis on the perils of stereotyping. But it is important that we do not allow the pendulum to swing too far the other way. One hazard of relying too heavily on stereotypes was nicely illustrated by the behavior of two subjects, Brad and Dan (not their real names), in a recent study in my lab. On the basis of Brad's genetic lineage, it was reasonable to expect that he would be more aggressive than Dan. But Dan had the history of violence. He had attacked several other individuals and had even got into trouble with the police a few times. When Brad and Dan came to us, we put them through a series of tests that confirmed Dan's aggressive tendencies. Dan became agitated when threatened. He was unfriendly to the graduate student who was testing him, and he even tried to bite her hand when she took his food away.

Did I mention that Brad and Dan were dogs? In our canine experiments, we have learned that, although breed information is a useful starting point, there is an enormous amount of information over and above what you might expect on the basis of breed alone. In this test, Brad the pit bull—a breed stereotypically thought to be aggressive—was less aggressive than Dan the Labrador—a breed widely supposed to be friendly. Even though breed is a useful preliminary guide to behavior—if you have that information and nothing else, use it—there's a whole lot more to be gained from interacting with the dog himself.

So as you snoop, remember to make judicious use of stereotypes. This means keeping the following four points in mind:

1. Stereotypes are just one of two ways to figure out what people are like from their stuff. We could guess that a snoopee is reliable either from a stereotype—perhaps the Chinese books by the bed activate a stereotype about Asians—or by using direct evidence of reliability, such as the carefully filled out desk calendar.

2. In our study of bedrooms, the stereotype that women are higher on neuroticism turned out to be valid, but the stereotype that women are more agreeable was wrong. So many stereotypes may help judgments, but others—the invalid ones—can lead us astray.

3. You can get the direction of the difference right—such as women having higher scores on neuroticism than men—but still get the size of the difference wrong, perhaps thinking the gap between men and women is much larger than it really is.

4. Before you demand the arrest of residents of Washington, D.C., for violent crimes they have yet to commit (based on the valid stereotype about people who live there), remember that the generalities conveyed by stereotypes neglect the variability within a group. It's true that the residents of D.C. are ranked fiftieth in agreeableness, but they're not all bad.

These four points combine to explain why, even when stereotypes have some validity, the information they convey is often dwarfed by specific, case-by-case facts. In our bedroom studies, for example, we found that even when the judges used valid stereotypes, they still gleaned more useful information from specific cues, such as the objects on the shelves. So the key to applying stereotypes successfully is to use them as working hypotheses, but be ready to drop them at a moment's notice as other information becomes available.

So be careful when you deduce from the preponderance of religious music on an iPod that the owner is rule-abiding, traditional, and politically conservative. But, let's face it, as an Englishman, when I go to a European beach, I cannot help but assume that those guys sunning themselves in the prime spots are Germans, not Brits.

EIGHT

When Good Judgments Go Bad

A FEW YEARS AGO, after my colleagues and I had finished reviewing the applications to our Ph.D. program, a student whom I shall call Cathy was near the top of our short list. Like all the applicants who made the first cut, she had outstanding credentials—several strong letters of recommendation from top-flight professors, a statement of purpose that was thoughtful and well researched, and her interests meshed nicely with those of our faculty. To top it off, her college grades were almost perfect and her GRE scores were through the roof. My colleagues and I eagerly looked forward to the interview weekend when we'd get a chance to talk with her and the other eight or so top candidates.

But to my surprise, Cathy's interview with me did not go well. She struck me as lacking interest in, well, anything. I asked her a few questions about topics in her statement of purpose, but even that failed to elicit a lively discussion. She also had an unpleasant and somewhat arrogant demeanor. Afterwards, I was confused. Given the glowing recommendation letters, the experience was far from what I was expecting. I wondered whether our personalities were just not meant to click. But when I compared notes with my colleagues, their interviews with Cathy had also been train wrecks. And this wasn't due to a lack of interest in our program, because Cathy was immensely disappointed when the inevitable rejection letter came, and she even asked to be put on the waitlist in case a place opened up.

Another Ph.D. program accepted her, and we breathed a collective sigh of relief at the bullet we had just dodged. But it turned out that the bullet was made of high-grade solid silver. Cathy went on to enjoy a phenomenally successful stint at graduate school. When she hit the academic job market, she was the "hot item." Now a junior professor, she is already making waves (the good kind) and poised to make a big splash in the field with any one of her several exciting projects.

How could we go so wrong? As psychologists, we should have known better; plenty of research has shown that, compared with the other items in students' application packets, unstructured interviews are surprisingly unhelpful. The uselessness of informal interviews is matched only by the unwavering confidence that most of us put in them. We consistently drag prospective students to Austin for interviews—even though we know all about the studies that say such interviews are ineffective.

Why aren't interviews more useful? One possible answer is that the information we need is there but we haven't quite figured out how to make good use of it. In an important study, Robert Gifford, of the University of Victoria, examined how good we are at picking up the right information and, crucially, how good we are at ignoring the wrong information. To do this, he drew on work conceptualized sixty years ago by the visionary psychologist Egon Brunswik. Brunswik's "lens model," as it is known, provides a way of understanding how good judgments go bad.

Brunswik's model—which strikes at the heart of the snooper's art—lays out the two ways you can make accurate judgments (using valid cues and ignoring invalid ones) and the two ways you can make faulty judgments (failing to use valid cues and wrongly using invalid ones). Brunswik's deceptively simple system can be applied to just about any situation—from customs officers' judgments about whether a person is carrying hidden contraband, to the likelihood of the stock market's taking a dive, to hunches about whether a particular neighborhood is safe at night or, indeed, whether a prospective graduate student has a promising career ahead of her. In each of these scenarios, we make judgments about something we can't perceive directly (contraband, the stock market's future, neighborhood safety, ability as a researcher) by using cues we can perceive directly (an overly casual walking speed, a comment from a financial heavyweight, the presence of street lighting, eye contact).

A job interview can be one of the most crucial thirty minutes of your career. Here, from a tiny behavioral synopsis, employers must decide whether to offer you a contract or to have security escort you from the premises. The wrong choice can cause a lot of grief. It is little wonder then that a good deal of business research has looked at behaviors that elicit favorable impressions. Studies have shown that to land a job you should engage in a lot of eye contact, smile often, and nod your head. People who do these things are perceived to have a host of positive qualities and to be good candidates to hire. But these findings miss a crucial element. Are gazing, smiling, and nodding actually diagnostic of desirable qualities on the job?

Judging a job applicant lends itself perfectly to Brunswik's system, and that is just what Gifford and his collaborators did. They analyzed thirty-four real job interviews for a research assistant position, coding each one for specific behaviors—including the time spent talking, looking directly at the interviewer, smiling, gesturing, leaning forward or back. They took note of whether the applicant was playing with his or her fingers or hair, or tapping a pen. They also assessed age, sex, formality of dress, and physical attractiveness.

Then Gifford showed videotapes of the interviews to experienced interviewers and asked them to rate the applicants' social skills and work motivation. Gifford evaluated how strongly each behavioral cue was associated with judgments of these two crucial traits. His analyses showed that the interviewees who spent more time talking, who gestured a lot, and who dressed more formally were judged to be higher on both social skills and work motivation. These findings were consistent with previous research.

However, when Gifford and his collaborators looked at the other half of Brunswik's model—the connections between what people were really like (not just how they were judged) and the behavioral cues—unexpected findings came to light. Brunswikian analyses showed that the talking, gesturing, and dress were indeed valid cues for social skills, but only the formality of dress predicted the applicant's work motivation; this finding mirrors the results of the Borkenau and Liebler studies (described in chapter 5), in which formality of dress was the one cue that signaled conscientiousness in their participants. Gifford's analyses also showed that the judges were good at estimating social skills in the interviews but miserable at estimating the applicant's work motivation. Gifford showed that instead of looking at the amount of gesturing to judge motivation, the interviewers should have paid attention to how far forward the applicants leaned. The more they leaned, the more motivated they were. From a snooper's perspective, Brunswik's model is important because it gives us a way to see when we're on the right track and when we are about to mess up.

A ROOM WITH A CUE

Consider the judgments of agreeableness made about the occupants of the bedrooms we studied. Recall that agreeableness is our Mr. Rogers dimension: People high on agreeableness are considerate, warm, and sympathetic; those low on this trait are harsh, critical, and quarrelsome. Our snoopers were not very good at figuring out occupants' agreeableness, but where did they go wrong? Are judges making mistakes at random or is something more systematic going on? A Brunswikian analysis can help address this question.

Our analyses showed that judges were consistently drawing on certain cues to form their impressions of the occupants' levels of agreeableness. Specifically, they thought people with organized, neat, clean, and comfortable rooms were agreeable. In fact, these cues provided absolutely no information about agreeableness.

Thinking about the kinds of actions that would result in clean, neat rooms suggests an occupant who is organized, methodical, and task-focused—that is, high on the trait of conscientiousness (the Robocop factor: orderly, time-oriented people). Indeed, our analyses revealed that a confusion between conscientiousness and agreeableness cues was at the root of the error. Judges incorrectly used conscientiousness cues to make judgments about agreeableness. Why did they do this? One possibility is that our judges found the messy, unclear, disorganized spaces to be unpleasant and inferred that the occupants must have been inconsiderate.

Our Brunswikian analyses show that another common snooping blunder is to judge cheerful, colorful rooms as occupied by agreeable, conscientious people. Again, there is no evidence that this is true. Observers will make this mistake even though—as you can see from the bedroom field guide below—there are plenty of cues that accurately reveal how organized you are. With the help of Brunswik's model we can look forward to the day when conscientious people will not be judged by the color of their walls but by the content of their calendars.

These findings are useful because they help us evaluate the quality of our judgments about others. If we are snooping in a place that is neat, clean, and organized, we can consciously overrule our natural tendency to judge the person as high on agreeableness. This is an important point to bear in mind as you think about yourself as a snoopee, and the impressions your own space conveys. You may not care that your messy office suggests to others that you have poor organizational skills (and, indeed, you may not be able to do much about the mess), but you should be aware that many observers will also infer, fallaciously, that you're not very nice either.

It is Brunswik's model that allows us to construct field guides such as the one depicted in table 8.1. It shows which clues people use when they form their impressions of various traits and which ones they should have used. The clues listed in bold are the ones that people should use and do use. The others represent either clues that are used and should not be or clues that should be used and are not.

Table 8.1 Bedroom Field Guide

When judging . . .	People actually rely on . . .	When they should rely on . . .
Openness	Decorated & cluttered, **distinctive,** quantity & **variety of books,** quantity of music, variety of **magazines**	A space that is **distinctive,** with a **variety of books, magazines,** & music. Books on art & poetry, art supplies
Conscientiousness	Cheerful & colorful Good condition, clean, **organized, neat, uncluttered, well lit,** clothing put away, **comfortable. Organized books, music,** & stationery	A space that is **well lit, uncluttered, organized, neat,** & **comfortable. Organized books,** magazines, & **music**
Extraversion	Decorated & cluttered	
Agreeableness	Cheerful & colorful Organized, neat, clean, clothing put away, good condition, comfortable, inviting	
Neuroticism	Stale air	Inspirational posters

The guide shows that the strongest cues in living spaces are for the two Big Five traits that clearly betray themselves in living spaces—openness and conscientiousness. If you walk into a house and it strikes you as distinctive—maybe the sofa is made from the hull of an old boat, or the paintings have been hung upside down, or there's graffiti spray-painted on the dining-room table—you've found a strong signal that the occupant is high on openness. The findings tell us that the snooper interested in openness should look for unusual and unconventional items, patterns of décor, or placement of objects. In our study of bedrooms, one of the occupants highest on openness had a desk lamp made from a bottle of vodka and old packets of Prozac. Another strong openness signal is the variety of books, magazines, and music; the definition of openness stresses the importance of breadth of interests and an appreciation of different ideas. Note, however, that it's the *variety,* not the *quantity,* of books, magazines, and music that's most important. Sure, a person with more books is likely to have a greater variety of books, but a person with ten books, each on a different topic, will be higher on openness than a person with fifty books on the structural properties of bridge rivets.

While looking over people's collections of books, magazines, or music, take note of how they are organized. Are CDs or other music media alphabetized by author or artist? Or thematically arranged by topic or genre? Are the book spines carefully lined up? Regardless of the book topics or the music genres, the arrangement of the items will give you clues to the occupant's level of conscientiousness.

Make sure you look very carefully, because having a system for organizing your belongings is not the same as being organized. Consider my collection of CDs. A cursory glance would suggest that I'm highly conscientious because the CDs are arranged in small drawers, each one labeled with the appropriate genre—"Dance," "Classical," and so on. However, expert snoopers would not be fooled by these superficial clues. They would know that it takes only one occasion to decide to organize one's CDs; a truly conscientious person does more than occasionally resolve to get organized. He lives the conscientious life, which means actually using a system day-to-day—putting the CDs back in their cases, putting the cases back in the right drawers and in the right place in the right drawers, and leaving enough space in the drawers for expansion.

A careful inspection of my superficially impressive organizational system would reveal that I stumbled at the next fence—the CDs were not in the right drawers, some were not even in the right cases, and I'd squeezed other CDs tightly into drawers because of my failure to foresee that I would be purchasing more in that category. An inspection of the books in my office would paint a similar portrait. Superficially, they seem organized, but a closer look reveals that I have not carefully aligned the books, nor have I always shelved them in the right categories, and I have even placed books horizontally on top of others, suggesting that I had failed to plan properly for expansion. In general, conscientious people have living spaces that are organized, neat, and uncluttered, and, perhaps more surprisingly, their living spaces tend to be well lit.

WHEN ENOUGH'S TOO MUCH

As we've seen, some people are automatically neat. Others worry about clutter, but they don't know what to do about it. Still others can tolerate a fair amount of extraneous material in the spaces of their lives. And then there are the hoarders—people who don't know when to stop gathering stuff.

In 2006, the chief of police in a small town in the state of Washington, got a call from a man reporting that his sixty-two-year-old wife (let's call her Alice), was missing. He sent a unit out to investigate. On stepping into the house, the police were greeted with a staggering sight—piles upon piles of clothing, dishes, books, boxes, and newspapers formed small mountains within the house. Alice had been hoarding stuff for fifteen years. The result was several tons of clutter piled so high that the police officers, their heads touching the ceiling, had to crawl on their hands and knees to find their way over some of the peaks. According to one report, they knew they were in the kitchen only when they saw the outline of a microwave.

Officers couldn't help from considering an alarming possibility— that Alice was still in the house, trapped under a collapsed pile of papers. They continued to search for evidence of Alice, but found nothing, so they left. But when she still did not show up, they went back. This time, after ten hours of searching, they found Alice buried under a pile of clothes. Apparently, she had fallen while searching for an old phone outlet and then suffocated to death under an avalanche of debris.

Few of us let the contents of our homes morph into mortally dangerous mountain ranges but, even within the normal range of behavior, there are vast differences in how much clutter we can tolerate. Of course, as with many disorders, Alice's symptoms were an extreme version of behaviors that many of us have in milder forms. In fact, when I was researching hoarding behavior, I was mildly alarmed to recognize in my own place many of the items collected by the super hoarders—fewer than half of the twenty or so pens in the cup on my desk are still working. I can't quite bear to throw them away.

I rely on the kindness of friends to take a firm hand to my closets and cabinets, pointing out that it's time I finally relinquished the jar of mustard with a sell-by date in the mid-1990s; and perhaps if I haven't used one of the airline freebie bags of toothbrush, blindfold, and socks for an unexpected overnight guest, it's likely I won't use the other fifteen, either. But, fortunately, like most of us with squirrelish tendencies, I am not compelled to hold on to these things. I can let go.

For our ancestors, hoarding—especially of food—made sense, and it still does for many animal species; it prepares them for times of scarcity. Studies of squirrels, ravens, rats, hamsters, as well as humans, suggest we have an ingrained disposition to collect stuff. We cache. If you're a squirrel, your life depends on it. Gather as many acorns, pecans, and hazelnuts as possible and save them for a snowy day. Of course, in most modern societies where humans have access to food and other commodities year round, the conditions that once drove this tendency are no longer present. But the tendency to collect remains, engrained in our brains after many millions of years of selection. This natural tendency has been co-opted and shaped by the context of modern culture to encompass all manner of collecting—from antiques and stamps to bottles of hot sauce and numbers from the sides of trains.

But there comes a time to stop caching, and that's why our tendency to collect stuff goes hand-in-hand with a way to stop. In normal people, the tendency to collect is governed by a neurological balancing act. Certain areas of our brain drive us to acquire items, and others, in particular the mesial (or middle) prefrontal region, stop us from going too far. If that area is damaged, our collecting tendency goes nuts (literally, for squirrels). People and other animals with damage to this area of the brain keep on collecting stuff.

In one study of brain-damaged patients by University of Iowa neurologist Steven Anderson, pathological collectors did not differ from a group of noncollectors (who had been assessed for the purposes of comparison) on a range of normal abilities, but all the extreme collectors had suffered damage to the mesial prefrontal areas of the brain. This region of the brain is easily injured in motorcycle accidents, so if you don't wear a helmet, you might consider clearing out some space in your closets.

People stash an enormously diverse range of items: receipts and bills, magazines and newspapers, letters and greeting cards, old clothes, old medication, old food, pens, paper bags, bars of soap, boxes, cardboard, combs, and just about anything else they can squeeze into their homes. In extreme cases, hoarders have been known to hang on to used toilet paper. Hoarding extends outside the house, too—we've all seen those broken baby swings and outdated oil burners littering people's backyards.

Extreme hoarding is a little-studied symptom, sometimes associated with obsessive-compulsive disorder. In a recent research paper focusing on fifteen extreme cases, Drs. Soraya Seedat and Dan Stein of the Department of Psychiatry at the University of Stellenbosch, South Africa, described hoarding as "the repetitive collection of excessive quantities of poorly useable items of little or no value with failure to discard these items over time." Seedat and Stein found that the most common motive the hoarders gave was the fear of discarding items of practical value. Sufferers often reported little or no control over their behavior. They seem to be saying, "But what if I need this one day? You never know, it might come in handy and if it does, I'll really regret throwing it away."

Eric Abrahamson, a Columbia University professor and the author of *A Perfect Mess,* has also noted distinctions between different kinds of hoarders, each one driven by a different motivation for holding on to things. The "I might use this one day" hoarders identified by Seedat and Stein are what Abrahamson terms "utilitarian hoarders." Based on his interviews with hoarders, Abrahamson found utilitarians to be either rational calculators ("What are the chances I'll need this again, taking into account the cost of replacing it and my chance of finding it again?"); overestimators of reuse ("I'm sure I'll get around to reading that old newspaper article, so I'd better hang onto it"); or people with deep-seated retention problems ("This seems very valuable to me").

If you discover when you're snooping that the hoarder's piles are largely comprised of old letters, bills, and receipts reaching back for years and years, then there's a good chance that you have what Abrahamson calls a "narcissistic hoarder" on your hands—he's thoughtfully hanging on to all this material in case it's one day useful to his biographers. Abrahamson notes in this context that Andy Warhol is said to have boxed each day of mess for posterity.

The "sentimental hoarder" is keeping things that help remind her of important times, events, or people in her life—parts of a childhood toy, the bus tickets from her vacation in Greenville eight years ago, the shards of a shattered teacup that belonged to a favorite aunt. It would be all too easy to see piles and piles of stuff, conclude the occupant is a hoarder, and leave it at that, but Abrahamson's insights direct the expert snooper to go further—to use the specific items to make inferences about the particular personality traits of the hoarder and thus to determine whether you're looking at the residue of a practical person, of someone smugly fond of himself, or just of a nostalgic softy.

Distinguishing between these different reasons for hanging onto stuff seems reasonable, but how much scientific evidence is there for different hoarding types? Stephanie Preston, a neuroscientist at the University of Michigan and an expert on hoarding, told me that although a lot of people talk about these different hoarding types there simply is no good research to support the distinction. Her own investigations suggest that the true hoarders—the ones, like Alice, who pile stuff up to the ceiling, are susceptible to all kinds of apparently good reasons for adding to their piles. To the might-be-useful, narcissistic, and sentimental types, she adds others, such as "environmentalist" and "cheapskate." Fellow hoarding expert Kevin Wu, a clinical psychologist at Northern Illinois University, agrees; he told me that he was not aware of any data supporting such categories. In fact, although he could understand the "might-use-it-one-day" and the "sentimental" types, the idea of a narcissistic hoarder ran counter to his own experiences with patients. His data suggest that hoarders are unusually low on entitlement and narcissism.

When I asked Wu about the difference between pathological hoarding and ordinary collecting, he shared this important observation with me: Collectors enjoy their collections. It gives them pleasure to collect and they savor their collections. Hoarders, on the other hand, find their situation distressing.

Although most of us are not likely to come across people who have reached clinical levels of hoarding, the distinction made by Wu (along with the data he has collected) suggests that hoarders and collectors have different personality profiles. Excessive hoarding tends to be associated with neuroticism, whereas meticulous collecting is more indicative of conscientious behavior. So as you snoop around a space and notice the large quantities of stuff, ask yourself whether it's the result of a carefully planned collection strategy, such as several sets of golf clubs each in a special nook, or a consequence of being unable to throw things away, such as that pile of old golf clubs stacked up against a garage wall.

OFFICES' MESS

One area of hoarding that has received more attention than most is the office desk. Mess meister Eric Abrahamson notes that when analyzing the state of a desk it is important to consider that two forces are at work—those that produce the mess, such as working toward a brutal deadline, and those that reduce it, such as tidying up. So your desk could be clear either because you've cleaned it up or because so little goes on that it never gets messy in the first place. Unfortunately, unless you catch the space at precisely the right moment, it can be hard to tell these two kinds of tidiness apart from just one visit. The exception would be if you just happened to show up right after the occupant had tidied the space; you might then be lucky enough to find the unusual combination of a tidy workspace along with overflowing wastepaper baskets. If you can, Abrahamson recommends a more dynamic approach, that is, observing the waxing and waning (or not) of mess over time.

Another Abrahamson tip for analyzing orderliness is to determine the different underlying mindsets that could have resulted in super-orderliness. Consider a former colleague of mine, whom I'll call Melody. She was smart and well read and an excellent writer, but she just couldn't finish her projects—her office contained a dozen of them in various states of progress. Melody held a black belt in procrastination. Part of how she avoided doing these tasks was by organizing. I once suggested to her that the project she cared so much about could be completed if she hadn't just spent three days creating a filing-card system to index all the research papers in her filing cabinet. But in her view, those three days would easily be recouped by her ability to locate all her papers much more rapidly. It's true that a minimal level of organization is needed for most people to operate effectively. But there's a limit. Is it really worth putting off adding that important paragraph to your report so you can pop down to Staples to replace your old single-section bulldog clip caddy with one that has sections for three sizes? I doubt it.

When I visited another university a few years back, one of the office staff members, Louisa, had heard about my research and came to ask me about her coworker in the next cubicle. That person, it seemed, was playing the office version of keeping up with the Joneses. Louisa said that every time she organized her own space, her neighbor would one-up her. Louisa added a paper wall calendar to her cubicle so that she could keep track of upcoming events. The very next morning, her office neighbor added a new wipe-board calendar complete with an array of colored sticky stars, circles, and squares to mark different kinds of events. Louisa's acquisition of a small plastic box for her backup CDs was promptly trumped by an impressive multitiered labeled CD rack next door. Eric Abrahamson calls these self-righteous people "order prigs"—they make it their goal to be the most organized person around. He gives the example of a colleague at a meeting who, when the boss starts discussing deadlines, pulls out his electronic organizer with a flourish and starts loudly tapping away. Whereas many orderly people are driven by a compulsion to make things neat, order prigs use their spaces as a weapon; their behavior is rather like trying to show up your daughter-in-law by wiping down her sink.

As you might expect, many of the cues in living spaces that signal certain personality traits turn up in workplaces. As shown in the field guide to offices below, clean, neat, organized, uncluttered offices tend to be occupied by people high on conscientiousness. And in offices, too, distinctiveness signals openness. When we visited the offices of an advertising agency, whose employees enjoyed unusually high levels of creativity and imagination (that is, openness), we saw unconventional furnishings—desks topped with stuffed piranhas, shelves made from skateboards, even a leopard-skin-print-covered box for holding receipts.

But there are also important differences between living and working spaces. As with bedrooms, our snoopers thought decorated offices were occupied by extraverts, but unlike in bedrooms—where level of decoration was a false clue—in offices it really did mark the extraverts. In offices (but not bedrooms), invitingness also signals extraversion—extraverts like hanging out with people, so they craft their spaces to lure people in and to encourage them to stick around. As bait, the extraverts might leave their doors open and place bowls of candy on their desks. You would want to linger in their offices, which tend to have comfortable seating and plenty of decoration.

Introverts, in contrast, are less enthusiastic about having people milling around their spaces. Should you find your way into the office of an introvert, don't expect to find your needs catered to. After a few minutes perched on a hard chair surrounded by gloomy, sparse walls, make your excuses and run for it—everyone will be happier that way. Although inviting offices usually signal an extraverted occupant, don't be too cavalier with your inferences. Our studies have shown that novice snoopers usually think that invitingness betrays high agreeableness, high conscientiousness, low neuroticism, high openness, and high extraversion. As a super snooper, you know that it signals extraversion only.

Table 8.2   Office Space Field Guide

When judging ...	People actually rely on ...	When they should rely on ...
Openness	Decorated, cheerful, colorful, inviting, cluttered, full, **distinctive, stylish, unconventional, varied books**	**Distinctive, stylish, unconventional, varied books**
Conscientiousness	**Good condition, clean, organized, neat, uncluttered,** comfortable, inviting, large, conventional	**Good condition, clean, organized, neat, uncluttered**
Extraversion	**Decorated, cheerful,** colorful, cluttered, full, **inviting,** distinctive, stylish, modern, unconventional	**Decorated, cheerful, inviting**
Agreeableness	Inviting	High-traffic location
Neuroticism	Uninviting	Decorated

To understand why invitingness should signal extraversion in offices but not in living spaces, contrast the natural ecologies of offices and homes. Offices are much more public than homes, and familiar people wander by on their way to drop off a report or make some copies. If you're an extravert, you could snag one of these passersby by making your space sufficiently appealing. In a living space, the goal is quite different. Not even an extravert is hoping that passersby will see the comfortable couch and decide to drop in. So invitingness serves a very different function in the two contexts and, as a result, is diagnostic of extraversion in only one of them.

As I've noted, one clue to an office occupant's agreeableness is where the workspace is located. Agreeable people tend to be put in the higher traffic areas, disagreeable people are kept at a distance. This is a valid clue that observers miss. Like extraverts, people high on neuroticism have decorated offices, but, as we saw, the content of the decoration is slightly different. Whereas extraverts keep pictures of people around them, those high on neuroticism use decoration, such as inspirational posters, to calm themselves.

Meredith Wells of Eastern Kentucky University has done extensive research on the ways people personalize their workspaces. One study, based on more than 230 workers in various settings, showed that the sheer amount of decoration and personalization signaled extraversion, and to a lesser extent openness. Extraverts were likely to display décor linking them to their friends and coworkers as well as reading materials related to their achievements and values; they also made the spaces comfortable with plants and music players such as iPods or radios. As we should expect for the Leonardo factor, people high on openness also displayed reading materials along with artwork and décor related to music and theater.

Wells discovered that women generally put up more stuff than men, and that they use different items. If you find yourself in an office with plants, knick-knacks, and symbols of personal relationships with friends, family, and pets, then you're more likely to be in a woman's office. Men's offices tend to display more items pertaining to sports and the occupant's achievements.

Wells's research suggests that personalization is generally good for both employees and employers. People who decorate their offices tend to have higher levels of job satisfaction and psychological well-being, and better physical health. So companies that allow their employees to personalize their workspaces should be rewarded with higher levels of employee morale and reduced turnover. Indeed, Wells showed that the degree of personalization in an office is a signal of how committed an occupant is to the organization. Particularly committed workers tend to display items pertaining to relationships with their coworkers and with their families and friends, and they have more artwork, trinkets, and mementos than noncommitted workers do. In other words, these dedicated workers integrate their private selves into their work lives, rather than keeping the two strictly separate.

I frequently meet people who claim vast differences between their offices and their living spaces. My friend Cameron, for example, insisted "my apartment is a mess but my office is immaculate." However, when I followed up, as is often the case, I discovered that the two spaces were more similar than Cameron himself believed; his apartment was perhaps a bit more organized, but not by much. In both his apartment and his office, all the books were on the shelves, the horizontal surfaces were generally clear, and the floor was clean. It's true that the spines of Cameron's books were lined up at the office and more haphazard at his home, but although these differences seem significant to Cameron they were minor compared to the differences between his office (or home) and the office (or home) of another of my friends, Amy, where there were more books under the desk, on the floor, or leaning against a plant pot than there were on shelves.

Still, it is not unusual for a person to be much more organized in one domain than another. Some people really do vary across contexts, so it is not surprising that these differences might be reflected in personal environments, too. A discrepancy between two environments belonging to the same person, should we be lucky enough to inspect both, could provide valid information on the occupant's personality and likely behavior. "Authoritarian" personalities are known to be sensitive to status, and they generally kowtow to people above them. Therefore, an authoritarian might have an exceptionally tidy space at work where there is a superior to suck up to, but may let things slide at home, where there is nobody powerful to impress. Such a pattern would be useful to a snooper because it would show that the tidiness at work was really driven by a higher-level characteristic—authoritarianism—and not an intrinsic appreciation

for order. Based on the office-home discrepancy, we could make behavioral predictions too—expecting the occupant to complete his latest work project on time but not be so confident that he'll get around
to cleaning the leaves from the gutter this weekend.

THE WISDOM OF BLOBS

We have now examined numerous snooping venues and have found
that different traits are revealed in different places. The "blob analysis" in figure 8.1 shows the accuracy of personality impressions based
on the various domains. My research has compared snoopers' impressions of people based on their bedrooms, Web sites, and so on with
what the people are really like. The domains, some of which we have
already discussed, were: (a) profiles on the social networking site
Facebook; (b) personal Web sites; (c) bedrooms; (d) offices; (e) CDs of
their all-time Top–10 songs; (f) records of their everyday social behaviors derived from micro-recorders attached to them for a few days;
and (g) brief face-to-face interactions. The figure shows how accurate
impressions were based on these domains—the bigger the blob, the
more accurate the impressions.

The blob analysis allows us to draw some broad conclusions that
are missed by looking at the studies in isolation. First, we must consider
the danger of drawing conclusions from just one domain; the field of
psychology has based the vast majority of its impression-formation
research on face-to-face interactions and has concluded that openness
cannot really be judged accurately. The figure shows that this conclusion is off target; indeed, openness can be judged accurately in many
domains; the problem was the field's overreliance on face-to-face
interactions.

Second, we've learned that some traits are easier to spot than others. My blob analysis shows that across domains openness is easier to
spot than agreeableness. Third, we can see that some domains provide
more information than others—Web sites provide a good general

Fig. 8.1   Blob Analysis: Accuracy of Impressions Across
            Snooping Domains

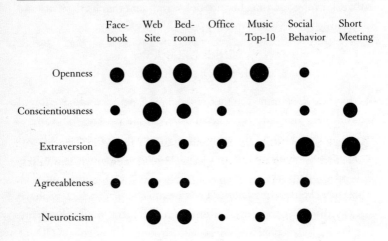

view of someone, offices are less informative. But these broad conclusions obscure an even broader and more important point—that different domains reveal different traits.

This observation has crucial implications for the snooper. It means
that the best portraits will be those that draw on several contexts. And
it means that the trait you're interested in learning about will determine where you direct your snooping attention. Using the blobs as
your guide, you can see that living spaces are great for learning about
openness, conscientiousness, and, sometimes, neuroticism; but if it's
people's extraversion or agreeableness you're after, a peek at the
"most played" list on their iPods is more telling than a bedroom visit.
As you decide where to look, let the blobs be your tutor—that's a lesson my colleagues and I wished we'd mastered several years ago as we
leapt to erroneous conclusions about Cathy's openness and agreeableness when she interviewed for graduate school.

NINE

Like a
Super Snooper

SUPER SNOOPING IS AN ART—albeit an art rooted in science—and before you can master it, you need to recognize certain quirks that, to the untrained eye, can render cues confusing or even misleading. Let's look at five quirks that combine to make super snooping such an interesting challenge.

QUIRK 1:
FIRST IMPRESSIONS COUNT

Guess the answer to this question: Is the Mississippi River longer or shorter than 5,000 miles? Now try this one: How long is the Mississippi? When I ask these questions in my class, the majority of students say (correctly) that the Mississippi is shorter than 5,000 miles, and when asked for the actual length, most of them give estimates in the 3,500-mile range. But sometimes I present a slightly different pair of questions. Question 1: Is the Mississippi River longer or shorter than 500 miles? Question 2: How long is the Mississippi? Again, nearly everyone gets the answer to the first question right—they say the river is longer than 500 miles. Question 2 is exactly the same as the second question in the first pair, but the students' answers are vastly different, averaging in the 1,500-mile range. What's happening here? It turns out that people use the information from the first question to anchor their estimates for the second question, even though most of them know the answer to the first is way off. (For an idea of how powerful this effect is, try it yourself. Give five friends the first pair of questions and five others the second pair and see whether you get a noticeable difference in estimates for the second question.)

Here's another example. Try it yourself and then share it with those ten friends of yours—before they've cottoned on to what you're doing, of course. I'm going to give you two multiplication problems, but instead of calculating the answer, take two or three seconds to make a rough estimate. Question 1: What is the product of $1 \times 2 \times 3 \times 4 \times 5 \times 6 \times 7 \times 8$? Question 2: What is the product of $8 \times 7 \times 6 \times 5 \times 4 \times 3 \times 2 \times 1$? If we put these questions side by side, the numbers are the same, so if we were truly logical beings our answer should be the same for both. However, we are psychological beings—without the pure logic or vast processing power of the computer—so we take shortcuts. When I ask my students to answer the first question by itself, the answer averages about 500. But when I reverse the order of the numbers, their answers average well above 2,000, more than four times higher than the first answer. Here again people estimate by calculating the product of the first few numbers and then projecting the total from there. In the second problem, the product of the first three numbers is high (336), and in the first it is low (6), resulting in hugely different projections. It turns out that in both multiplication problems, people vastly underestimate the correct answer, which is 40,320. Oh, and the Mississippi is 2,320 miles long.

These examples illustrate a principle called *anchoring,* meaning that the first information we encounter has an unduly large influence on what follows. We use anchoring in all sorts of real-life settings. When you offer $600,000 for a house you know is worth more than a million, you are hoping to anchor the negotiation in a range favorable to you. And your teenaged daughter is using anchoring when she calls to report vaguely that she's been in an accident, and only after a suitably dramatic pause, during which you inevitably conjure up images of various ghastly scenarios, does she reveal that the door panel has a small dent in it—which suddenly seems minor next to the possibilities running through your mind.

Anchoring plays a big part in how we form impressions of other people. In an experiment similar to the multiplication problems above, Solomon Asch, one of the pioneers of social psychology, gave participants six-word descriptions of target people—the words were *intelligent, industrious, impulsive, critical, stubborn,* and *envious.* He then asked the participants to generate a broader description of those people on the basis of the six words. As you can see, Asch included both negative and positive words. But for one group of participants he presented the positive words first; for the other, he reversed the order. For both groups, the words were exactly the same. Yet Asch found striking differences in how the participants characterized the target person, depending on whether the first words they encountered were positive or negative. Here are some excerpts from the responses of participants who were given the positive words first (that is, *intelligent, industrious, impulsive, critical, stubborn, envious*):

A person who knows what he wants and goes after it. He is impatient at people who are less gifted, and ambitious with those who stand in his way.

Is a forceful person, has his own convictions and is usually right about things. Is self-centered and desires his own way.

The person is intelligent and fortunately he puts his intelligence to work. That he is stubborn and impulsive may be due to the fact that he knows what he is saying and what he means and will not therefore give in easily to someone else's idea which he disagrees with.

The participants who heard the negative words before the positive terms had a significantly different take on the imagined person:

> This person's good qualities such as industry and intelligence are bound to be restricted by jealousy and stubbornness. The person is emotional. He is unsuccessful because he is weak and allows his bad points to cover up his good ones.

> This individual is probably maladjusted because he is envious and impulsive.

Just changing the order of the words was enough to drastically alter the participants' final impression. The first word anchored the description and colored how they interpreted the rest of the words. In bedrooms, offices, and even on Web sites we find the same phenomenon. Recall Fernando's bedroom, where the rater noticed a pair of stilettos on the floor, decided the occupant was female, and, as he formed his impressions, proceeded to interpret all the other cues—some of which indicated the room belonged to a man—as though the occupant was female.

Attention-grabbing items are a mixed blessing for the snooper. They might provide a key piece of evidence or they might lead you down the wrong path. In our original Berkeley bedroom study, the items in Room 40 and their arrangement appeared to say "a responsible, conventional, smart student lives here." The books were well organized. The well-lit desk area was tidy and obviously used. The items on the bulletin board—schedules, sensible phone numbers (such as the library and whom to call in case of a blackout) and a realistic to-do list—reinforced the initial impression. The décor on the walls and the content of the bookshelves suggested a person who was far from wild or even irresponsible. The CDs, featuring healthy helpings of Van Morrison, Sting, and Joan Baez, supported this view.

But one element stood out as incompatible with this chorus of consistency. Behind the bookshelf in an old milk crate was a bong for smoking marijuana, an activity that usually does not coincide with the behavior of a conventional, dedicated, successful student. My diligent observers did not overlook the bong, but they should have, because the bong was saying something markedly different from the message sent by the rest of the room. And this was for good reason—the bong's owner was a different person. I later learned that it belonged to a friend who had left town and requested temporary storage. (True to form, the occupant had responsibly put her friend's belongings in a milk crate and stored them behind the bookshelf.)

Unusual messages can easily trip up our attempts to figure out what someone is like. If we're interested in personality, we should focus on clues to behaviors, attitudes, feelings, and thoughts that are consistent, not the ones that appear to buck the trend. To be sure, the outliers can contain valuable information about passing fancies or one-time behaviors—but in all likelihood, as with the stilettos and the bong, they don't add to our understanding of the occupant's personality. Unfortunately, by their nature, these inconsistent bits of information stick out, so they are hard for even seasoned room readers to overlook.

To get a more accurate picture, the super snooper must find a way to allow these attention-grabbing features to fade a bit, giving the other objects their moment to shine. When I first began my bedroom-snooping project, I decided to consult the people who do this kind of thing for a living. Although my teammates and I couldn't cordon off a space and dust it down for fingerprints the way FBI crime scene investigators would, I figured we could still learn something from them. And I wasn't wrong—although the information turned out not to be exactly what I had expected.

An investigator from the local FBI branch agreed to come in and talk to our research group about the work of the Evidence Response Team. Most of what he had to say was straightforward and useful, with tips about how to photograph rooms and diagram the space (fortunately, we had no use for his tips on measuring blood-spatter traces). However, one thing he said puzzled me. He told us that when he is investigating a crime, he liked to just sit in the space for a while.

Although he didn't give a reason for this, I later realized that it was his way of allowing the attention-grabbing clues to fade in salience and the other items to show themselves. The super snooper would be wise to follow his advice: When you are examining a space, dwell a little and see what the room has to tell you. It may not be quite the same thing it told you when you first walked in and zoomed in on the stilettos in the middle of the floor.

QUIRK 2: CUES DERIVE PART OF THEIR MEANING FROM OTHER CUES

When we form impressions of others in everyday situations, we do not treat each cue as an isolated element but instead combine the information to form an overall impression. Suppose I want to fix you up with Benny, a friend of mine, and I tell you he is quick, skillful, and helpful. Now suppose that your coworker wants to set you up with Bjorn, a friend of hers, whom she describes as quick, clumsy, and helpful. You would have slightly different expectations about what Benny and Bjorn would be like. But your expectations would extend beyond the one different word—either skillful or clumsy—and those expectations would also affect how you interpreted the other words in the set.

This phenomenon was confirmed by one of Asch's experiments. When *quick* was paired with *skillful* and *helpful,* the target's quickness was described by one research participant as "one of assurance, of smoothness of movement" and by another as "fast in a smooth, easy-flowing way." But when *quick* was paired with *clumsy* and *helpful,* the descriptions of *quick* were noticeably different: "a forced quickness, in an effort to be helpful" and "quick in a bustling way— the kind that rushes up immediately at your request and tips over the lamps." The meaning of *quick* is modified by *skillful* and by *clumsy* so that *quick* contributes in a different way to each impression. This quirk, where one word is seen differently according to the words that accompany it, is different from anchoring (Quirk 1), which refers specifically to how our *first* impression affects our subsequent thinking.

Most species have an interest in forming accurate impressions of others. Gazelles, for example, are particularly motivated to form accurate impressions of the creatures that can harm them, such as lions—is Simba looking hungry? The same goes for humans, but our primary threat comes from other humans. So we have become particularly attuned to the actions of our fellow Homo sapiens, many of whom also provide us with crucial benefits, such as opportunities for mating and companionship. And we have evolved a drive to rapidly assimilate the information available to us (as we saw in chapter 7 in the context of stereotypes). Making sense of people is thus a survival skill, and we'll go to great lengths to combine bits of information into the integrated package—a whole person—that we typically encounter in day-to-day life. Our ability to do this comes so naturally that we rarely give it any thought. But if you look closely at this process, you see that it requires great ingenuity—albeit beyond conscious awareness.

It was Solomon Asch's studies of impression formation that first drew systematic attention to the ways by which we instinctively combine discrete elements into a unified impression of a person. Imagine that I tell you a little about the personality of a woman—let's call her Agnetha—whom I met at a party last night. I say that she was sociable and lonely. If you're like most people, you'll integrate this apparently discordant information to yield a single psychological impression, perhaps of a social butterfly who has many acquaintances but no real friends.

Here are some more pairs of superficially inconsistent characteristics: brilliant-and-foolish, hostile-and-dependent, cheerful-and-gloomy, strict-and-kind, generous-and-vindictive. Try to imagine the pairs of traits coexisting in the same person. Chances are you will be adept at creating a story that connects them. This task demonstrates the resourcefulness of the human mind in combining information about people, something snoopers must also do when they draw conclusions from the clues in living spaces. One of the bedrooms we inspected contained items that might seem incongruous—a small plaster statue of the Virgin Mary somberly watching down from her ledge above the window, and a large, bright plastic pineapple on the bedside table. So was the occupant serious and pious, or frivolous and goofy? Other items in the room resolved the issue. When we combine the statue and pineapple with the faux Elvis Presley bedspread and the string of Christmas lights in the shape of cows wearing Santa hats a broader impression emerges: that of a kitsch collector who is conscientious and has a keen and playful sense of aesthetics. The crucial conclusion for those of us interested in combining information found in bedrooms, music collections, and elsewhere is that the impression we form is more than the sum of its parts. An approach that weighs information without considering context is neglecting potentially important social information. If we imagine that the statue of the Virgin Mary from the kitsch collector's room was instead accompanied by a bible, a biography of Pope Benedict XVI, and a cross on the wall, then the meaning of the statue would be quite different—now suggesting a pious Catholic.

Similarly, a life-size model of a human skull on a bedside table could be integrated with a set of carefully annotated medical texts on the bookshelf, literature on social causes pinned to the bulletin board, a binder left over from a recent stint volunteering for an immunization program in South America, and an array of happy pictures taken during the trip. Together, these clues yield a coherent portrait of a dedicated, engaged, smart, left-leaning, upbeat person. Had the skull been paired with a whole wall inscribed with T. S. Eliot's "The Waste Land" and a wardrobe in seven shades of black, a very different, yet internally consistent, image would emerge.

As we saw in chapter 1, discrepancies—such as those between self- and other-directed identity claims or between front and back yards—

can provide useful keys to the occupant's underlying motivations. The office may look clean, but how deeply does the orderly streak run? To be certain that the organization is authentic, not just a show, you'll want to check inside the desk drawers. Often you will find that what appears to be a beautifully clear desk space or a tidy bedroom is a façade—the desk drawers are a chaotic mishmash of pens, pencils, Post-its, clips, sticky-tape, stamps, and calculators; the closets contain heaps of winter coats, pants, sneakers, purses, and gloves. Your snoopee is trying to reduce clutter, but the tidiness is only skin deep. Someone tidy to the bone cannot live in peace until even the things that are out of sight are in their rightful places. The expert snooper combines information to create a richer portrait of this snoopee, who is what mess expert Eric Abrahamson would call an "order phony," a person who creates the appearance of shipshape while harboring a shipwreck.

Consider again the room of Frida, the thrill junky mentioned in chapter 1. That room had a snowboard, a surfboard, and a skateboard all stacked up against one wall—evidence of a sensation-seeking, highly energetic person. In a cabinet, my assessors discovered a trove of liquor—several bottles of tequila, vodka, gin, and Jagermeister. Taking into account the other items in the room, we could infer that the occupant uses alcohol in the service of getting wild and ramping up the energy level. Had the room also included a comfy armchair next to a reading lamp and a pile of books, and if contemplative jazz music was playing on the stereo, we could have guessed that the occupant uses the alcohol for a different purpose—to relax and calm down.

QUIRK 3: WE MAKE USE OF CUES THAT SEEM UNRELATED TO THE TRAIT WE'RE JUDGING

When I first analyzed the snooping data gathered from bedrooms, I was intrigued to discover that, after just a few minutes in a room, our snoopers could judge with remarkable accuracy how attractive the occupant was. They had never met or even seen the occupants, so they couldn't have been using direct clues. And they weren't drawing on photos because we had covered those up. We could also rule out age as a possible clue because all the targets in this study were about the same age. So how were the observers doing it? Before you read on, take a guess.

The snoopers were not allowed to open drawers or closets, but clothing was often visible, draped over a chair or lying on the floor or stacked on shelves or in a closet with the door left open. So you might guess that the size, style, and cut of clothing provided some information about attractiveness, but that's not the whole story. The answer lies in how we concealed the photographs and in what psychologists have discovered about patterns of human mating.

We didn't want to simply remove the photographs, because we knew we could learn a lot from the quantity, placement, and type of photographs people display of themselves. A framed snapshot of the occupant as a child with her parents sends a very different signal from a wall's worth of glossy glamour shots. And the topic of the photo is informative. Do you display a picture of yourself peacefully meditating on a misty mountaintop in India or do your photos distill those buoyant moments when you and your trusty band of friends are up to a night of mischief on the town?

We knew that people form impressions of others purely from their physical appearance, so we couldn't let the observers see what the people whose spaces they were judging looked like. Our challenge was to provide observers with information about what the occupants were doing without letting them see the occupants directly. Our solution was to leave the photos where they were but to carefully cover just the occupants' images. The snoopers could still see the other people in the photos. And they could easily tell from the poses and activities that some of these characters were the occupants' romantic partners; a photo in a heart-shaped frame of a (concealed) occupant kissing another person was a dead giveaway.

When observers combined this information about who the occupant was with what we knew about human mating patterns, clues to attractiveness began to emerge. It's a well-documented phenomenon that people tend to mate with people who match them in attractiveness. So I believe that our bedroom snoopers were successfully deducing how good looking the occupants were simply by looking at the pictures of their boyfriends or girlfriends. If the photos revealed that an occupant's love interest looked like Brad Pitt, it was a pretty good bet that she was also easy on the eye.

We have yet to test these ideas experimentally, but the example is interesting because it shows how subtle cues (information in the photos) are seamlessly combined with implicit knowledge—that people seek mates who are as attractive as they are—to form impressions of others. For attractiveness, the impressions tended to be accurate. But the broader lesson for the super snooper is that if you are resourceful you can make good use of these kinds of indirect clues when you are scoping someone out.

Consider again the study of faces by Little and Perrett (introduced in chapter 5). Recall that these psychologists found that judgments of personality based on composite faces were generally accurate, especially for women; the judges rated the composite face derived from fifteen extraverts as more extraverted than the composite face derived from fifteen introverts. They also found that some traits could not be judged accurately—agreeableness in men, for example. Yet the canny judge could make personality inferences based on other facial cues—features superficially unrelated to personality could be used as a backdoor method for acquiring information about people based on their faces. Specifically, Little and Perrett found that agreeableness in men (along with low extraversion) was actually signaled by faces rated as low on masculinity, although the judges did not make this connection. Similarly, agreeableness in women was, unbeknownst to the judges, associated with facial attractiveness.

Quirk 4: Mind the Gap

Information about people can vary along two dimensions—and as a super snooper you should consider both of these. One dimension refers to the amount of control people have over their environments. You have a lot of control over your Web site, your e-mail signature quotation, your voicemail message, your book preferences, your blog entries, the contents of your wallet, the cut of your underwear. But you have much less control over your nationality, your language style, and your dreams. The second dimension reflects how public or private the form of expression is. Some things, such as physical attractiveness, language style, geographic location, bumper stickers, and Web sites, are available for just about anyone to see. Others—dreams, thoughts, journal entries, passwords, underwear—are much more private.

Understanding where items sit along these two dimensions can help determine where you search for clues. For example, if you are trying to discover how the person wants to be seen, you should choose items that are both controllable and public. Web site profiles and bumper stickers are good examples. But if you are concerned that your snoopee is trying to dupe you, then you'll want to compare the messages sent by the items known to be public with those believed to be more private (should you be lucky enough to gain access to them). If you found a Web site that suggests its owner has an abiding admiration for classical works of art, music, and literature but then you discover nothing but trashy fiction on the bookshelf in his house, you should be on guard for a possible wool-over-eyes puller.

This general snooping strategy—contrasting the easy-to-control items (which tend to be identity claims and feeling regulators) with things that are difficult to control (which tend to be behavioral residue)—captures many of the specific examples we have examined so far, such as comparing front and back yards, or offices and bedrooms, or books on the coffee table versus books in the bedroom.

What makes this two-dimensional system useful is that it reminds you of the important questions to ask yourself when making your comparisons. Is this object in a public or private context? And how much control does the snoopee have over it? Whereas a novice snooper might just take note of the snoopee's music collection, a super snooper would need to distinguish between music that is public (a collection of vinyl sitting out in the living room) and music that is private (a playlist on a computer at work). A beginner would note the snoopee's photos or paintings, but an advanced snooper would want to determine the difference between art the snoopee had control over (taped to the refrigerator door) and art that was out of his hands (pictures on the office wall identical to those in the offices nearby).

Advanced snooping requires that you are aware of varying degrees of control even within the very same context. Facebook profiles are a good example, because although the owners have full control over the bulk of the information on their profile pages, they have less control over the messages posted by others on their profiles and the photos of them flagged by others. Technically, profile owners could delete the uncool posts and unflag the unflattering pictures, but, as anyone knows who's had repeated unwanted postings, that's generally considered bad form. The snooper will jump on this opportunity to find potential schisms between approved and unapproved content. Sharp snoopers will have noticed that the sensible staid persona I portray in my own Facebook profile is somewhat undermined by the more risky frisky pics of me flagged by my friends.

QUIRK 5: KNOWING ME KNOWING YOU

My research on bedrooms has always relied on the goodwill of volunteers to allow my team and me into their personal spaces. So I needed to make sure that all eight judges were well trained and ready to go before we arrived at the first bedroom. I decided to offer my own place as a "practice room." I didn't tell the team it was my room, and I followed the usual precautions, covering photos of me and any sign of my name. All went well with the training, but when we were finished, a couple of male judges took me aside and said they had realized it was my room. Really? How had they figured it out, I asked them. They said they knew what kind of car I drove and they saw manuals for that car on the bookshelf. A few minutes later, a couple of female judges took me aside and said that they, too, knew it was my room. Really? Again, I asked how they had figured it out. They said they recognized my clothing on the floor.

This early experience foretold a lesson I was to learn again and again: Expertise plays a crucial role in a judge's ability to figure out what someone is like. When I look through a woman's apartment and find a tube of lipstick, I see a tube of lipstick. Many women looking at the same evidence would see a tube of *MAC* lipstick, or *Covergirl* lipstick, or . . . well, as a reflection of my low level of cosmetic expertise, I have already run dry on lipstick brands. Not only would a woman be more sensitive than I to the brand of lipstick, but she would probably know the connotations of each—whether it was expensive or cheap and what image was associated with it. She might also be able to figure out things about the owner from the shade of the lipstick and how it had been used—was the lipstick itself in a pattern that suggested hasty application or a more careful approach? This kind of information, combined with other clues in the space, could make her assessment richer than mine.

Similarly, our student judges were experts at decoding the stuff in the dormitory rooms; they saw distinctions that I would miss, and they drew conclusions where I would be at a loss. One student judge spotted a button with the emblem, unknown to me, of an ultrareligious campus group, from which he inferred the occupant was opposed to gay rights and held pro-life attitudes. In another room I didn't recognize the bands in the posters above the bed, but the judges quickly identified them as contemporary rock musicians, allowing them to boost their ratings of the occupant's openness levels.

The question that Quirk 5 addresses is this: How can you sharpen your expertise to become a better snooper? The answer lies simply in increasing your dedication to your art. First, you must become an expert in the language of your snoopee. I don't own a television set, which puts me at a disadvantage when I have to snoop around students' rooms. So I have enlisted the help of natural experts—other students. But if I were charged with assessing dorm rooms myself, I would need to do my homework—get a television, find out about what programs are popular. I'd also have to make sure I was up-to-date on students' music preferences.

It's not easy to become an expert in a domain with which you're unfamiliar, but there are shortcuts. Begin with a quick reconnoiter in comparable spaces. Before I analyze an office, I try to take a look at other offices in that same institution to scope out the language of the place. If I learn, for example, that company policy prohibits altering the computer display settings, I'll realize that the lack of personalization—no photos of loved ones on the screen saver, no idiosyncratic color scheme on the computer desktop—says more about corporate preferences than it does about the occupant's personality.

Once, when I was inspecting an office, I noticed a Filofax on the desk under the computer monitor, leading me to upgrade my rating of the occupant's organization levels. In the office next door I was intrigued to see an *identical* Filofax on an empty bookshelf. And another in the third office. I quickly realized that the company issued them to all the employees and I soon found myself playing find-the-Filofax in the remaining offices. More important, I downgraded the upgraded organization rating of the first office, realizing that the personal organizer there did not tell me nearly as much about the occupant as I had originally thought.

The second way you can improve your expertise is to bring a guide with you. If you're a man surreptitiously snooping around a woman's house during a cocktail party, then grab a woman as your helper. Under your direction she can interpret the cryptic clues scattered around. With her help, you'll find out that's not just a pair of shoes on the closet floor; it's a pair from Marc Jacobs's latest collection, and the crumpling at the back and the stretch marks on the instep strap are indicative of hastily squeezing her feet into them rather than meticulously unbuttoning them in preparation for their next outing. Once, while snooping in the bathroom of a woman for whom I was rapidly developing a soft spot, I was alarmed to notice some mysterious prescription medications on a shelf above the towels; since I had no idea what they were for, I had to text-message my expert, who assured me my new crush was not crazy; she just had bad allergies.

The last thing you can do to hone your craft—and this will help with all aspects of snooping—is simply to ask questions. Whenever I am in a space for the first time I ask the occupant about the stuff in it. The knowledge gained, especially if combined with other information, helps me make sense of other clues, too. So I might ask, Why do you keep your beer in the microwave? Why is that seagull hanging so close to your desk? What does that Hemingway book mean to you? Who are the people in the photos on your fridge? Even when you are not snooping, you should ask questions, because every time you do so you will extend your domains of expertise just a little bit further. In time, you will become a better snooper.

In chapter 10, I describe a unique chance I had to put this chapter's "quirk lessons" to good use.

TEN

An Office and
a Gentleman

IN JANUARY 2006, I received an unusual snooping assignment—to inspect the television studio offices of two presenters from ABC's *Good Morning America:* I would be a private eye in the public eye. I thought it would give me a terrific opportunity to demonstrate how I piece together information—figuring out which objects are important and which to discount—to create a personality portrait of an office occupant.

GOOD MORNING, AMERICA

I would be presenting my findings live on air, but because my travel schedule didn't allow me time to inspect the GMA offices in person, the producers sent me photos of the offices instead. My targets were Charles Gibson, a longtime news anchor, and Mike Barz, a young correspondent who had recently joined the show to report the weather and present human-interest features. A reasonable concern would be whether my current knowledge of these men would affect my judgments. Fortunately, as a night owl who doesn't own a television, I had never seen the show (although it was gently suggested that I not share my ignorance with the people whose offices I would be evaluating).

Relying on photos rather than offices that I could touch, kick, and smell was an impediment, but there was an even bigger challenge.

My job was to look for differences between two people working for the same network, on the same show. By its nature, a morning show tends to attract dynamic, enthusiastic, socially facile people at the top of their game. And a high level of success in most fields requires organizational skills and an ability to plan and stay the course; therefore, these guys were bound to share a substantial number of characteristics, more than would be expected between a television anchor and, say, a librarian or an architect, or even a correspondent on a local evening show. So as I agreed to take on the task, I wondered how much I'd be able to discriminate between these two people. As soon as I saw the photos, my concern disappeared.

I examined Charles Gibson's office first, and here's what I saw: To the right of the door was a low bookshelf with a television set on it. A small plush tiger and a key were on the top shelf next to the television. Quite a few books sat on the lower shelves, so inspecting them seemed like a good place to start. The books had a lot to say. Most obviously, they provided clues to Gibson's specific interests. What were the exact topics? Were they books on the military? On science? Religion? The Icelandic avant-garde art movement? From the photos, most of the books appeared to be written by popular authors such as Tom Clancy and Dan Brown. Under most circumstances, this would suggest conventional taste, but I held this opinion only tentatively because those books were probably there by virtue of Gibson's job, which required him to interview authors. That alone was not grounds to dismiss the book information altogether; after all, this *was* his job. If the writers did not appeal to him, how successful would he be? And if he wasn't interested in the books, would he have kept them?

The breadth of topics of a book collection is particularly revealing. As we saw in chapter 8, a varied book collection (even if it's a small one) is a strong clue to a person's openness to experiences. The books on someone's shelf capture the person's general intellectual style and outlook. People high on openness tend to enjoy abstract thought and to be broad-minded, creative, imaginative, and philosophical (after all, openness is the Leonardo factor). So the apparent variety of books on the shelf caused me to raise my estimate slightly of Gibson's levels of openness. He was probably a little less conventional than some of the books might suggest.

In addition to topics themselves and their variety, we can distill information from the way books are arranged. Or, in this case, the way they were not arranged. Gibson's books appeared to be on the shelves in no particular order. Some were vertical, some were stacked untidily, and some were on their sides. They were not arranged by topic or author's name, or the color of the jacket, or size, or any other obviously discernable system. I suspected that Gibson followed the most-recent-ones-on-the-top rule. The spines were not lined up neatly, but at least most of the books were in the bookcase, which is more than can be said of many offices. As an office snooper, I set my initial estimate to medium-low on organization.

At this point, I didn't know how heavily to weigh the books as measures of Gibson's interests. Had I been able to engage in some in-person advanced book snooping, I would have pulled out several books and inspected them more closely. Whether they were well thumbed or pristine would tell me whether Gibson had read the books. And I might find other clues, such as muffin crumbs between the pages or notes in the margins (revealing his thoughts and suggesting he was focused on his task but had a casual attitude about the sanctity of books).

If my inspection suggested that the books were unread, I would wonder why. Various possibilities jump to mind. Perhaps, as suggested earlier, the books had accumulated as part of the job; a scan for similar collections (recall Quirk 5) in other offices might resolve this question. Or Gibson might genuinely be hoping to read these books but had not gotten around to it. If so, this would raise the possibility that he is an unrealistically optimistic planner. He may be busy, but he should know this, and if he is realistic, he should calibrate his book acquisitions accordingly. Or he might have a collection of unread books on a bookshelf to create a good impression. To evaluate this, I would need to look at how the books are arranged: Are the impressive ones all pulled to the front where visitors will see them (remember Quirk 4, "Mind the Gap")? Although people often try to create positive impressions in this way, as we saw in chapter 6, it's much harder to pull that deception off than one might imagine.

When I compared photos of Gibson's office with those of Mike Barz's, I was struck first by how sparse Barz's office is. This suggests someone whose perspective is more functional than aesthetic. Compared with Gibson, if Barz were faced with a tradeoff between function and looks, I suspect that he would lean toward function more than Gibson would. "Does it work? Yes. Then I'll take it. No, I don't care that it's ugly."

Witness, for example, the unsightly (but highly efficient) scrunched-up wires at the foot of Barz's lamp. I saw few attempts to make the space pleasing to the eye. And the bookcase was empty, suggesting that Barz is a more concrete, conventional person than Gibson.

On Gibson's desk I found evidence to solidify my initial appraisal of his organizational style. The rubber bands were not in the rubber-band container, the items in the desk area were arranged chaotically, the daily desk calendar hadn't been updated for twenty days, and only some of the pens were in the pen jar. Consistent with the signal sent by his haphazard way of displaying his books, the desk suggested that his life is not dominated by order, at least in contrast to Mike Barz's.

But by objective standards, Gibson's office was in pretty good shape. I could learn more about him if I delved a little deeper and investigated the reasons underlying the (dis)organization. He might be disorganized because he doesn't care about being organized. Or he might care, but be incapable of maintaining an organization system. The arrangement of items in Gibson's office suggested the latter to me. He had the trappings—a desk organizer (with its rubber-band section), a calendar, a pen jar, and so on—which is far more than you would find in many offices. So he has organizational ambitions, but he just didn't execute them in the way intrinsically organized people do. He isn't time-oriented enough to turn the pages of his calendar regularly. (A deeply organized person would consider a calendar that showed the wrong day—or, heaven forbid, the wrong month—an alarming sign that order is breaking down. Today, the wrong date; tomorrow, rioting in the streets.)

The filing drawer in the desk was not closed fully; if Gibson were a true neat freak he would be unable to focus on what he's doing with a half-closed drawer in his peripheral vision. There were Post-it notes on his desk but, significantly, they were out of reach. All these items suggest that, at heart, he does have organizational aspirations; that is, he does see the value of being organized. So I wouldn't be surprised if he was a sporadic organizer (someone who lets things get out of hand and embarks on a major clean-up when the mess is no longer tolerable). I also noticed some boxes on the desk. If they contained stationery items, that would be another indication of Gibson's noble intentions to become organized.

There was an inbox on the desk, too. In it was a green baseball hat. Otherwise, it was empty, which could indicate that everything had been handled. Or would the dust patterns underneath it show that Gibson doesn't use the box at all. On the basis of the hat-holding function of the box, along with the other evidence, I would guess the inbox goes unused.

So what's the point of discriminating between the possible reasons for Gibson's disarray? The result—a mildly disorganized desk—is the same in either case. The payoff comes in learning about what he might value in other contexts, which could influence how we relate to him. For example, I felt sure that Gibson sees the value of order. So if someone should ask him to do something—finish a report at work or clean out the garage—it would make sense to appeal to this appreciation of order. People who let their desks disintegrate into chaos because they don't value order would not find order-based appeals compelling.

Not everyone aspires to be organized, and not everyone who wants to become organized fails to do so. We can use the concept of an "aspired self" to help distinguish those who are disorganized but wish they weren't from those disorganized folks who are not bothered by it. Knowing something like this can help you in your everyday interactions. For example, it could motivate you to clean up your office when you are hosting a meeting with a disorganized person who appreciates organization. Someone who couldn't care less about being disorganized may prefer a loosely structured meeting that goes with the flow. One of my colleagues falls into the category of people who simply don't care. Her office has always been a disaster zone, but one day, when I commented mildly on the sorry state of her workspace, she told me that she had let it get so bad only because she knew she would soon be moving. Her new office would look much better, she assured me. I was not convinced, though, because I could tell that office organization was the farthest thing from her mind. And sure enough, her new office is no better than the old one.

Unlike my colleague, Charles Gibson is not dismissive of order. As I began to piece together a sharper picture of him, I realized that he seems to have an "I really must get around to that" personality—that is, his actions typically lag behind his good intentions. This character configuration was suggested by the way the desk and books were organized (and perhaps also from the books themselves if close inspection revealed them to be unread but not placed there to impress others). What other evidence would help support or reject this working hypothesis?

Lined up along one wall was a row of grocery boxes, and they appeared to be full of files and papers. Did this mean that Gibson was in the midst of getting organized? Having that stuff in boxes is a good start, but a deeply organized person would find a permanent place for things, and might even have special organizing boxes with color-coded tabs. Many of us would soon stop noticing the boxes, but the fastidiously inclined would find them a constant reminder of all the things that were not yet where they ought to be.

I found another clue to Gibson's really-must-get-around-to-that personality in the pictures in his office—in particular, their placement. There were two paintings—one a blown-up detail (I later learned) of a painting he has at home, and the other a framed painting of a building at Princeton University. Interestingly, neither of them was hung up. The enlarged reproduction leaned against a wall and the Princeton picture was balanced on the printer. For Gibson, like many of us, that was good enough. For people on the top end of the orderliness scale or those who care deeply about aesthetics, it wouldn't be. Had I been inspecting the premises in person, I would have quickly scanned other offices to make sure that some people did have their art work hanging up and thus rule out the possibility that the company had a policy against putting hooks on walls—think Quirk 5 again.

GOOD INTENTIONS GONE BAD

As I did in Gibson's office, I occasionally find evidence of good intentions gone awry—all those things we say we ought to do but, given our personalities, we don't. These unrealized aspirations are usually actions we really want to take—"get in shape," "get organized," "take time to relax." A good snooper would unearth evidence of these failed resolutions: the unopened package of swimming goggles collecting dust behind the desk, the out-of-date schedule for water aerobics classes, the recently expired gym membership card. Optimistic (but unrealistic) office organizers give themselves away with an impressive but unused haul of stuff from Staples. Accumulating evidence for these aspirations is easy, but carrying them out is hard.

Many of us see a change in circumstances—a new job or even a new office—as a chance to make big changes. A few years ago, when the psychology department at the University of Texas moved into a new building, I conducted a small study to see whether people would really be true to their aspirations. We examined the old offices before the move, the new offices afterwards. Here was an opportunity for those whose offices had drifted into disarray to turn over a new leaf.

I could just imagine my colleagues saying, "Boy, this new office is going to mark a new era of organization for me." Except, of course, it didn't. The chasm was too great between their aspirations and the lifestyle dictated by their personalities. In the new offices, the evidence was all there: color-coded files arranged willy-nilly; the Post-it notes still in their packets, business cards stuffed randomly into the box for some mythical day when there would be time to alphabetize them.

It was no surprise that the personality impressions of observers who saw only the old offices correlated strongly with the impressions of observers who saw only the new offices. And I would expect these correlations to increase if we compared the impressions after a year or two. This is because most people did show a bit of progress in organizing their new offices. They started out by making logical use of the folders and labels and boxes. But after a while, things began to break down. Again, I imagined their voices: "Damn, I didn't get enough red folders, so a yellow one will have to do!"

Offices are not the only site of failed aspirations. Snooping in someone's home can reveal many signs of good intentions gone bad. For example, an unrealized relaxer might have stocked up on scented candles, foot massage cream, bath oil, and an iPod playlist titled "Soothing Sounds"—but you'll find the jar of cream still nearly full, the candles hardly used, and the gentle songs missing from the "most played" list. Those moments of solitude and reflection are unlikely to happen because of the relentless pressure exerted by our personalities and the lives we create for ourselves.

Real change is possible, of course, but it's hard to achieve because you have to contend with your underlying biological predisposition as well as the pressures and daily obligations you have built into your routines. It is hard to conjure up a daily self-pampering hour without making big changes to all the other things you do. That's why personality change is most clearly seen at times of major life change—conscientiousness tends to increase when parenthood and professional duties demand that you ramp up the responsibility levels.

Considering aspirations, realized and unrealized, reminds us once again that you cannot equate a simple clue with an element of personality. As we learned from Quirk 2, cues derive part of their meaning from other cues. Candles alone are not enough to signify their owner likes to relax. A sharp snooper needs to take into account the condition of those soothing items and where they're placed; and you need to consider the surrounding features in the snoopee's bathroom: If you find a burned-down candle on a bathroom shelf, and it's accompanied by other candles in a similar state, a jar of bath salts, an eye mask, well-worn exfoliating gloves, and residue of wax around the bathroom, this is a good sign that the person values taking time to relax—and actually does it. You can then build on this foundation to learn more. How else does your self-pampering snoopee indulge herself? Do you find magazines on celebrity gossip, on gourmet cooking, or books about travel to exotic locations, or erotica? Again, each item provides valuable information that can guide your interaction with the snoopee. A good snoop before Valentine's Day might help you decide whether to make reservations at a four-star restaurant or surprise your love interest with a trip to Zanzibar.

PICTURING CHARLES

Returning to Charles Gibson's office, I searched for clues to his values and identity in the pictures in his office. Of all the images he could choose, why were these particular ones here? The Princeton painting propped on the printer was interesting because there was other

Princeton memorabilia around—including the plush tiger. I assumed the display meant that this elite university was Gibson's alma mater—and I'd attempt to make inferences about him from his Ivy League identity claim. But as I've noted earlier (recall Stephanie's seagull), a good snooper must be sure about the provenance of objects before drawing conclusions. Maybe his daughter was a student at Princeton; perhaps a guest on the show had given the picture to Gibson.

Other information told me that Gibson himself laid claim to Princeton's prestige. When I later watched the show on which my segment was aired, he referred to his time at Princeton twice. More interestingly, though, it was clear that his memories of that experience continue to be integrated into his sense of who he is. Not all that many grown men—Charles Gibson is in his sixties—continue to advertise their collegiate connections. Obviously, he was proud to have gone to Princeton, and that fact raised my snooping antennae. What was it about that experience—the high status, the superior academic standards, or more simply his attachment to an unusually important life transition—that continued to drive this bond? Had I been able to get to know Gibson better, I would have liked to probe his Ivied past and its connection to his personality.

Like Gibson, each of us integrates connections like these into our sense of self. In my adopted city, Austin, a huge number of the people derive pride from their association with Texas, and they can be alarmingly enthusiastic about communicating this pride through bumper stickers, flags, T-shirts, store names, dress, and tattoos; indeed, one visitor remarked to me that he had never been in a state where it was harder to forget exactly where you were. Keep a snooping eye out for these types of clues; in the offices we studied there were plenty of symbolic ties to moments, places, and groups from the past. In one office, a small Hungarian flag had been pinned to the wall above the desk; in another, a crystal glass sphere with three Greek symbols announced an ongoing allegiance to a sorority.

Also on Gibson's wall, above the printer, was a map of a foreign country. Our research shows that maps tend to be kept by people with diverse interests and are a clue to open-mindedness. But here it wasn't clear that the map was really there to satisfy Gibson's intellectual curiosity: It was pinned right next to the printer, where it could easily be referred to (rather than in a spot that favored sitting back and getting lost in a reverie, contemplating all the opportunities and excitements travel to that place would bring). This placement made it seem that the map was there for business reasons, perhaps because Gibson needed to keep track of the geography for a story. If so, this would dampen the clue's diagnosticity for open-mindedness. Sure enough, the map depicted Afghanistan, which at that time featured prominently in the news; Gibson is a news man, and he needed to know the relationship of the places he was reporting on.

The art also provided clues to complement the impressions I had gotten from the books in Gibson's office. The paintings were a bit unusual, but they were reproductions, not originals. This suggests an interest in the arts and signifies someone only slightly elevated on the trait of openness. But mostly, the walls in Gibson's office were empty—and this brings me to a fundamental facet of snooping: It is as important to pay attention to what is absent—an empty wall, a bare windowsill, or a mantelpiece with no photos on it—as it is to note what is there.

When weighing the significance of a blank wall or a clear surface on top of a filing cabinet, look around at other similar spaces that can act as your on-the-fly yardstick. In one of the offices we looked at we saw four postcards on the wall along with some stickers and a couple of posters. Had this been a retail-banking office, it would have been among the most decorated places we assessed; but it was in the building housing the advertising agency, where its décor appeared positively anemic next to the extensive and elaborate decoration in the neighboring offices.

MIKE BARZ:
THE SEDIMENT OF SENTIMENT

When I compared Gibson's art with that in correspondent Mike Barz's office, one feature of the décor set them apart: the presence of family photos. Barz's office was adorned with pictures of him, his kids, and his wife. Contrast Barz's arrangement with Gibson's office, where there was not one family photo. This suggested to me that Barz maintains less separation between his work self and his home self than Gibson does.

One of the most interesting things I saw in Barz's office was the way he arranged his photos. On the windowsill were several nicely framed family photos in which everyone was beaming beautifully at the camera. But who is supposed to see these photos? From his desk, Barz would have to turn around to see them; but a visitor sitting across from Barz would see him flanked by the photos of his wife and kids in the background. These are classic other-directed identity claims. Not only is Barz telling us about his values but he is giving us a glimpse into his personal life, and this itself suggests a more permeable border between his family and work life.

Yet not all the photos were for the benefit of others. On the bulletin board to his left, Barz also displayed about a dozen pictures of his children; the photos were pinned in a narrow vertical column running down the right rim of his bulletin board, giving it an unbalanced look. What could account for this unusual uneven display? I realized that Barz placed the photographs there so that he could see them as he works. And this told me something important about Barz—he's a snacker. But he doesn't hunger for food. He hungers for connection with his family. The photos are social snacks that tides him over until he can reconnect with his loved ones in person.

Wendi Gardner, a professor at Northwestern University, has studied social snacking and has provided compelling evidence to suggest that these psychological snacks—photos in wallets, letters from lovers—soften the pain of social isolation. In a clever set of studies, Gardner and her collaborator asked one group of research participants to bring in a photo of a friend and another group to bring in a photo of a favorite celebrity. The participants put the photos on the desks in front of them and were then asked to recall in vivid detail an experience of being rejected by other people. Normally, doing this exercise makes you feel bad, and that's exactly what happened for the people who had a picture of a celebrity in front of them. But the people who were looking at a friend's image did not experience a drop in mood. Gardner showed that this buffering effect of social snacks was specific to feelings about being separated from others.

When she did the same experiment but asked people to recall a failure instead of a rejection, all the participants felt equally bad, regardless of whether they had photos of celebrities or friends in front of them. These effects may explain why, according to Gardner, as many as 85 percent of adults have photographs or mementos of loved ones on their desks at work or in their wallets. And it's a good thing they do because loneliness has been linked to a host of serious health problems, from poor sleep and cardiovascular disease to compromised immune systems and increased blood pressure. Reminders such as photos, wedding rings, or e-mails from intimate others can fend off isolation and enhance well-being and productivity.

In Barz's office, every photo and poster depicted a person. This suggests he is extraverted. Introverts tend to display fewer depictions of people. They go for a quiet landscape or a still life. If introverts do display portraits, they are often of calm, restful people. An introverted graduate student of mine adorned her walls with pictures of doors. I'm relatively extraverted and when I was in her office I would keep glancing at those doors, half expecting to see an actual person walk out of one. (Extraverts are so drawn to other people that they are more likely than introverts to prefer music with vocals.) Further supporting Barz's extraversion were his comfortable chair and sofa with cushions. Although it is not a conscious strategy, as we saw in chapter 8, an inviting office layout is implicitly designed to encourage people to come in and linger.

The photos in Barz's office and their arrangement suggest that he is especially concerned with social connectedness. People vary in how much they have this "need to belong," but we all have it to some extent. As a social species, we have long been dependent on the groups in which we live for benefits that range from the protection afforded by numbers (and numbers of vigilant eyes) to the efficiency of hunting in packs. So in our evolutionary past we needed a mechanism that ensured that individuals stayed near one another; without group cohesion, people (or zebras or hyenas) might wander off, diminishing the integrity of the group and leaving its members unprotected.

Our ancestors felt compelled to hang out together. Those who didn't either perished or became the ancestors of a solitary species. The mechanism that held them together wasn't part of a conscious strategy; they just felt better in groups than when they were alone. You can see something similar in action if you watch a pair of ducks quietly dabbling in a pond together; one moves away a bit, perhaps to chase a bug, but sooner or later the other one will move closer. As they dabble around, they engage in a delayed dance that maintains their proximity—sometimes one leads and the other follows; sometimes the roles are reversed. It would be anthropomorphic to describe this as "love," but at a very basic level we can assume that the ducks are more comfortable when they're near each other than when they're apart.

Like the ducks, those of our ancestors who stayed together over time accrued the advantages of group living. They survived to pass their genes on to you and me. The result is that, as a rule, we humans like to be with and interact with others. Even though humans are more social than octopuses or orangutans (which are solitary species), there are still big differences within the human range. For some of us being alone, even for a short while, is unbearable; but for others, a week or two without human contact sounds just fine.

Obviously this need to affiliate is associated with extraversion—people high on this trait tend to be sociable and to enjoy interacting with others, and they have more close friends and a more active social life than people low on this need. They also tend to be higher on the trait of agreeableness and disclose more about themselves (I noticed this difference between Barz and Gibson, even during my brief encounter). And, crucially, people high in the need for affiliation are unhappier when they are alone than people low on this need. Recall from chapter 5 that, according to David Winter's analysis of his inaugural address, George W. Bush is unusually high on this need. In general, people like Barz, with a high need for affiliation, are more dependent on others than people low in that need.

The need to be with others feeds into a more specific need, the need to belong, which has been studied extensively by Mark Leary at Duke University. He found that people with a strong drive to belong form social bonds easily and are reluctant to break bonds, even if those bonds are no longer needed or cause them pain. They also become more distressed than others when relationships end. They are much more likely to engage in hello and good-bye rituals, they like to interact just for the sake of it, even when there's no real purpose ("I just called to say hello"), and they spend lots of time and energy thinking about their relationships. People with a strong need to belong are also particularly attentive to social cues. So based on the evidence in their offices, guess which man—Barz or Gibson—looked at me and which one looked away, when he shook my hand. If this seems easy now, that's because you've become an accomplished snooper. Barz looked, Gibson looked away.

*   *   *

Most of the people we have looked at so far, such as Charles Gibson, Mike Barz, and the dorm occupants in my study, inherited the spaces they decorated. They were given a standard box and did what they could and what their personalities compelled them to do with it. But what would happen if they could start from scratch—crafting the basic parameters of the space itself rather than altering what a previous occupant or an architect had left behind? What if, instead of trying to change a place to fit the personality of the occupant, we began by trying to figure out what the occupant is like—and then designed a space to match that person's personality? This intriguing proposition is the subject of the final chapter.

ELEVEN

Bringing It Home

NOT MANY KITCHEN appliances would inspire a photograph, but on more than one occasion visitors to my apartment have been sufficiently amused by what they found inside my refrigerator to whip out their camera phones. There are no gory body parts or rare wines in the fridge; it's the arrangement of items that grabs their attention. When you open the door, you face shelves and shelves of perfectly regimented beverages. On the bottom shelf you'll find the beers and sodas, several different kinds stretching in perfect rows all the way to the back. On the next shelf are the mixers—small bottles of tonic, soda, ginger ale, tomato juice, V8, and orange juice. The top shelf holds the bottled water, Red Bull, fancy lemonade, and Guinness. That row doesn't go all the way across because I need to leave at least half a shelf for all the other things that people ordinarily store in refrigerators. The door compartments are full of wine, champagne, cider, larger bottles of water, and backup beers.

The drinks are not for show. My guests and I do consume them. But the shelves are rarely less than fully stocked because right next to the refrigerator is a tall cupboard that contains my backup hoard, always on standby for replenishment emergencies. I'll casually offer someone a drink and affect a calm demeanor, apparently unfazed that the ginger ale row is now one bottle short; but as soon as the guest takes a bathroom break, I head straight to the storage cupboard and restore balance to my beverages. What makes the arrangement particularly odd is that my OCD tendencies stop at the refrigerator door.

My desk is typically in disarray, and the organization of items in my bathroom cupboard is determined by the order in which they were chucked in there. So the fridge has always puzzled me.

Even the snooping I did while researching and writing this book didn't shed light on my strange beverage behavior. It was not until I met a man named Chris Travis that I began to solve the mystery of my chilly little universe. It was through Travis that I learned how the unique needs we seek to satisfy with our physical spaces are rooted deeply in our past experiences.

Travis, a builder and designer who also heads up an architecture firm, contacted me when he heard about my snooping studies because he recognized the connections between his work and my research. I am interested in how people's personalities leave their imprint on the spaces in which they live, and he is interested in creating homes perfectly matched to his clients' personalities.

I soon discovered that Travis is no ordinary builder. Over the last twelve years he has been developing an innovative system, which he calls the Truehome workshop, to help people identify their emotional and psychological associations to places and to integrate those associations into the design of their houses. In a sense, Travis is focusing on the processes I have been studying—identity claims, self-regulators, and behavioral residue—and taking them to the extreme. I look at how people affect their existing spaces with their deliberate and inadvertent reflections of who they are—putting up posters, playing mellow jazz, leaving magazines scattered across the floor. Travis goes to a whole new level. He doesn't wait until people move to a new place and then use posters and music and magazines to shoehorn their personalities into it. He considers people's personalities so early in the design process that he can make the house fit the occupants, not the other way around. This technique requires coaxing out the idiosyncratic psychological connections between people and their places that typically go unexamined—the kinds of links that might even shed light on why some people hoard their beverages; indeed, it was by chance that Travis himself stumbled on the realization that our feelings about places are rooted deeply in the past.

YOUR TRUE HOME

It was winter 1992 and Travis had just about had it. After some disastrous entrepreneurial ventures, he was bankrupt. At that point, he decided to return to what he knew best: renovating old houses. He chose as his base a tiny central Texas town called Round Top. Still stinging from his losses and far from his family, whom he was trying to support, Travis had every reason to be blue. Yet, one evening as he strummed his guitar in a rocking chair on the balcony of a house he was restoring, he was surprised to find himself overcome by a sense of warmth, wellness, and tranquility.

Travis is a reflective man, so he intuitively started thinking about the roots of this unexpected state of mind. He allowed himself to associate his current feelings to earlier experiences. Before long, he was remembering his great-grandfather's house, where Travis, his mother, and his sister had sought sanctuary during hard times. He recalled sitting on his great-grandfather's knee as the old man rocked back and forth humming a song. Now, more than three decades later, as Travis rocked back and forth on the balcony in Round Top, he felt connected to this earlier time, when he had felt loved and appreciated. This realization—about the connection between his present feelings and those from a happy childhood memory—precipitated an epiphany in Travis. It became clear to him that we all develop emotional associations with places that affect how we later respond to our surroundings. As a result, our long-term emotional well-being can be profoundly affected by how well our surroundings match our ingrained psychological needs.

Was there some way, Travis wondered, to incorporate people's psychological needs into the design of their homes? For more than a decade, making that match would become the goal of his Truehome project and, indeed, of his life. Travis's method goes much deeper than conventional question-and-answer exercises, from which an architect might learn that, for example, his client "likes trees." The Truehome system would find out why—because they afford seclusion, or because she enjoys the sound of the wind blowing through the leaves, or because they remind her of the house she lived in as a little girl. Each of these reasons for liking trees suggests a different architectural solution.

The Truehome method focuses more on some levels than others in Dan McAdams's three-tiered system of describing personality. Recall that Level 1 traits, such as sociability and curiosity, are the most superficial. Then as we get to know people better, we learn about their personal concerns (Level 2), and we may even glimpse their identities (Level 3), the stories they tell about themselves to give their lives purpose and narrative. Travis's system is tapping something much deeper than McAdams's Level 1 traits: He is touching Level 2 constructs, such as roles and goals and values, and even delving deeper to matters of identity at Level 3.

In one exercise, Travis encourages clients to list "special furnishings that follow you through your life." Everyone has these. They can be as simple as a tattered concert poster or as meaningful as a grandparent's heirloom hope chest. Albums of photos from vacations or holidays are "special furnishings," and so are awards and medals, religious icons, old tools, campy signs, and cowboy paraphernalia. In my bedroom there's a table that stood in the hallway of the house where I was born and a lamp that my mother made from industrial resin and a pair of my old work boots. "Special furnishings" are symbolic threads that bind us to our past selves and maintain continuity through the present into the projected future. So if Travis designed a home for me, in addition to probing my emotional association to the objects, he'd be sure to take the practical steps of getting the exact dimensions of the table and lamp so that they could figure prominently in the plans.

When I visited Travis and looked at some of the plans he had created for his clients' houses, I quickly saw how his understanding of the functions of a living space differs from that of a conventional architect. One plan was stretched out on a long table. Whereas a conventional architect might use labels such as family room, back porch, and master bedroom, Travis's labels denote the feelings each space must evoke for the home's owners. Here the kitchen was labeled "warmth and companionship," the dining area "friendship," the pantry "abundance," the master bath "rejuvenation," the laundry area "productivity," the gun room "safety and adventure," the rear porch "friendship," the front porch "community," the living room "relaxation and family," and the master bedroom "privacy, passion, and reflection."

Of course, Travis's designations are customized for each client. On another plan I looked at, the spaces were labeled quite differently: the kitchen was "central and functional," the rear porch "invitation to beautiful vistas," and the master bedroom "tranquility heaven." Clearly, Travis does not view homes simply as places in which to eat and sleep and work; rather, he looks at how they can help provide feelings of safety, social stature, and comfort.

The case of his clients Jenni and Sanjay showed how Travis's uniquely psychological perspective gets translated into design features. When he first met this couple they had been arguing constantly about the design of their new home. The apparent cause was that Sanjay wanted a basement in their house and Jenni had what seemed an irrational negative reaction to it. They were deadlocked until Travis began exploring their associations with the basement. Jenni expressed negative reactions to closed spaces, such as closets and small rooms, and it soon became apparent that she was claustrophobic; oddly, neither she nor Sanjay realized this, even though she literally had to hold her breath when she needed to enter a walk-in closet. When the couple did Truehome's My Family exercise, it emerged that closets had figured in traumatic experiences that Jenni had suffered when she was a young child.

As Travis explained: "Not only could she not abide dark or enclosed spaces, but she also took her husband's desire for that type of space as evidence that he did not care about her or appreciate her needs. In her eyes, he was trying to force her to live through that trauma again." The impasse was creating a major rift in their marriage. Once Jenni and Sanjay were able to see the psychological roots of their conflict, finding an architectural solution was possible. Travis included plenty of shallow but ample closets and fitted the house with windows galore. And he designed the space so Jenni could surround herself with her own "special furnishings," so she would feel safe and secure. Sanjay's need for a personal place in which to hang out and tinker was met by a large back porch that reminded him of loving times he had spent with his mother when he was a kid.

In the everyday give-and-take of a relationship, even couples who have spent many years together may lose sight of each other's likes and dislikes. In our own snooping work, interpreting shared spaces is one of the greatest challenges because it's so hard to know who is responsible for what. Does that ghastly picture in the living room reflect his tastes or hers? Or perhaps it's just the result of an unhappy compromise suiting neither person well. So when my colleagues and I are snooping, we look for a place—such as a study or a basement—that is primarily the province of one person.

MY OWN PRIVATE MYSTERY BOX

I began this book with a "mystery box" that sparked my search for the links between people and their surroundings. However, only when I met Chris Travis did I begin to solve the puzzle of my own mystery box—my refrigerator. As I reflected on how Travis and his clients resonated with memories of their parents' or grandparents' homes, my mind wandered back to my own experiences at my grandmother's house. I recalled summers playing in the garden with my brother; whenever we felt like it, we could dash into the living room, go to the drinks cabinet, and grab a bottle of tonic water or bitter lemon. What felt so good was that we didn't have to curb our thirst— the great tonic fount never seemed to run dry. This may not seem extravagant or luxurious to modern readers, but my parents grew up in England during the severe rationing of World War II; excessive consumption (or even thirst-quenching) was discouraged. We were not poor, but my father famously (in our household at least) would add milk to the ketchup when it got low so that we could extract every last dreg of the precious tomato-flavored gold. The abandon with which my brother and I could plunder Grandma's trove of mixers seemed to us like the delicious pinnacle of self-indulgence.

Now as an adult, without quite realizing it, I have re-created my own bottomless mixer wellspring. Were I to design a house with the aid of a conventional architect, I doubt I would think of mentioning this deep-rooted need for abundance. But I am sure it would have emerged with Travis's expert probing. And I am sure he would have devised a brilliant solution—perhaps my own glass-fronted "mixers fridge" and a matching storage cabinet so that I could admire the rows of drinks and relax in the knowledge that I had on hand enough tonic to manage a medium-sized outbreak of malaria.

Travis's work provides a fascinating extra dimension for the snooper. Of course, not everyone can have a house custom designed for them or have the opportunity to bring their unconscious associations to the surface in the process of creating their home. But many of these implicit connections will find ways to express themselves in the spaces you create, even if you're not quite sure what it is that's driving your preferences. When one of Travis's clients fondly recalled sitting in an adult chair where her feet couldn't touch the ground, he responded by building in a kitchen counter for high stools so she could swing her legs as she did when she was a child; without Travis the client might never have discovered the root of her preference, and the counter might not have figured so prominently in the design. But it's likely that her preference for stools or oversized chairs would have found expression in her space one way or another. Being aware of the principles that Travis employs will direct you—as it did me, in the case of my refrigerator—to ask the right questions about the psychological functions that spaces serve.

SNOOP DREAMS

So we have come full circle, from discovering how we leave personality footprints on the spaces we inhabit to learning how spaces can be crafted to realize our personality potential—and how knowing about this process can help us when snooping.

As I've demonstrated in this book, when it comes to the most essential pieces of our personalities—from friendliness and flexibility to orderliness and originality—snooping has the power to uncover truths about us that are hard to detect in any other way. This observation is important because so much of living life successfully involves getting to know what people are like. That's why we have been endowed with a fundamental need to figure others out—to size them up as a prospective mate, to decide whether they've got the goods for a particular job, or even to deduce what kind of closets would suit them best.

What is clear from my studies, from Travis's distinctive approach to home design, and from the rich lode of psychological research that I've mined here, is that our personalities are inextricably linked to the places that surround us. Every time we hang a poster on a wall or toss a coffee cup in the trash or download another album from iTunes, we leave clues about who we are. We broadcast our traits and values, our goals and identities for people to see and perhaps to judge. And although we may attempt to arrange our stuff to outfox others, our true personalities inevitably leak out, especially under the scrutiny of sharp-eyed sleuths.

A core goal of this book has been to provide the tools that will turn you from an ordinary observer into a savvy snooper. If I've succeeded, you will have learned something that has been overlooked by a century's worth of psychological research: that snooping gives all of us unique insights into ourselves and sharpens our perceptions of others.

There's another benefit too: Your enriched knowledge of how people relate to their spaces, deliberately and inadvertently, will help you investigate domains of expression that have yet to be studied scientifically—from the contents of wallets, purses, suitcases, or Facebook wall posts, to preferences for pets, tattoos, cocktails, and vacation spots. So the next time you start to poke around a friend's medicine cabinet or surreptitiously review the stuff stuck on his refrigerator door, I hope you will revel in the realization that you are poised at the edge of a new frontier in the understanding of human behavior. And after just a little bit of reveling, I trust you'll get down to some serious snooping.

ACKNOWLEDGMENTS

THE IDEAS AND information in this book are drawn from many sources, including my own research, my close reading of the work of other academics, and discussions with my research team and with the participants in my studies. In order to provide the richest possible perspective on the connections between people and the places they inhabit, I have used this book as an opportunity to go well beyond summarizing findings to include stories and examples from my own experience and that of colleagues and collaborators. When I describe rooms and offices in which I've snooped, I've changed some names and details to protect people's anonymity and in a few cases have combined examples to improve the efficiency of exposition and the flow of the narrative.

Below I thank many of the people who have contributed in one way or another to this book. For the sake of simplicity I have spliced my gratitude into various paragraphs consisting of students, friends, teachers, editors, and so on; in truth, of course, most of the people thanked belong in multiple categories, but I figured life was complicated enough without trying to mix things up.

Among the many people whose work I have drawn on, I am most indebted to my former and current students, especially the dynamic trio of Jason Rentfrow, Simine Vazire, and Matthias Mehl. It was an enormous privilege to be associated with these brilliant young scientists. Our discussions and work together provided the foundation for much of what is contained in this book.

Before that, my early development as a scientist was strongly influenced by my two main advisors at graduate school: Oliver John and

Kenneth Craik. They created an enormously rich intellectual climate in which I was able to explore my wacky ideas rigorously and systematically. They gave me the latitude and support that allowed me to nurture the projects that would later come to define my major research programs. I am pleased to be able to dedicate this book to them.

Several other faculty and graduate students at Berkeley were important in shaping my thinking, including Jerry Mendelsohn, Ravenna Helson, Phil Tetlock, Tom Tyler, Steve Glickman, Rick Robins, Mark Spranca, Jeffre Jackson, Jen Beck, Jen Pals, Brent Roberts, Virginia Kwan, Aaron Ware, Cameron Anderson, Veronica Benet-Martinez, Sanjay Srivastava, Eric Knowles, and Jenni Beer. At the University of Texas I have benefited from my fantastic colleagues: Bill Swann, Bob Josephs, David Buss, and James Pennebaker.

Many people contributed to this book by talking ideas through with me and telling me about their research. Most important among these were Daniel Ames, John Jost, and Del Paulhus. I also benefited from the input of Eric Abrahamson, Kevin Wu, Stephanie Preston, Gary Marcus, Mike Norton, Christine Chang-Schneider, Pranj Mehta, Tony Maxwell, Malcolm Gladwell, and Charles Siebert and from fruitful collaborations with Dana Carney, Jeff Potter, Tom Mannarelli, Sei Jin Ko, and Margaret Morris.

I am deeply indebted to Chris Travis, who generously taught me about the Truehome system and answered my incessant questions with great patience and thoughtfulness. I also thank his clients who gave up many hours to show me around the magnificent houses Chris designed for them and to share their experiences with me.

I am grateful to the scores of dedicated undergraduate students who were research assistants on the studies reported here, especially the two trailblazing groups who worked on my first studies of offices and bedrooms: Lauren Altman, Patricia Baker, Allison Bonburg, Jenni Brelsford, Keren Brooks, Alice Chuang, Erica Dolor, Garin Ekmekjian, Manjit Gill, Dorothea Ho, Linda Huang, Lane Johnson, Beth Jones, Cohav Kimmel, Adam Klinger, Lawrence Lee, Monica

Lee, Peter Lwin, Kevin Murray, Sun No, Susan Orgera, Michelle Pryor, Rachelle Robles, Jenny Vuong, Alex Wang, Elisa Wong, Mei-Ling Woo, and Marisa Yee.

During the last three years my friends have played a vital role in maintaining my sanity. Those who bore the brunt of my impossible behavior are Brad Love, Cindy Meston, Stefan Cohrs, Mark Sellman, Amanda Merchant, Christina Jarrous, Chris Marcazzo, Tom Barlow, Elise Ballard, Sadie Rossow, Lisa Simmons, Jo Carten, Amber West, Sara Vig, Laura Kressel, Marcia Mitchell, Mubeyyet Ozgen, and William Lamb.

There's nothing like writing a book to work up a good appetite. And nothing like Lou Miller's catering and Mike Morris's and Shula Melamed's all-round New York hospitality service to satisfy the hunger. It's thirsty work too, and I'd like to thank the staff and patrons who created the (café) spaces where most of this book was written in Austin (Little City, Spiderhouse, Epoch, Jos, Halcyon, Progress, JPs), New York (Verb, Think, Doma, Cake Shop, Read), Exeter (Boston Tea Party), and Stanford (CoHo).

I am grateful to the Center for Advanced Studies in the Behavioral Sciences, where I sketched out the basic ideas for this book during a sabbatical year. I also benefited from the superb insights of Daniel Crewe at Profile Books and Svetlana Katz at Janklow and Nesbit Associates, from Kay Mariea's expert copy editing at Basic Books, and the sharp eyes of Lauren Dolinksy.

Finally, the two people who contributed more than anyone else to transforming a hopeless to-do list into a book are my agent, Tina Bennett, at Janklow and Nesbit Associates, and my editor, Jo Ann Miller, at Basic Books. When people in the know learn that I am represented by Tina, the most common response is that I've got the best agent in the business. They are right. Tina is a model of integrity, insightfulness, and brilliance. I have benefited from every interaction with her. I feel guilty that I have had the good fortune to be represented by Tina while other writers have to be satisfied with mere mortal agents. I especially appreciate the support, advice, and advocacy she provided as we navigated complex issues at the beginning of this project. And she has been amazing throughout.

Quite simply, without Jo Ann Miller this book would never have been written. I learned so much from her. I now look back with great fondness on the many hours we sat side-by-side writing, rewriting, and excising, and on our shift-work schedule that allowed us to keep this book moving forward twenty-four hours a day. Jo Ann contributed so much that in my mind she is a co-author. To the extent that you can make your way through this book without tripping over my "throat clearing" and "belaboring," you have Jo Ann to thank. The single sad thing about finishing *Snoop* is finding that my work with her is over (at least for now).

NOTES

PROLOGUE: THE ARRIVAL OF THE MYSTERY BOX

The "bedroom study" along with my research on office spaces is reported in: Gosling, S. D., Ko, S. J., Mannarelli, T., & Morris, M. E. (2002). A room with a cue: Judgments of personality based on offices and bedrooms. *Journal of Personality and Social Psychology, 82,* 379–398.

Our work on the clues to political orientation can be found in: Carney, D. R., Jost, J. T., Gosling, S. D., & Potter, J. (in press). The secret lives of liberals and conservatives: Personality profiles, interaction styles, and the things they leave behind. *Political Psychology.*

CHAPTER 1: LESS THAN ZERO ACQUAINTANCE

My research on living spaces is described in: Gosling, S. D., Ko, S. J., Mannarelli, T., & Morris, M. E. (2002). A room with a cue: Judgments of personality based on offices and bedrooms. *Journal of Personality and Social Psychology, 82,* 379–398.

I am grateful to Joe McCarthy for bringing to my attention some of the work on personalization of office spaces, including the survey on worker comfort and engagement in the Gallup management journal (which was written about by J. Krueger and E. Killham and can be accessed at the Gallup management journal Web site: http://gmj.gallup.com/content/21802/Why-Dilbert-Right.aspx). For some of Joe's thoughts, check out his blog at: http://gumption.typepad.com/.

The "I am . . ." twenty statements test was originally published in: Kuhn, M. H., & McPartland, T. S. (1954). An empirical investigation of self-attitudes. *American Sociological Review, 19,* 68–76. The photographic version of the test was developed much later and is described in: Combs, J. M., & Ziller, R. C. (1977). Photographic self-concept of counselees. *Journal of Counseling Psychology, 24,* 452–455.

For more on iPods, see: Levy, S. (2006). *The perfect thing: How the iPod shuffles commerce, culture, and coolness.* New York: Simon & Schuster.

The study of the effects of Christmas decorations on perceptions of homeowners can be found in: Werner, C. M., Peterson-Lewis, S., & Brown, B. B. (1989). Inferences about homeowners' sociability: Impact of Christmas decorations and other cues. *Journal of Environmental Psychology, 9,* 279–296.

The classic work on unobtrusive measurement of behavior is: Webb, E. J., Campbell, D. T., Schwartz, R. D., Sechrest, L., & Belew Grove, J. (1981). *Nonreactive measures in the social sciences.* Boston: Houghton Mifflin.

The garbage project is described in: Rathje, W. L., & Murphy, C. (1992). *Rubbish! The archaeology of garbage.* New York: HarperCollins.

Music is so powerful at affecting mood that it sometimes is used to induce various moods in psychological studies. For a review of the studies, see: Västfjäll, D. (2002). Emotion induction through music: A review of the musical mood induction procedure. *Musicae Scientiae, 6, Special Issue 2001/2002,* 173–203.

Chapter 2: Ocean's Five

For a good brief introduction to the Big Five, check out Sanjay Srivastava's Web site: http://darkwing.uoregon.edu/~sanjay/bigfive.html. For a more advanced treatment, see John, O. P., & Srivastava, S. (1999). The Big Five

Trait taxonomy: History, measurement, and theoretical perspectives. In L. A. Pervin & O. P. John (Eds.), *Handbook of personality: Theory and research* (2nd ed., pp. 102–139). New York: Guilford Press. Or McCrae, R. R., & John, O. P. (1992). An introduction to the five-factor model and its applications. *Journal of Personality, 60,* 175–216.

Details regarding the brief test of the Big Five can be found in: Gosling, S. D., Rentfrow, P. J., & Swann, W. B., Jr. (2003). A very brief measure of the Big Five personality domains. *Journal of Research in Personality, 37,* 504–528.

To calculate where your Big Five scores fall in relation to the broader population, you can convert your scores to "t-scores." The t-scores show you where you score on each dimension relative to the other people who took the test. As you examine your scores you should bear in mind that the comparison sample provided here may not be representative of the population as a whole (so your scores would be slightly different if you compared yourself to another comparison sample).

To create your t-scores from the scores you computed in chart 2.2, use the following formulas:

FEMALES
Openness t-score = 50 + (((Your openness score − 0.8) ÷ 2.12) × 10)
Conscientiousness t-score = 50 + (((Your conscientiousness score − 11.0) ÷ 2.22) × 10)
Extraversion t-score = 50 + (((Your extraversion score − 9.1) ÷ 2.94) × 10)
Agreeableness t-score = 50 + (((Your agreeableness score − 10.6) ÷ 2.22) × 10)
Neuroticism t-score = 50 + (((Your neuroticism score − 6.7) ÷ 2.90) × 10)

MALES
Openness t-score = 50 + (((Your openness score − 10.7) ÷ 2.18) × 10)
Conscientiousness t-score = 50 + (((Your conscientiousness score − 10.4) ÷ 2.30) × 10)
Extraversion t-score = 50 + (((Your extraversion score − 8.5) ÷ 2.82) × 10)
Agreeableness t-score = 50 + (((Your agreeableness score − 10.1) ÷ 2.20) × 10)
Neuroticism t-score = 50 + (((Your neuroticism score − 5.7) ÷ 2.62) × 10)

To interpret your t-scores, refer to the graph below. The midpoint of the horizontal axis (labeled "50") represents the average score for members of the comparison group. The shape of the curve reflects the fact that most people tend to be near the average point (i.e., the curve is highest at the midpoint) with fewer people scoring very high or low on the trait (i.e., the height of the curve diminishes as it gets further from the midpoint).

To find out how you compare to others on a particular trait (e.g., extraversion), locate your t-score for that trait on the horizontal axis of the graph. If you got a t-score of 50 for extraversion, this means that half the people in the comparison group (50 percent) were rated as higher on extraversion than you and half were rated as lower. If you got a t-score of 60, then about 84.13 percent of the comparison group were rated as lower on extraversion than you (i.e., the 50 percent below the average plus the 34.13 percent between 50 and 60). If you got a t-score of 55, then between 50 percent and 84 percent of the comparison group were lower on extraversion than you. If you got a t-score of 30, this means about 2 percent (i.e., the 2.14 percent between 20 and 30 plus the 0.13 percent below 20) of the comparison group were rated as lower than you. Note that, by definition, t-scores have a mean of 50 and standard deviation of 10. Thus, most people (68.26 percent) fall within one standard deviation above or below the mean so most of your scores will probably be between 40 and 60.

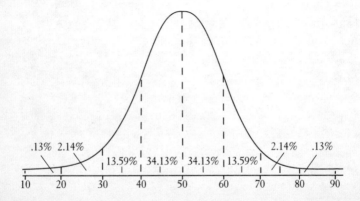

The descriptions of the Big Five and their facets were adapted from John A. Johnson's excellent descriptions of the dimensions. They can be found at: http://www.personal.psu.edu/faculty/j/5/j5j/IPIPNEOdescriptions.html.

For papers reviewing some of the ways personality is linked to important life outcomes, see: Ozer, D. J., & Benet-Martinez, V. (2006). Personality and the prediction of consequential outcomes. *Annual Review of Psychology, 57,* 401–421. And Roberts, B. W., Kuncel, N. R., Shiner, R., Caspi, A., & Goldberg, L. R. (2007). The comparative predictive validity of personality traits, SES, and cognitive ability for important life outcomes. *Perspectives on Psychological Science, 2,* 313–345.

CHAPTER 3: GETTING TO KNOW YOU

Dan McAdams's account of Lynn and the three levels of personality can be found in: McAdams, D. P. (1995). What do we know when we know a person? *Journal of Personality, 63,* 365–396.

Allport and Odbert's attempt to identify all the words in the dictionary related to personality is described in: Allport, G. W., & Odbert, H. S. (1936). Traitnames: A psycho-lexical study. *Psychological Monographs, 47* (No. 211).

Arthur Aron's "sharing game" procedure for generating closeness in studies is described in: Aron, A., Melinat, E., Aron, E. N., Vallone, R. D., & Bator, R. J. (1997). The experimental generation of interpersonal closeness: A procedure and some preliminary findings. *Personality and Social Psychology Bulletin, 23,* 363–377.

Richard Slatcher used Aron's procedure to generate closeness between sets of couples. That work is described in his dissertation: Slatcher, R. B. (2007). Party of four: Creating closeness between couples. Doctoral dissertation. University of Texas at Austin. Some of the findings were reported in a conference presentation: Slatcher, R. B. (2008, February). *Effects of couple friendships on relationship closeness.* Paper presented at the annual meeting of the Society for Personality and Social Psychology, Albuquerque, NM.

The work Jason Rentfrow and I did examining topics in getting-acquainted conversations is described in: Rentfrow, P. J., & Gosling, S. D. (2006). Message in a ballad: The role of music preferences in interpersonal perception. *Psychological Science, 17,* 236–242. Figure 3.1 is reproduced, with permission, from that article.

A good source for Jefferson Singer's work on self-defining memories is: Singer, J. A. (2005). *Memories that matter: How to use self-defining memories to understand and change your life.* Oakland, CA: New Harbinger.

CHAPTER 4: BELGIAN SLEUTHS AND SCANDINAVIAN SEABIRDS

A fascinating account of the Office of Strategic Studies (OSS) assessment program can be found in: OSS Assessment Staff. (1948). *Assessment of men: Selection of personnel for the Office of Strategic Services.* New York: Rinehart.

Richard Slatcher and Simine Vazire's work on IM is reported in: Wang, J., Slatcher, R. B., Vazire, S., & Pennebaker, J. W. (2006, January). *Predicting relationship satisfaction and stability from couples' instant messages.* Poster presented at the annual meeting of the Society for Personality and Social Psychology, Palm Springs, CA. And in Slatcher, R. B., Vazire, S., & Pennebaker, J. W. (2007). *A view from the inside: Predicting relationship stability from couples' everyday interactions.* Manuscript submitted for publication.

CHAPTER 5: JUMPERS, BUMPERS, GROOVERS, AND SHAKERS

Halsman's jumping celebrities can be found in: Halsman, P. (1959). *Jump book.* New York: Simon & Schuster.

For an excellent review of the scientific status of projective tests see: Lilienfeld, S. O., Wood, J. M., & Garb, H. N. (2000). The scientific status of projective techniques. *Psychological Science in the Public Interest, 1,* 27–66.

Many of the papers describing Oliver Schultheiss's work on the Picture Story Exercise (PSE) and the analysis of motives can be found at: http://www-personal.umich.edu/~oschult/index.htm and http://www.psych2.phil.uni-erlangen.de/.

David Winter's analyses of George W. Bush's inaugural speeches can found in: Winter, D. G. (2001, Spring). Insights and observations about political psychology. *International Society of Political Psychology;* and Winter, D. G. (2005). Continuity and change in George Bush's motive profile. *International Society of Political Psychology News, 16,* 10–11.

To get the latest on Karl Grammer's research at the Ludwig Boltzmann Institute for Urban Ethology, check out his papers, available at: http://evolution.anthro.univie.ac.at/institutes/urbanethology/staff/grammer.html.

More information on the research at Georgia Institute of Technology identifying individual walking patterns can be found at: http://www.cc.gatech.edu/cpl/projects/hid/ and http://www.cc.gatech.edu/cpl/projects/hid/#Gait_Recognition.

Borkenau and Liebler's work on walking signatures is reported in a series of articles published between 1992 and 1995. The findings are complex, so to get the full picture you really need to read all of them:

Borkenau, P., & Liebler, A. (1992). Trait inferences: Sources of validity at zero acquaintance. *Journal of Personality and Social Psychology, 62,* 645–657.

Borkenau, P., & Liebler, A. (1993). Consensus and self-other agreement for trait inferences from minimal information. *Journal of Personality, 61,* 477–496.

Borkenau, P., & Liebler, A. (1993). Convergence of stranger ratings of personality and intelligence with self-ratings, partner ratings, and measured intelligence. *Journal of Personality and Social Psychology, 65,* 546–553.

Borkenau, P., & Liebler, A. (1995). Observable attributes as cues and manifestations of personality and intelligence. *Journal of Personality, 63,* 1–25.

An earlier article reporting a correlation between the feature of "babyishness" and agreeableness was: Berry, D. S., & Brownlow, S. (1989). Were the physiognomists right? Personality correlates of facial babyishness. *Personality and Social Psychology Bulletin, 15,* 266–279.

The work by Anthony Little and David Perrett on personality traits associated with faces can be found in: Little, A. C., & Perrett, D. I. (2007). Using composite images to assess accuracy in personality attribution to faces. *British Journal of Psychology, 98,* 111–126. Other thought-provoking work by Little and his collaborators on the links between personality and facial features can be found in: Little, A. C., Burt, D. M., & Perrett, D. I. (2006). Assortative mating for perceived facial personality traits. *Personality and Individual Differences, 40,* 973–984; Little, A. C., Burt, D. M., & Perrett, D. I. (2006). What is good is beautiful: Face preference reflects desired personality. *Personality and Individual Differences, 41,* 1107–1118; Little, A. C., Burriss, R. P., Jones, B. C., & Roberts, S. C. (2007). Facial appearance affects voting decisions. *Evolution and Human Behavior, 28,* 18–27.

The research reporting associations between facial lines and personality in older people is reported in: Malatesta, C. Z., Fiore, M. J., & Messina, J. J. (1987). Affect, personality, and facial expressive characteristics of older people. *Psychology and Aging, 2,* 64–69.

The work by Nathanson and colleagues on tattoos, body piercings, provocative dress, and other expressions of cultural deviance can be found in: Nathanson, C., Paulhus, D. L., & Williams, K. M. (2006). Personality and misconduct correlates of body modifications and other cultural deviance markers. *Journal of Research in Personality, 40,* 779–802.

The study testing whether observers could match drivers to their vehicles is reported in: Alpers, G. W., & Gerdes, A. B. M. (2006). Another look at "look-alikes": Can judges match belongings with their owners? *Journal of Individual Differences, 27,* 38–41.

Some interesting findings on the stereotypes associated with drivers of different car types are provided in Davis, G. M., & Patel, D. (2005). The influence of car and driver stereotypes on attributions of vehicle speed, position on the road and culpability in a road accident scenario. *Legal and Criminological Psychology, 10,* 45–62.

Handshaking was mentioned in Allport and Vernon's classic: Allport, G. W., & Vernon, P. E. (1933). *Studies in expressive movement.* New York: Macmillan.

Then in the 1990s there was a spate of work by a Swedish group: Astroem, J. (1994). Introductory greeting behavior: A laboratory investigation of approaching and closing salutation phases. *Perceptual and Motor Skills, 79,* 863–897.

Astroem, J., & Thorell, L. (1996). Greeting behavior and psychogenic need: Interviews on experiences of therapists, clergymen, and car salesmen. *Perceptual and Motor Skills, 83,* 939–956.

Astroem, J., Thorell, L., Holmlund, U., & d'Elia, G. (1993). Handshaking, personality, and psychopathology in psychiatric patients: A reliability and correlational study. *Perceptual and Motor Skills, 77,* 1171–1186.

Then came William Chaplin's study: Chaplin, W. F., Phillips, J. B., Brown, J. D., Clanton, N. R., & Stein, J. L. (2000). Handshaking, gender, personality, and first impressions. *Journal of Personality and Social Psychology, 79,* 110–117.

Raymond's day is recorded in Barker and Wright's classic volume: Barker, R. G., & Wright, H. F. (1951). *One boy's day: A specimen record of behavior*. New York: Harper & Brothers.

Ken Craik's "lived-day" approach, where he videotaped participants for a full day, is described in: Craik, K. H. (2000). The lived day of an individual: A person-environment perspective. In W. B. Walsh, K. H. Craik, & R. Price (Eds.), *Person-environment psychology: New directions and perspectives* (2nd ed., pp. 233–266). Hillsdale, NJ: Erlbaum.

The work done using the EAR by Matthias Mehl, James Pennebaker, and myself is described in: Mehl, M. R., Gosling, S. D., & Pennebaker, J. W. (2006). Personality in its natural habitat: Manifestations and implicit folk theories of personality in daily life. *Journal of Personality and Social Psychology, 90,* 862–877; Mehl, M. R., & Pennebaker, J. W. (2003). The sounds of social life: A psychometric analysis of students' daily social environments and natural conversations. *Journal of Personality and Social Psychology, 84,* 857–870.

To find out more about the obtrusiveness of the EAR and participant's compliance in using it, see: Mehl, M. R., & Holleran, S. E. (2007). An empirical analysis of the obtrusiveness of and participants' compliance with the Electronically Activated Recorder (EAR). *European Journal of Personality Assessment, 23,* 248–257.

James Pennebaker and Laura King's research on how personality is reflected in the words we use is reported in: Pennebaker, J. W., & King, L. A. (1999). Linguistic styles: Language use as an individual difference. *Journal of Personality and Social Psychology, 77,* 1296–1312.

James Pennebaker's text analysis software program for analyzing language, "Linguistic Inquiry and Word Count," can be found at: http://www.liwc.net/.

A preliminary report of Christine Chang-Schneider's work on e-mail addresses can be found in: Chang-Schneider, C. S., & Swann, W. B., Jr. (2008,

February). *Wearing your self-esteem like a flag.* Poster presented at the annual meeting of the Society for Personality and Social Psychology, Albuquerque, NM.

Tsutako Mori's research on Japanese mobile phone e-mail addresses was reported in a series of poster presentations:

Takahira, M., & Mori, T. (2005, September). *Can we detect personalities from mobile phone email addresses?* (I). Poster presented at the annual meeting of the Japanese Society of Social Psychology, Hyogo, Japan.

Mori, T., & Takahira, M. (2005, September). *Can we detect personalities from mobile phone email addresses?* (II). Poster presented at the annual meeting of the Japanese Society of Social Psychology, Hyogo, Japan.

Mori, T., & Takahira, M. (2005, November). *Impression management through email addresses of mobile phones.* Poster presented at the annual meeting of the Japanese Society of Personality Psychology, Iwate, Japan.

CHAPTER 6: SPACE DOCTORING

Amis's story of the manipulative Charles Highway is: Amis, M. (1973). *The Rachel papers.* New York: Vintage International.

Del Paulhus's over-claiming technique (OCQ) is described in: Paulhus, D. L., Harms, P. D., Bruce, M. N., & Lysy, D. C. (2003). The over-claiming technique: Measuring self-enhancement independent of ability. *Journal of Personality and Social Psychology, 84,* 890–904. That article will show you how to generate more accurate scores for the OCQ. Also, for an interesting list of people ranked by sheer fame, see: Paulhus, D. L., Wehr, P., Harms, P. D., & Strasser, D. I. (2002). Use of exemplar surveys to reveal implicit types of intelligence. *Personality and Social Psychology Bulletin, 28,* 1051–1062.

Goffman's classic volume on how we present ourselves in daily interactions is: Goffman, E. (1959). *The presentation of self in everyday life.* New York: Doubleday.

An example of research showing that people with different personalities (in this case, high neuroticism) respond to the world differently from others can be found in: Schneider, T. R. (2004). The role of neuroticism on psychological and physiological stress responses. *Journal of Experimental Social Psychology, 40,* 795–804.

You can find out all about Daniel Ames's terrific studies on personality and interpersonal perception at: http://www0.gsb.columbia.edu/whoswho/full. cfm?id=56194.

Self-verification theory, developed by Bill Swann, is described in: Swann, W. B., Jr., Rentfrow, P. J., & Guinn, J. (2002). Self-verification: The search for coherence. In M. Leary and J. Tagney (Eds.), *Handbook of self and identity.* New York: Guilford Press. And in Swann, W. B., Jr., Chang-Schneider, C., & Angulo, S. (2007). Self-verification in relationships as an adaptive process. In J. Wood, A. Tesser, and J. Holmes (Eds.) *Self and relationships.* Psychology Press: New York.

For details on the study in which self-esteem affected how people responded to pay raises, see Daniel Schroeder's dissertation: Schroeder, D. G. (2002). *Self-esteem moderates the effect of wage trends on employment tenure.* Doctoral dissertation. University of Texas at Austin.

The research by Mehta and Josephs on how dominant and submissive people react to wins and losses in a rigged competition is reported in: Mehta, P. H., & Josephs, R. A. (2006). Testosterone change after losing predicts the decision to compete again. *Hormones and Behavior, 50,* 684–692. The "mismatch" hypothesis is described in: Josephs, R. A., Sellers, J. G., Newman, M. L., & Mehta, P. H. (2006). The mismatch effect: When testosterone and status are at odds. *Journal of Personality and Social Psychology, 90,* 999–1013.

The work I did with Simine Vazire on how people project identities through personal Web sites is reported in: Vazire, S., & Gosling, S. D. (2004).

e-Perceptions: Personality impressions based on personal Web sites. *Journal of Personality and Social Psychology, 87,* 123–132.

CHAPTER 7: IN DEFENSE OF STEREOTYPES

Robert Levine's research examining various indicators of the pace of life in different countries is reported in: Levine, R. V., & Norenzayan, A. (1999). The pace of life in 31 countries. *Journal of Cross-Cultural Psychology, 30,* 178–205.

Richard Florida's fascinating and important research program on how values, taste, and personality influence where people choose to live is described in his books:

Florida, R. (2002). *The rise of the creative class.* New York: Basic Books.

Florida, R. (2005). *The flight of the creative class.* New York: Collins.

Florida, R. (2008). *Who's your city.* New York: Basic Books.

The work I have done with Jason Rentfrow on how personality is reflected in location is reported in: Rentfrow, P. J., Gosling, S. D., & Potter, J. (in press). The geography of personality: A theory of the emergence, persistence, and expression of regional variation in basic traits. *Perspectives in Psychological Science.*

Our work predicting voting patterns from geographic differences in personality is reported in: Rentfrow, P. J., Jost, J. T., Gosling, S. D., & Potter, J. (in press). Statewide differences in personality predict voting patterns in 1996–2004 U.S. presidential elections. In J. T. Jost, A. C. Kay, and H. Thorisdottir (Eds.), *Social and psychological bases of ideology and system justification.* New York: Oxford University Press. And the paper describing the connections between political orientation, personality, behavior, and living spaces is: Carney, D. R., Jost, J. T., Gosling, S. D., & Potter, J. (2006). The secret lives of liberals and conservatives: Personality profiles, interaction styles, and the things they leave behind. *Political Psychology.*

The research on brain differences associated with political orientation is reported in: Amodio, D. M., Jost, J. T., Master, S. L., & Yee, C. M. (2007). Neurocognitive correlates of liberalism and conservatism. *Nature Neuroscience, 10,* 1246–1247.

Important work on validity of stereotypes (e.g., about sex) can be found in: Swim, J. K. (1994). Perceived versus meta-analytic effects sizes: An assessment of the accuracy of gender stereotypes. *Journal of Personality and Social Psychology, 66,* 21–36.

Hall, J. A., & Carter, J. D. (1999). Gender-stereotype accuracy as an individual difference. *Journal of Personality and Social Psychology, 77,* 350–359.

Eagly, A. H., & Steffen, V. J. (1986). Gender and aggressive behavior: A meta-analytic review of the social psychological literature. *Psychological Bulletin, 100,* 309–330.

Eagly, A. H., & Crowley, M. (1986). Gender and helping behavior: A meta-analytic review of the social psychological literature. *Psychological Bulletin, 100,* 283–308.

Eagly, A. H., & Karau, S. J. (1991). Gender and the emergence of leaders: A meta-analysis. *Journal of Personality and Social Psychology, 60,* 685–710.

For work documenting differences in the contents of rooms occupied by males and females, see: Gosling, S. D., Craik, K. H., Martin, N. R., & Pryor, M. R. (2005). Material attributes of personal living spaces. *Home Cultures, 2,* 51–88.

The classic study examining the effects on stereotype use of being cognitively "busy" is: Gilbert, D. T., & Hixon, G. J. (1991). Cognitive busyness task: The trouble of thinking: Activation and application of stereotypic beliefs. *Journal of Personality and Social Psychology, 60,* 509–517.

The work by Michael Norton and his colleagues on our super-sensitivity to stereotypes is reported in:

Norton, M. I., Sommers, S. R., Apfelbaum, E. P., Pura, N., & Ariely, D. (2006). Colorblindness and interracial interaction: Playing the political correctness game. *Psychological Science, 17,* 949–953.

Norton, M. I., Vandello, J. A., & Biga, A. (2007). Colorblindness inhibits the expression—but not the formation—of racial preferences. Manuscript under review.

Other work by Norton and his collaborators suggests that children develop this sensitivity around the age of ten: Apfelbaum, E. P., Pauker, K., Ambady, N., Sommers, S. R., & Norton, M. I. (2007). Learning (not) to talk about race: When older children underperform in social categorization. Manuscript under review.

The research on judging people by their music preferences is described in: Rentfrow, P. J., & Gosling, S. D. (2006). Message in a ballad: The role of music preferences in interpersonal perception. *Psychological Science, 17,* 236–242.

And our research on the stereotypes of fans of different music genres is in: Rentfrow, P. J., & Gosling, S. D. (2007). The content and validity of music-genre stereotypes among college students. *Psychology of Music, 35,* 306–326. Charts 7.1–7.4 are reproduced, with permission, from that article.

Chapter 8: When Good Judgments Go Bad

Research on the effectiveness (or lack thereof) of unstructured job interviews can be found in: McDaniel, M. A., Whetzel, D. L., Schmidt, F. L., & Maurer, S. D. (1994). The validity of employment interviews: A comprehensive review and meta-analysis. *Journal of Applied Psychology, 79,* 599–616.

Robert Gifford's analysis of behaviors during an interview can be found in: Gifford, R., Ng, C. F., Wilkinson, M. (1985). Nonverbal cues in the employment interview: Links between applicant qualities and interviewer judgments. *Journal of Applied Psychology, 70,* 729–736.

Brunswik's classic work on perception is: Brunswik, E. (1956). *Perception and the representative design of psychological experiments.* Berkeley: University of California Press.

The hoarding work referred to here is described in:

Anderson, S. W., Damasio, H., & Damasio, A. R. (2005). A neural basis for collecting behavior in humans. *Brain, 128,* 201–212.

Seedat, S., & Stein, D. J. (2002). Hoarding in obsessive-compulsive disorder and related disorders: A preliminary report of 15 cases. *Psychiatry and Clinical Neurosciences, 56,* 17–23.

Research describing the connections between hoarding and personality is described in: LaSalle-Ricci, V. H., Arnkoff, D. B., Glass, C. R., Crawley, S. A., Ronquillo, J. G., & Murphy, D. L. (2006). The hoarding dimension of OCD: Psychological comorbidity and the five-factor personality model. *Behaviour Research and Therapy, 44,* 1503–1512.

Eric Abrahamson's work on mess can be found in: Abrahamson, E., & Freedman, D. H. (2006). *A perfect mess.* New York: Little, Brown.

Meredith Wells's research on workplace personalization can be found in:

Wells, M. (2000). Office clutter or meaningful personal displays: The role of office personalization in employee and organizational well-being. *Journal of Environmental Psychology, 20,* 239–255.

Wells, M., & Thelen, L. (2002). What does your workspace say about you? The influence of personality, status, and workspace on personalization. *Environment and Behavior, 34,* 300–321.

Wells, M., & Thelen, L., & Ruark, J. (2007). Workspace personalization and organizational culture: Does your workspace reflect you or your company? *Environment and Behavior, 39,* 616–634.

The blob analysis correlations for brief interactions were taken from Kenny's meta-analysis of zero-acquaintance research: Kenny, D. A. (1994). *Interpersonal perception: A social relations analysis.* New York: Guilford Press.

CHAPTER 9: LIKE A SUPER SNOOPER

Solomon Asch's classic work on how information is combined when impressions are formed is: Asch, S. E. (1946). Forming impressions of personality. *Journal of Abnormal and Social Psychology, 41,* 258–290. Research building on the original work is described in: Asch, S. E. & Zukier, H. (1984). Thinking about persons. *Journal of Personality and Social Psychology, 46,* 1230–1240.

CHAPTER 10: AN OFFICE AND A GENTLEMAN

Our research on correlations between impressions based on offices before and after a move is described in: Gosling, S. D., Gaddis, S., & Vazire, S. (in press). First impressions from the environments that we create and inhabit. In J. Skowronski & N. Ambady (Eds.), *First impressions.* New York: Guilford Press.

The work on "social snacking" is reported in: Gardner, W. L., Pickett, C. L., & Knowles, M. L. (2005). Social "snacking" and social "shielding": The satisfaction of belonging needs through the use of social symbols and the social self. In K. Williams, J. Forgas, & W. von Hippel (Eds.), *The social outcast: Ostracism, social exclusion, rejection, and bullying.* New York: Psychology Press.

One good source on the "need to belong" by Mark Leary and Roy Baumeister is: Baumeister, R. F., & Leary, M. R. (1995). The need to belong: Desire for interpersonal attachments as a fundamental human motivation. *Psychological Bulletin, 117,* 497–529.

CHAPTER 11: BRINGING IT HOME

You can learn all about Chris Travis and the Truehome workshop at www.truehome.net.

INDEX